Anna,
Grandmother of Jesus

Anna,
Grandmother of Jesus

A Message of Wisdom and Love

Claire Heartsong

HAY HOUSE

Carlsbad, California • New York City
London • Sydney • New Delhi

Published in the United Kingdom by:
Hay House UK Ltd, The Sixth Floor, Watson House,
54 Baker Street, London W1U 7BU
Phone: +44 (0)20 3927 7290
www.hayhouse.co.uk

Published in the United States of America by:
Hay House LLC, PO Box 5100, Carlsbad, CA 92018-5100
Tel: (1) 760 431 7695 or (800) 654 5126;
www.hayhouse.com

Published in Australia by:
Hay House Australia Publishing Pty Ltd, 18/36 Ralph St, Alexandria NSW 2015
Tel: (61) 2 9669 4299;
www.hayhouse.com.au

Published in India by:
Hay House Publishers (India) Pvt Ltd, Muskaan Complex, Plot No.3, B-2,
Vasant Kunj, New Delhi 110 070
Tel: (91) 11 4176 1620; www.hayhouse.co.in

A catalogue record for this book is available from the British Library.

ISBN: 978-1-78180-908-2

16 15 14 13 12 11 10 9 8 7

Interior images: Claire Heartsong

Printed in the United States of America

This product uses responsibly sourced papers and/or recycled materials. For
more information, see www.hayhouse.com.

This book is dedicated to the return of the Divine Mother,
Birthing the compassionate Christ in every heart.
May all beings know freedom and union.
May all beings be at peace.
In the Oneness
I AM
Om

✒ Contents ✒

BIBLICAL PALESTINE

0 5 10   20   30
        Miles

Tyre

Mt Herman

Akko

Capernaum   Bethsaida
Magdala   SEA
             OF
Mount   GALILEE
Carmel

Sepphoris • Cana
Nazareth   Mt Tabor

Dor
        GALILEE

Caesarea

                Beth Barah

SAMARIA

Joppa

JUDEA

            Jericho

            Qumran

Jerusalem ●
Bethlehem Bethany
            Etam

Hebron

THE GREAT SEA

PLAIN OF SHARON

Jordan River

SALT SEA

Map by Claire Heartsong
and Aaron Abbasson

✍ Acknowledgements ✍

M y eternal gratitude to the Father–Mother of Life, who hearing my childhood cries continues to answer my prayers: 'Who am I?' 'What is my purpose here in this strange land?' 'How do I return Home?' 'Open me to love and wisdom so that I may bring compassion to myself and others!' To Anna, Yeshua, Mother Mary, and the Councils of Light, I AM yours in service to the upliftment of all life, as we continue to collaborate in Oneness. My innermost heart ever acknowledges the eternal Friend and Beloved on the inner planes whose company and nondual embrace sustain me.

I wish to acknowledge my parents, who are no longer available for hugs, and my brother for being a constant support. My four daughters and seven grandchildren are precious jewels shining in my maternal heart. A warm thank you to my life partners and beloved friends who have gifted me with your love and presence. Heartfelt gratitude to my large spiritual family for all the championing encouragement and tangible support which has manifested this book into the earthplane. Thank you, dear Virginia Essene (who has since passed on), for following your inner guidance and choosing to publish Anna's messages in 2002.

We are all fortunate at this time to have Anna's story being told through a new format and expanded outreach. Immense gratitude to Hay House Publishers in the UK! Thank you for hearing the call and bringing your collective creativity and resource together for this purpose. And thank you for always inviting my input.

A heartfelt thank you, dear friend, for calling Anna forth in this form. May her words of love bring you deep inner peace and her life of wisdom inspire your way. May you realize your own nondual nature which you will find Anna always pointing out. Who you truly are is beyond your limited intellect, so please pause often, go within, and find an expansive warmth in the centre of your heart space. Allow your heart of love to open to all that is showing up in your ordinary life in this and every here and now. In this effortless way, you'll realize the enlightenment you seek has been here all along! Blessed journey without distance!

Thanks to one and all!

✍ Foreword ✍

There are those among us who serve as celestial historians and storytellers, bringing to light inner perceptions long hidden within the human psyche, as well as information that helps explain our life on Earth with its mysteries great and small. If it is higher consciousness you seek, we invite you to bring your spiritual nature and an open mind as we go journeying into nontraditional concepts that continue to influence human lives today.

Anna was first introduced by S.E.E. Publishing Company – part of the nonprofit SHARE Foundation. She was an extraordinary, powerful woman, who light conceived her daughter, Mary, and taught her the Essene way of life so Mary could fulfil her role as mother for the expected Messiah, Jesus.

Although readers of the Edgar Cayce materials may know something of the Essenes and Anna's spiritual importance to Mary, her grandson Jesus, Mary Magdalene, and others, one must wonder why bibles and history books rarely mention her essential role. How is it possible that Anna has been forgotten or ignored by two major religions for so long? It is for this reason that we introduce you to Anna and a small, secretive group of Jews who deliberately created a holy community of light servers capable of supporting the divine plan known as 'the greatest story ever told'.

In looking at Judaic literature for an answer, we find that it totally ignores the vital role Anna played in those profound biblical times before the birth of Jesus. Whether earlier mainstream Jews rejected the importance of the entire Essene group at large, or just Anna because she was a woman, is not known. Perhaps, like the Roman Catholic Church that eventually sainted Anna as St. Anne, they were both merely ignorant of her true role in the Holy Land events of 2,000 years ago. Unbelievably, the recent Catholic Encyclopedia dismisses Anna with the following comment: 'Of the mother of Our Lady nothing is certainly known: even for her name and that of husband Joachim we have to depend upon the apocryphal

Protevangelium of James which, though in its earliest forms is very ancient, is not a trustworthy document.'

Although officially sainted, Anna's importance seems greatly diluted within the Roman Catholic Church until later in the 6th century when the Emperor Justinian I dedicated a shrine to her. Then in the early 700s, Pope Constantine is said to have introduced devotion to her in the church in Rome. Further silence about her life continues until the 14th and 15th centuries when her popularity seems to have brightened again. This touching appreciation of Anna is artistically expressed by world famous artist, Leonardo Da Vinci (1425–1519), in his drawing entitled: 'The Virgin and Child with St. Anne and St. John the Baptist' now in the National Gallery in London. In this group portrait, Anna is shown just behind her daughter Mary's side, with Anna's hand obviously pointing upward to a sketch of the Holy City, perhaps acknowledging her recognition of the family's spiritual source as well as the importance of the baby Jesus and John the Baptist.

As the centuries passed and the Catholic Church's motives became more and more unethical, certain theologians and philosophers openly accused the Church and challenged their behaviours. As the Reformation movements continued their accusations, it was Frederick the Great, himself, in 1790, who wrote: 'Jesus really was an Essene: he was imbued with Essene ethics.' Less than a century later, as the religious questioning and fervour continued, Earnest Renan wrote a book suggesting that 'Christianity is an Essenism that has largely succeeded.'

Whatever the reasons for this scarcity of past information, we now invite you to open a new chapter in biblical history by meeting both Anna and the Essenes. It is time to acknowledge that a complex plan of assistance from celestial realms required incarnation of embodied spiritual volunteers to help anchor and fulfil the ancient prophecies of bringing a Messiah into physical life. It is our contention that Jesus' grandmother, Anna, willingly cooperated with many celestial beings to assist in the divine event of bringing Mary, Jesus, Mary Magdalene, and others, onto planet Earth. However, only by having the disciplined and devoted members of the Essene community at Mount Carmel, Israel as a receptive matrix of energy, was this possible (*see map, page ix*).

Who were these secretive Essenes? is the question. The only commentaries the early western world had about the existence of the Essenes came from classical writers such as Josephus, Philo, and Pliny the Elder. Unfortunately, although their comments are interesting, I believe these authors were describing a different Essene settlement at Qumran, not Anna's community in Mount Carmel. Although the Essenes had their common characteristics of living as a disciplined spiritual, agricultural community of ascetic, reclusive, pacifist individuals, divorced from the mainstream of social, political, and Judaic religious practice, there were major differences as well as commonalities.

The Mount Carmel Essenes were said to maintain a strict, ritual purity, to share their possessions in common, to work hard and keep no slaves. They did not seek pleasure and wealth and they elected their own leaders from among themselves. Because they had strict dietary and health habits, refused to offer animal sacrifices as other Jews did, and used a solar not a lunar calendar, they were considered very odd by their contemporaries. It was reputed that some of the Essenes could even foretell the future.

What these early writers failed to realize was that there were several Essene communities and it was the members of a small mystical group at Mount Carmel who were intensely devoted and involved in bringing a Messiah to planet Earth. None of the writers apparently understood that the wisdom Anna shared with her daughter, Mary, and later with her grandson, Jesus, were profound spiritual teachings and initiations whose influence would help formulate later Christian belief.

Within the pages of this book, you will come to know Anna in her role as headmistress of the Essene spiritual community at Mount Carmel, the secret enclave of the School of the Prophets, which allowed her to share her celestial knowledge with all those entrusted to her tutelage. An extraordinary woman, able to extend her physical life for over six hundred years, Anna reveals the intimacy of the Essene community and their personal relationships against the backdrop of the Roman occupation of the holy lands. You will discover her unusual abilities and responsibilities, including the light conception and birth of Mary, and Mary's own light conception, birth and upbringing of Jesus. This panorama explaining what the Essenes had to do for Jesus, Mary Magdalene and a host of other well-known disciples and helpmates of the Christ drama, emphasizes their essential role in assisting Jesus fulfil his part as the Messiah.

We see how Jesus' resurrection allowed the formation of a church that deified Jesus as a saviour – not as an Essene teacher and healer who taught each person to express their own inner Christ. Thus the growth of Christianity as both a theology and an organizational entity began and Essenism was set aside.

It is interesting that until 1928 there was little information describing the Essene teachings for the contemporary public to read. Then a dedicated linguist and researcher named Edmond Bordeaux Szekely, PhD, was able to find and translate a startling third century Aramaic manuscript and Old Slavonic text. This material contained extensive information about an unusual spiritual group called the Essenes, focusing on their profound dedication to the health and healing practices as epitomized by Jesus. For 50 years Dr Szekely continued his life work of translating and publishing these actual Essene writings, in 26 different languages, mostly in small inexpensive booklets. His work brought the Essene beliefs to greater world attention and he was able to cofound an international Essene organization with 20th Century mystic and Nobel Prize winner, Romain Rolland.

Even so, no particular mention was made of Anna and her daughter Mary in Dr Szekely's writings. Rather, it was the focus on Jesus' teachings and healing practices contained in the Essene gospels that would now capture public attention. In one of his books, *The Gospel of the Essenes*, he related the following Prologue to the Essene Worship.

'When God saw that his people would perish because they did not see the Light of Life, He chose the best of Israel so that they might make the Light of Life to shine before the sons of men. And those chosen were called Essenes because they taught the ignorant, healed the sick, and gathered on the eve of every seventh day to rejoice with the Angels.'

It was not until the 1930s and 40s in America, however, that the first fascinating description of the Essene community at Mount Carmel was revealed. Through his self-induced trance-like states, psychic Edgar Cayce discussed both Anna and the Essenes among his 14,000 'readings'. He described the Essenes as members of a small spiritual Jewish sect that began a hundred years before Jesus' birth in the 2nd Century BC and continued some 68 years after the crucifixion of Jesus and the destruction of the Jewish temple. Cayce's readings about the Essenes confirmed there was a definite connection between Jesus' family and friends and the Essene communities.

After defining the term Essene as 'expectancy', Cayce clarified that divisions had arisen among the Jews into various sects such as the Pharisees and the Sadducees, and also to a small group called Essenes. This latter group represented those Jews who cherished individuals who had been visited by the supernatural or who had unusual experiences in their dreams, visions, or inner voices. Cayce reported that these designated Essenes were an outgrowth of the teachings of Melchizedek, as propagated by Elijah, Elisha, and Samuel, and that they consequently offered themselves as channels to receive spiritual information of divine origin. They joined together in a community of love and devotion, living a holy life of performing good deeds, honouring women equal with men. Above all, the Essenes believed in a divine plan for human evolution and deliberately prepared themselves to be worthy of hosting a Messiah in the world.

Mr Cayce specifically mentions Anna as being in the Promised Land in the days preceding and just following the entrance of the Prince of Peace into the physical world. He describes her as being a seeress and prophetess among an organization that could interpret time and place according to the stars and could calculate numerological effects upon physical life. She was apparently highly regarded among the Essenes, and initiated innumerable people, including the 12 maidens whose purity was high enough to receive the light conception energies needed to conceive the Messiah. Anna, herself, birthed Mary via the light conception process and also helped Mary do the same. In this way, and many others, she was a holy woman actively involved in the preparation of the Messiah's arrival.

It is fascinating that part of what Mr Cayce's readings described would be physically discovered in Israel in 1947. Indeed, because of the discovery of the Dead Sea Scrolls at Qumran, Israel, archaeologists have uncovered a female skeleton there, just as Cayce's reading said they would. This scientific evidence corroborated Cayce's remarks that there really were Essenes and that women were part of the community, even at Qumran.

It has taken nearly 2,000 years to find the Dead Sea Scroll evidence proving that the Essenes really existed and that they played a dramatic role in human history. Like voices from the past, this 800-piece archaeological discovery in modern-day Israel proves there were Essenes living in the community at Qumran.

You may have heard or read about the Dead Sea Scrolls that are now considered the oldest biblical evidence in existence. If not, I recommend them as proof that the Essenes existed. However, they are primarily focused on the community at Qumran and do not necessarily identify the work of the Mount Carmel community. Among the treasure trove discovered in the jars found in the first explored cave near the former Qumran community, there were seven nearly intact scrolls ready to translate. One of these was an entirely readable scroll containing the Old Testament scripture of the book of Isaiah that predated the earliest Jewish example of that same biblical source! So there was great excitement and fear among theologians and historians as to what this would mean to our present religious understandings. (When I visited Jerusalem in 1984, a handsome building called the Shrine of the Book had been built to keep the scrolls safe and to display the wonderful ancient Isaiah manuscript behind humidified glass in one continuous roll all around the circular room. It was thrilling to see a piece of such ancient writing even though I couldn't read the words.)

The curious part of this extraordinary find is that it has been a continuing and laborious translation process by many professionals of different nations and religions. Both the secrecy of the scrolls' content and the lengthy process of translating the materials have caused scholarly outrage, accusations and arguments worldwide, coloured by competitive and often uncooperative attitudes among those involved. Nonetheless, today the public can finally read some of the translations of what the Essenes scribed those 2,000 years ago, including actual contents of some gospels contained in the scrolls. Regrettably, the scrolls were not individually signed by their scribes, neither was the location or date of their work given. So many mysteries still remain. For anyone interested, however, a profusion of information is available on this topic in books, in countless articles and in over 19,000 website listings about the Dead Sea Scrolls!

In spite of all this information, I am saddened to say that nowhere in the Dead Sea Scrolls research have I seen mention of Jesus' grandmother, Anna, and very little about his mother, Mary. This suggests to me that the truth about the esoteric Essenes and Anna, who helped bring forth the Messiah, remains hidden in the earlier School of the Prophets community at Mount Carmel. Perhaps through other inspired authors, including information contained in this volume, or from a still-hidden archaeological find at Mount Carmel's physical site, we may finally know and appreciate what has gone before. In the meantime, the implications and meaning of the Essene topic invites us, these two thousand years later, to interpret their historical and religious value, as always, by our own individual opinion, perception and conclusion.

It is our hope in presenting this book about Anna and the Essenes that you may find something inspiring that raises your consciousness and gives you courage and commitment to fulfil the particular soul purposes you wish to complete. If the material we share gives you new insight and increased willingness to be the finest spiritual human you can be, then we rest content.

Before I go, I would like to leave you with one short commentary from a real scroll fragment taken from the Essene Book of Revelation.

> *I have reached the inner vision*
> *And through thy spirit in me*
> *I have heard thy wondrous secret.*
> *Through thy mystic insight*
> *Thou hast caused a spring of knowledge*
> *To well up within me,*
> *A fountain of power, pouring forth living waters:*
> *A flood of love and of all-embracing wisdom*
> *Like the splendor of Eternal Light.*

Virginia Essene

Chapter 1

A Letter from Anna of Mount Carmel

My dear friend,

I bring you greetings of love and peace this day. I am Anna, also known as the mother of Mary and the grandmother of Jesus. The fact that you are reading this letter, as an introduction to my story, is something of a miracle. For I send this message to you across great spans of time and space. And yet, I am here, closer than you might think.

I extend to you a personal invitation to come and embark on a journey with me that will follow the hidden initiatory path that my family and I walked 2,000 years ago. Our meeting and travels together will be accomplished through your imagination as you read the pages upon which I reveal myself. The only difference between my path and yours today, is that your present daily life is the temple and mystery school, and you are your own master teacher and guru. Then, when you come together in masterful equality, the power of your individual influence can be amplified through beneficent group intention.

I offer you my version of a complex, compelling, and life-transforming story, among many, that presents Jesus, the human, and Jesus, the Christ. Along the circuitous path that leads us to meet with the Christ 'face to face', much will be revealed about the ancient Essene initiations that I mastered. These same initiations I facilitated for Mother Mary, Yeshua ben Joseph (Jesus), Mary Magdalene, and others adepts who embodied and exemplified the Christ or the 'Way of the Teacher of Righteousness', (the way of rightful use of energy). I gave these wisdom and high alchemy teachings (internal energy practices) to many, and now I pass the secrets of physical and spiritual immortality, resurrection, and other mysteries on to you. This I do because, you, my dear friend, have asked for freedom and empowerment. You are well prepared to use these gifts for the benefit of all as we move through a perilous passage during Earth's birth changes.

I realize that times of irreversible change, such as you are encountering now in your world, can be harrowing to entrenched beliefs and dogmatic protocol that have previously pointed the way to God and how to relate to 'Him'. I am available to meet you wherever you are. Then, together we will travel to a meeting place where the known and unknown court one another and begin to merge. This mystical courtship of consciousness is a mysterious walk between the worlds. It is the rendezvous point where the intuitive, unconditionally loving Divine Feminine is found. In Her embrace all polarities meet, heal into wholeness, and become empowered, balanced and harmonious expressions of love.

You may find that travelling with me involves becoming something of a metaphysical sleuth: digging, probing, exposing, examining, and offering up the old cosmological Creator/Creation and saviour/victim/tyrant paradigms to a clearer light. Understand, my friend, my purpose in bringing greater clarity to the path that the Christ initiate takes is not to contend or to prove that I know the truth about 'what really happened' 2,000 years ago, nor is it my intention to make another's viewpoint wrong.

With much soul searching, I look out upon great vistas of the Earth's historical landscape. I see a wilderness riddled with endless rounds of suffering and littered with tattered, dramatic scripts. As I feel humanity's heartache, I ask these poignant questions: Are we finished with our gathering of wisdom through duality? Have we had enough repetitions of our favourite melodramatic roles? Can we embrace both polarities as equally divine and know that God–Goddess expresses in all forms? Can we be content to simply rest in love, having known love's opposite?

I give you my experiences in the context of the old, esoteric (hidden) paradigm of 2,000 years ago. As we proceed together, I invite you to examine, question, and restructure all that I share with you in such a way that you feel acknowledged, empowered, and supported as you pass through the sometimes arduous Christ initiations that are occurring in your life, even as we speak.

How do we go about restructuring paradigms that no longer serve us? First of all, an understanding of old belief structures, such as the one I present in my story, is required. Next, the vision of a new harmonious form of true individual and global empowerment is called forth and allowed to manifest. As these old and new paradigm lenses merge, important questions arise. What eternal principles empower life's greatest potential and provide a sense of continuity and stability during a time of great transition and change? Are there perspectives within the old way of relating to Creator and Creation that enhance our collectively chosen vision, and what tenets of the past clearly do not work and must be discarded?

Allowing these questions to be our signposts, I invite us to have the courage to be simple, open-minded, optimistic, appreciative, and childlike adventurers. As we visit a broad spectrum of venues, topics, and perspectives, I would rather that we keep questioning as we go along, instead of taking positions that defend answers. Have we not had enough 'holy' wars fought over 'right answers?'

I invite you to join me in a most timely exploration of these pivotal questions, trusting that the answers are already present, simply awaiting unveiling. I offer my story as a threshing board for winnowing the wheat of eternal wisdom and releasing useless, encumbering chaff. I hold up a mirror to you so that you may behold yourself in greater clarity, knowing that you are the answer to your mind's most perplexing questions and the fulfilment of your heart's deepest longing.

Please note that I address you as 'my friend' instead of 'my child', because now is a time of empowerment, in which you and planet Earth are passing through a Rite of Passage and are coming of age. While I have played a maternal role for eons in the affairs of humanity, I desire that we meet this day as peers and friends. You have matured sufficiently so that childish temper tantrums and adolescent power games no longer hold your interest. While I gladly offer you my unconditional maternal love, comfort, and example, it is time to be your own Messiah.

We have heard each other's request to meet. And so it is that I will come to your abode where we will embark on our journey without distance. Its location does not matter; whether in a secluded mountain hermitage, austere desert cave, monastery, sophisticated urban apartment, city ghetto, prison, or sprawling suburban estate, as long as you meet me in your feelings of the present moment. Likewise, my appearance is of little importance. Any caring, strengthening image you may have of me can serve as a sense of initial connection. I assure you, you will recognize me when you see me across the threshold of your open door. My preference is that you might eventually come to know me as I AM, beyond all images that would distance me from you in a hierarchical manner, or that might perpetuate our old dysfunctional relationships.

Remember this, my friend, it is not my story's cast of characters that is important. It matters little that you know who I have been, even though I have served as an emissary of the celestial realms involved in the original creation of this planet, and my incarnations representing the Divine Mother have been numerous. I would have you know that my journey with you and this beloved jewel of the heavens – Earth – has bequeathed me with great treasures of compassion and wisdom. Neither is my version of the Christ story important, nor is any contending to prove it right or wrong. What is infinitely more important is the life transforming and enhancing energy of love that is carried within and beyond my words.

Although I have made my ascension, I have freely chosen to return into the earthplane from time to time so that I can continue to participate in Earth's evolution. My profound love for every particle and expression of life moves me to remain close. I have returned at this time so that I might take this long awaited and most extraordinary journey with you. This I do, not as a sacrifice, but because I deeply know that my complete Union in God is inseparable from yours and that of Mother Earth's. It is reward enough to know that my words have catalysed your memory of us walking this way before, dreaming our vision of a New Earth, and that our love has brought us together again. We can be comforted in knowing that all our adventures, both past and future, have prepared us for this consummating finale we promised to celebrate.

I gladly serve you as a paradigm shifter, life coach, midwife, and as a very accessible friend. I accompany you side by side on the path that leads to the knowing that you are the beloved Christ you seek. I offer you my hand in full fellowship so that we can remember the enduring thread of light that is the path that weaves all life together into a seamless, ever-changing, impeccable tapestry that reveals Mother–Father God's infinite love and grace. Regardless of its name, that eternal light reveals your destination to be closer than any limiting thought you may think. You, my eternal friend, are the Path, the Light, and the Way.

Let the door to your Christ heart be open. Enter in and *'Know Thy Self!'*

Enjoy your homecoming journey of remembrance.

Anna

❦ Chapter 2 ❦

Anna Comes Forth Near Bethlehem

Ah, my beloved friend, we are together at last, just as I promised before you took this incarnation. You see it is destiny and a deeply resounding resonance that draws us to be together this hour. You are coded in your DNA to hear my Call. In truth, it is your own Self who is calling you Home, not me, although your Self is also who I AM. You thought you would never find me, and I wondered when you would invite me in. But, joyfully, we are here together. You are sufficiently prepared for our journey. Fear not, you have everything required to move gracefully along the way.

As we begin our journey, I will tell you, and remind you often, to breathe, relax, and open your heart. With the turning of the pages, you may move more deeply into a greater awareness of your self. There may be a sense that your experience of present and past time is blending and merging. With this shift in your perception, it is possible that your imagination will use my words to actively evoke emotions of all kinds. I recommend that you breathe, open your mind and heart, and become receptive to your internal experience as my words move upon your soul. If you are resisting your feelings that may come with the words, images, and remembrances, there could be some discomfort. My story, in a sense, is the Journey Perilous taken by the Grail Knights. Remember this, my friend: you determine the timing and the pace of our mutual adventure.

One of the requirements I ask of you, as I suggested in my letter, is to be willing to let go of any preconceived notions you may have of me or of the characters represented in my story. First of all, I suggest that you remove me from any pedestal that you might have placed me on, as St. Anne. I do not consider myself a saint. That exalted station distances me from you. I am here. I am your friend.

Secondly, allow the possibility that I lived far longer than you have ever likely considered possible. To those I knew intimately, I revealed myself as an immortal who maintained a physical body, (albeit with some changes) for over six hundred years. I tell you this, at the outset, so that you can relax into my unfolding story, as it becomes increasingly complex.

The third requirement I ask of you to understand is that I was not above human discord. I felt and came to understand the extreme polarities of the human condition and human emotion because I chose to experience life's full spectrum. I immersed myself into the physical plane, as does any soul who desires to attain self-mastery. There were times of exquisite beauty and ecstasy. There was also severe tribulation and heartbreak. In truth, beloved, my physical life was little different than yours, except that my long years in the same body was something you have not yet experienced. I share this with you so that you may come to know you can also accomplish all that I did, and even more.

Anna continues.

(For purposes of simplification, the commonly used Gregorian calendar will be used for dates instead of the Hebrew calendar.)

It was in December of the year 612 BC, that a child had been born in the village of Etam, just three miles south of Bethlehem, in Judea. A descendant of the tribes of Judah, Levi, and Joseph, this child was named Hannah, after the mother of Samuel the Prophet. Her birth took place about 358 years after the reign of David the King and some 110 years after the Kingdom of Israel had been conquered and carried away into captivity by the Assyrians.

Hannah was the physical aspect of my multidimensional soul who prepared the body through which I, Anna, chose to reenter the drama of Earth on the twenty-third day of May in the year 596 BC. And a sore drama it was; for Babylon was now coming forth to rule the hearts of men and women who had forgotten their innocence before the Lord.

In 597 BC, while I still abided in the light realms shortly before I requested permission from the Councils of Light for my return to Earth, the Babylonian soldiers of King Nebuchadnezzar swept through Etam. They laid siege to Jerusalem for the second time, and carried away thousands of hostages into captivity. It was in May of the following year during a 'near-death experience' that Hannah and I voluntarily exchanged places through a process of blending and merging, which I will now briefly explain.

You may well ask, 'Why would an adept such as I choose to come into a challenging circumstance like Hannah's?' While you may perceive tribulations as unpleasant, even dangerous, the opportunity for expansion and empowerment of consciousness is greatly enhanced. Please allow me to explain this 'easier said than done' answer more fully. Consider the possibility that an over-soul level exists, where many aspects of consciousness focus collectively. Here, a much broader perspective offers the possibility of assessing many different time-lines, realities, and dimensions. Within this holographic realm of consciousness there is an awareness of simultaneous, interactive experiences functioning together with every possible cause and effect.

From such a place it is easy to view the potentials that will facilitate the greatest growth and evolution for the interconnected wholeness of life. Although the painful growth experiences of human life may seem unbearable on a personal level, the end result fulfils a benevolent Creator's desire for ever-expanding personal growth. As you are learning, the ultimate purpose of life is to know itself as love. Rather than feeling hopeless and powerless, you can choose to realign with your soul's original intention and recreate your present challenges into a more harmonious and joyful design. In the more coherent and refined realms of consciousness, the highest possible outcome is always chosen. An impeccable 'blueprint' is securely held in place within the blissful realms of sound and light. In every moment, there is an opportunity to remember your soul's empowered design and to receive guidance from a more inspired choice.

So it was with my experience as Hannah. As all factors, including genetic potentials, were considered from the over-soul perspective, a choice was made to project an aspect into the earthplane. You might think of this aspect, the personality called Hannah, as a facet of the 'Anna over-soul', or group soul collective consciousness, immersed in the illusion of separation. Hannah's limited point-of-view veiled her awareness of having made a choice to incarnate, as well as her true relationship to her 'Anna over-soul'. Nevertheless, the connection was always there. Also the potential for consciously co-creating the highest outcome or destiny through her free-will choices was available to Hannah.

You have heard stories of individuals who died, 'went into the light', and upon regaining consciousness, had a greater awareness and faith in their Creator Source. Such ones often return with many more abilities, even miraculous powers, than they had before they died. So it was with Hannah as I came forth. When she was 'out of body', Hannah awakened and remembered her pre-incarnation choices. These choices were: prepare a physical body that could hold specific DNA coding, live in a precise geographical location and time period, and have experiences that would provide a strong foundation for self-mastery. All of these choices would fulfil an even greater purpose at the appropriate timing. Just as we had agreed, at the precise moment of her awakening, even though she seemed to be dying, there was a powerful 'downloading' and merging of Hannah's human consciousness with the 'Anna over-soul' consciousness.

Understanding Hannah's relationship to her over-soul could assist you to make a deliberate connection with your own over-soul or higher self through meditation and other methods for enhancing consciousness. With this preliminary explanation about why Hannah and I, her 'higher self' called Anna, 'exchanged' places, let us return to my story.

I now found myself in Hannah's body, disoriented and near unto death from the wounds and infections that occurred during childbirth. There happened to be an old seeress, named Naomi, who heard the mewing cries of my newborn while giving oxen, camels, donkeys, and goats their ration of water and feed. These were corralled in pens and caves behind the wayside inn where her son-in-law presided over guests. She ran for the help of a midwife who lived nearby, and together they quietly and gently washed and restored my infant and me to health.

Naomi then took me into her humble abode next to the inn, where I remained until my child could walk. She asked after me, 'Who was I? What had befallen me that I would choose to be alone without adequate shelter for the bringing forth of my labours in childbirth?' I was hard pressed to remember right away. For many days I was delirious, and the suckling of my child the only thing I knew how to do. I was young of body as I looked upon my form – perhaps sixteen, at the most.

With patient understanding, Naomi nursed my mind and body. She knew the human psyche, could read my palms and face, could look into the past and future, and could commune with my soul across time and space. Thus, this dear one read my Book of Life, and though she did not 'Know' as one who is an adept, her intuition was highly developed. Over the following weeks, she and I began to solve the mystery of why I had chosen to be alone within a stable cave to bring forth my child.

Over the next few months I, Anna of the higher realms of light, and the embodiment of Hannah merged as one. As I grounded into the simple tasks of caring for my baby daughter and assisting Naomi with the affairs of her hearth, my memory slowly returned. I recovered quickly, once I got my bearings, for indeed, the energies I brought were of a much higher dimension. Naomi and I gradually pieced together the story of Hannah and how she had come to be with child. And I was then able to heal the wounds that tore at her heart and soul. Briefly now, I will tell you the story, though upon the details I shall not linger.

Several weeks before her scheduled wedding, Hannah and her childhood sweetheart, Tomas, came together in the heat of their youthful passion, and Hannah conceived in her womb. They held secret their tryst. However, before a marriage ceremony could take place, Tomas was captured and carried away. Soldiers of Babylon poured into the villages, taking women and children hostage. Many men lost their lives trying to protect home and family. Those who resisted were brutally killed. The remainder was taken into captivity. The blood and carnage that spilled upon the ground were raw and devastating.

Hannah was attending to the care of her two younger brothers while her parents were away gathering food and water. The soldiers found her and her brothers lying huddled beneath their parents' bed. They tore the two boys from her arms and killed them mercilessly, while forcing Hannah to watch. Something in her mind gave way; Hannah would never be the same. Then, after taking their pleasure at the expense of her body and soul, they laid her aside, bruised, unconscious, and wasted. She lay on the muddy street while they set her childhood home on fire. Thinking her dead from a blow to her head, they walked away.

At that point, Hannah was lifted up into the celestial realms, where she met her over-soul who told her that her body could now serve as a vehicle through which miracles would occur to lift Israel from its dark night. So she and I, who were aspects of the same over-soul, communed, and she agreed to allow that higher dimensional aspect of her soul, which I am, to come into her physical form at a later date.

Thus it was, in those days of the second Babylonian siege of Jerusalem, that I inherited the lot of Hannah, who was orphaned, widowed, stripped of all worldly possessions, and left behind by the Babylonians as one who was dead. Returning to consciousness, Hannah suddenly found herself in the position of an outcast, the poorest of the poor, even though she had been born into the royal lineage and House of David. Her mind was besieged by demons. Most of those who would have sheltered her had been carried away, and those relatives of a higher class who remained in Etam scorned her as one defiled, justifying their indifference by the Law of Moses. Thus, wandering in the wilderness of her soul's dark night, Hannah carried Tomas' secret child until the appointed hour, when her purpose for being would be fulfilled.

During the remaining months of her pregnancy, we continued to commune and merge in the higher dimensions. As the babe grew within Hannah's womb, the young mother received comfort and increasing self-awareness from her over-soul's deep caring. When her labour began, I, Anna, incarnated fully into Hannah's embodiment through the crown. I entered into the body just as the child came forth.

I named my little one Aurianna. A golden gift of light from the Great Mother was she. Her little face shone with the brilliance of the sun, and her large brown eyes held the twinkle of starry reflected seas. Her personality was almost always serene and calming. Aurianna's presence was a blessing through all the days she lived near me. During the thirteen years after her birth, I walked from place to place within the villages of Etam and Bethlehem, offering myself to households to be hired and taken in. There were many families that required ones such as I who knew something of midwifery, medicinal herbs, the care of small children, and how to create a peaceful sanctuary within an orderly home.

During the thirteen years Aurianna and I lived within the vicinity of Bethlehem, I met with several wise teachers who were able to recognize my unusually high energy. Some knew me better than I knew myself at the beginning of my reentry into the earthplane. For it requires a period of time to make the necessary attunements, adjustments of mind and body, and transmutations of karmic patterns within cellular memory, before the higher consciousness can fully be present in awareness. This is also true for every soul who comes through the birth canal. And for the few who 'walk in', as I did, it is no different, except that the body is already fully developed and there are fewer veils.

I would have you know that my teachers were among an ancient order that lived in secluded hermitages secreted away in the hills and among the populace of towns and cities. These obscure mystics recognized one another even though they usually appeared as quite ordinary to the uninitiated. It took several years of probationary effort on my part and the patient understanding of my mentors to lift the veils of forgetfulness I had inherited, so that I could remember more fully why I had come again.

༄

๑ Chapter 3 ๑

The Essenes of Jerusalem and Mount Carmel

As the years passed and I entered fully into my human journey, I experienced much testing of my soul, during which I occasionally faltered. My steady progress prompted my wise teachers to pass me on to a mystic who resided within the walled city of Jerusalem. My new teacher's name was John. That name will do for now, though in time I knew him by another. He took my now thirteen-year-old daughter and me under his protective wing. His jovial and devoted wife, Hannah Elizabeth, made space for us in a small storage room located on the roof of their stone dwelling. To be in the clamour of Jerusalem was something of a rude awakening, yet I relished the opportunity to go deeper into the mysteries of my soul, to awaken, remember, and fulfil my part.

What had once been a proud city was now a broken city, its former glory but a fading memory. Having ignored the repeated warnings of Jeremiah the Prophet, Jerusalem had been devastated by the Babylonian soldiers of Nebuchadnezzar during the course of three successive sieges.

The suffering that our people had experienced during those twenty years from 605 to 585 BC is beyond description. Many had died. Many more were taken into captivity. Others had fled for their lives. Only the poor remained. Such was the situation in Jerusalem when Jeremiah the Prophet wrote his Book of Lamentations. And such was still the situation in Jerusalem when I arrived on the scene in 583 BC.

Now, it was twenty-four years that I remained in Jerusalem. I thrived within the city, even though there was much unrest and violence from time to time. The Temple lay in ruins, and the streets strained with the return of those who had fled. Yet, I learned how to remain calm and centred within my being, regardless of what my senses perceived was occurring on the outer screen.

John was a stonemason by trade and also a scribe/reader of the Temple library. He was esteemed by most of his peers with whom he worked because he had a way of smoothing the feathers among the many discordant factions of Jews and Gentiles. John was, for the most part, a very gentle and unassuming individual, devoted to God. He could also be unbending about certain principles of the Law, as he understood the ancient writings, which he shared with the priests and young men who came for schooling and training to become rabbis. He reminded me in some ways of my father, and thus a need was fulfilled by his attention and care of Aurianna and me.

John worked upon the restoration of the Temple library that had been destroyed by the Babylonian conquerors, whose continuing presence was felt as a bed of thorns. He always seemed to have boundless energy, sleeping little, and rarely was he heavy with fatigue. I desired to know his secret. As if knowing my readiness, John began to appear in my dreams. These dreams felt as real as my waking life. He would take my arm and lead me through doors and passages into great halls of learning, where there were white robed beings of such light-filled countenances that at first it was difficult to comprehend their human features. How wondrous were these encounters! How thankful I was to be with such a master teacher! How grateful I was for the wise ones who first directed my path to Jerusalem.

As the weeks and months went by in this manner, I, too began to experience that I required little sleep. I would awaken after just a few hours of sound rest. Sitting upright upon my pallet, I felt fully enlivened, my heart beating strongly my soul's ancient rhythms. I would meditate on the light and sound current charging every cell, and soon John would etherically appear and escort me to one of the many Halls of Records. Sometimes before I met John, I experienced myself floating up and looking down on my body lying asleep or sitting in meditation. I noticed an elastic-like silver cord attaching me to my body. I was free to go anywhere! You would call my 'out of body' experiences astral travel.

In the Hall of Records John would open scrolls and begin to teach me how to decipher the symbols and languages. Thus, my etheric training as a scribe had begun in earnest. My daily chores of helping Hannah Elizabeth with her busy household seemed to pass easily, my meditation upon highly refined and subtle light and sound currents sustained my strength of body. I found little time for socializing. That was all right as far as I was concerned. My desire was for the greater wisdom that was opening up to me.

Although there were not many women in my outer life with whom I could share my most intimate thoughts, there were, within the inner retreats, many females whom I came to love. I relished their companionship, even though uninitiated eyes could not see my companions. Some of these I will introduce to you as we continue our walk together, for they are key characters in our unfolding story.

Few women I came across in the marketplace or synagogue had access to the learning I was receiving from the Great Ones. While remaining closely tied to their hearths, most women seemed to be invested in acquiring social graces and status. Frankly, I found their gossip and mundane interests boring and tedious. Even Hannah Elizabeth, though a most caring and gentle soul, could not meet me where I yearned to go.

In those first years, I only found two women in all of Jerusalem who carried the same vibrational resonance and desire for the hidden wisdom teachings. With these sisters of the immortal soul, a pact was made to support each other in all manners, as our circumstances would allow. These two courageous women, Ruth and Mariamne, would grace my life through many years. Fortunately, the number of such women increased, as souls beyond the veil came forth in flesh to play their sacred parts with me.

At the age of sixteen, Aurianna married a man called James, and right away was pregnant with my first grandchild. I, of course, was thrilled by the opportunity to prepare her for giving birth. I had mastered midwifery, having been taught by my mother at a very young age, during the births of my younger brothers. She had taken me with her to attend other women when their hour came. Because of my disposition, which was naturally maternal, I enjoyed the gathering of wisdom that made the passage of the soul into newborn flesh one of love and welcoming.

I assisted the labour through certain sounds or combinations of sounds that would flow from my lips while massaging the mother's great belly, heaving with contractions. Watching the energies with clairvoyant vision, how the colours and thought forms would shift with her breath, I advised the mother in breathing and sounding the names of the One God. I also called forth the angels to be present throughout her labour. I had learned the way of herbs for relieving pain, infection, swelling, and the bringing in of the milk. In Jerusalem, my two friends and I kept gardens for such medicinal purposes. We walked out into the fields and pasturelands during the appropriate seasons to gather and replenish our herbal supplies.

So it was that I delivered the first of my many grandchildren. To Aurianna would be born eight children altogether. Because of my calming presence, midwifery skills, and herbal knowledge, both the poor and the wealthy sought me out. Welcoming the souls who would take part in Earth's drama warmed my heart. Thus I was engaged in my outer life. And together with the learning in the night from the secret masters of the Brother–Sisterhood of Light, my days were full to overflowing.

Now that I had a means of livelihood, I took residence in an upper room near the home of Aurianna and James in the Valley Kidron near the old city of David. What a delight to be close to my grandchildren as they grew over the years. For those who showed promise and the desire for esoteric learning, I created a school where they could learn at my knee. Quick they were to learn, and later they followed me to the sands of Egypt. Those whose interest lay in other walks of life came and gathered around me to be entertained and to gain some preparation for life's many lessons. All of my grandchildren enjoyed my stories and our walks within the beauty of Nature's halls of wisdom.

By this time, John had become fully established within the library of the Temple, and his stonemasonry no longer took up as much of his attention. When possible, he would bring me into rooms hidden away, where he and a group of master masons, who belonged to a secret order, had access to subterranean passageways which led to ancient catacombs and archives. Not often in the physical did I go into the vaults, yet enough to establish in my mind and heart a knowing that I would do whatever was necessary to learn how to read the ancient texts and share the hidden knowledge. Strong was my desire to bring the fountain of enlightenment to each one who chose to quench their thirsty soul.

Many years before I met him, John had joined a sect of Judaism called the Essenes. These, the most enlightened and uncorrupted of Judaic Hebrews, traced their origins back to the ancient mystery schools of Moses and Akhenaten and beyond. Derived from the root words 'esse' (being) and 'ene' (source), Essene means 'Source of Being' or 'Holy One'. We addressed one another as Son or Daughter of the sun, as those who kept the way of healing we were also known.

Every Sabbath and high day, members of the Essene Brotherhood would come to John's household to pray, read, and discuss matters of spirit. Hannah Elizabeth graciously attended to feeding us and then would retire to the hearth to mend, embroider, or rock a child. She would tune in when there was a topic of interest; otherwise, she felt her place was to provide a household of order and serenity.

Our communions were rich and full, providing me with a family in the outer world who took on the luminescence that I witnessed in the inner planes. Of this community, my two women friends, Mariamne and Ruth, were also faithful disciples. So began my walk with the Faithful, the Chosen, or the Elect as some called themselves within the Essene Brother–Sisterhood. I continued in the fellowship of the Essenes throughout the remainder of my long days.

James, Aurianna's husband, was one of these brothers who hailed from Mount Carmel. The stories he told about Carmel quickened my spirit, and I felt called to go to the mount where Samuel and Elijah had taught – there to establish myself as a full initiate within the ancient Essene mysteries. So it was that, with Aurianna, James, and five of my eight grandchildren, I left Jerusalem in 559 BC to begin a new life. Later, Mariamne and Ruth also joined the Mount Carmel community. My soul was at peace, and I looked to the future with a glad heart.

Just as you heard your soul's call and we have come together to enter upon this journey to *'Know Thyself'* more deeply as a living Christ, so did I respond to my heart's call to enter into the Mount Carmel Mystery School. Carmel, as we called our monastery, is one of the most ancient mystery schools that survived numerous rises of civilization. It has preserved the lineage that holds the Grail codes of ascension and incarnation through which the Divine Mother brings forth Christ Consciousness during cosmic, solar, and planetary cycles.

Now I shall share my memories of Mount Carmel by the sea with you, my friend.

In joyful gratitude, I walked the beauteous hillsides of Carmel gathering the sweet lilies of the field and collecting a variety of herbs with which I prepared medicines for our monastic community who kept the Way of the Teacher of Righteousness. For we strived with great discipline and dedication to fulfil the power of God within us through the rightful use of energy, by acting upon God's word with forthrightness and compassion, thereby bringing an aura of peace to a war-ravaged land.

My years at Carmel accumulated to thirty-nine before I went to Egypt to undertake advanced initiations and specialized training. During that time, I took my probationary initiations under the tutelage of Solomon and Eloise. These were a couple dedicated completely to the Creator. They entreated me to calmness when my heart raced with fear for my people whenever troops of soldiers came to the mount. They instilled forgiveness and compassion in my breast when the savage memories of my youth tore through my mind. They opened my Book of Life and assisted me to remember the Law of One, the One God I AM. They trained my mind, body, and soul to be aligned to the greater good of our community. So it was with great love that I dwelled and learned within my beloved Carmel.

There were, at that time, relatively few couples compared to single individuals who chose to be celibate. I was one of the sisters who chose to hold the life force within my bowels and lift it through the fires of my soul into the wholeness of my greater being. Whether married or single, we sanctified our sexual energy and looked upon this great force with reverence and awe. We studied the forces of nature and called them the agents by which we could know God as both Father and Mother – Spirit and Matter. We were attuned to the spirits of plants, minerals, fire, water, and air. These we called angels, to whom we prayed for grace each night and day. The cyclic seasons were honoured, as was Mother Earth and Father Sky, through songs, dances, and feasts.

We bowed to the Law of Life and partook of those laws that replenished and sustained our physical expression of spirit. Through much training in the alchemy of transmutation, we transformed our animal natures. We uplifted our senses to perceive beyond the physical veils of lust, anger, and dualistic needs. We participated in ritual washings and cleansings of our inner and outer minds and bodies. There was much understanding of herbs, simple raw foods, and practices of horticulture that sustained us throughout the seasons.

When I was not engaged in transcribing records at the library, assisting with the ill at the infirmary, or practicing midwifery, I would range over the hillsides, gathering herbs and seeds. These I planted in our community gardens. Each who lived within our compound laboured for the benefit of all according to each one's disposition and talents. Often, to my delight, a flock of youngsters would gather around me to hear stories of the prophets, our people's history, and folklore. Among these children were my grandchildren and great-grandchildren. These precious moments I treasured and stored up in my heart. How I loved Carmel and the life we created there!

As I matured in wisdom, rituals and ceremonies were taught to me and to others as we advanced through the degrees of our mystery school initiations. When we were sufficiently prepared, these practices facilitated the activation of psychic abilities and the rejuvenation of our bodies. These rituals, if I were to describe them to you now, would most likely be misunderstood. Therefore, I shall prepare the way, so that you may in due time receive according to your allowing.

The processes for rejuvenation are very ancient practices, and it was in Carmel that I first became aware of these inner secrets for sustaining my body. Truly, I developed the skills and disciplined my mind to recreate my body every month. Although my first sixty years reflected typical aging of mind and body, once I began to regenerate myself, I looked and felt like a thirty-five year old woman. However, there were times over the following centuries when my appearance varied according to the requirements of the situations in which I found myself.

Even as Solomon and Eloise taught me The Way of the Teacher of Righteousness (the rightful use of energy), so shall I share with you, that you may accomplish your purpose for coming to Earth. There are a variety of purposes, to be sure; yet, it is the 'Great Work of the Soul' that we are destined to finish when all is brought together. Therefore, we shall open the gates that lead to the One who knows the truth beyond the shadows. When you have come to the understanding that all paths converge within the heart of the One, the purpose of this writing shall be fulfilled.

So, I now leave you to contemplate the feelings in your heart. Is the 'Great Work of the Soul' that for which you have come? If so, then our story shall unfold according to divine decree, that you may receive the energies of transmutation and ascension. You shall be directed from within; for I would have you receive according to your capacity to know Mother–Father God as your infinite source of supply. Your journey is yours to create. Divine are your choices, every one.

I am here to comfort you during your passage of birth, even as I hold all life. I represent the Mother of Mothers. In some ways you are always my child, yet, more so at this time of self-empowerment, I call you my beloved friend. Together, we shall merge at the ending of time. Are you ready to remember who you really are and be finished at last with the drama that has held you apart from your true Self? If so, read on. Be prepared to exchange your old identity for one far vaster. And those of you who have long trod the Way of the One, I welcome your countenance and offer mine as your mirror. Greater effulgence is the gift I give to all who persevere through my many words and enigmatic phrases.

We have now completed the first circle from where we started when first we began the story of Anna of Mount Carmel. Yet other circles await us, as we walk the terrain of my life until all is gathered up and brought to completion. Next to come is the story of my sojourn in Egypt where I became a high priestess of Isis and Hathor, which prepared me for my work in the Essene and Magdalene Orders at Mount Carmel.

‿

∾ Chapter 4 ∾
Anna's Initiations in Egypt

As we pick up the thread of my life just before I departed Mount Carmel for Egypt, I hasten to remind you that I had already begun the process of youthening my body by disengaging from the collective consciousness that believed in aging and dying. I had participated in most of the initiations into self-mastery that the Mount Carmel Mystery School could offer me. My incessant desire was to expand my awareness and innate capacities, as well as to know union in God, while still retaining my physical body. There had been ones who had gone to Egypt and upon their return to Carmel shared their increased wisdom, motivating me to leave and trust my destiny to the gods and goddesses who had prepared Moses.

So it was that I arranged to travel by foot, cart, and camel with several of my Essene brothers, my daughter Aurianna, and some of my descendants. We joined a caravan of traders, and together with other immigrants, made our way by land to the Nile's delta. Our destination was On, a temple complex mostly in ruin, around which many Hebrews still remained since the Exodus. They lived in clustered village homes made of sandstone and mud bricks. You know this area by its Greek name Heliopolis. Very little of ancient On remains in your day because it lies buried below the Cairo airport and is engulfed by Cairo's sprawling metropolis.

During the next 303 years of my long life, I lived and worked in the ancient underground city of Tat, whose subterranean passages stretch all the way from the Great Pyramid to the seaside port you now call Alexandria. I also had access to a portion of the greater labyrinthine passages that are a part of the Inner Earth network some have called Agartha. To be sure, my friend, this is a truth that soon may be uncovered in your day. And even as I can see your generation, so shall you see the hidden events of my experience long ago, as we continue our walk together.

I invite you to join with me now as one who is prepared to labour within the vaults of time. I gladly do this because, as I have said before, I would have you succeed in your journey through this world of illusion and know the blessings of true vision as you behold your eternal Self. (My words in this chapter will refer to terms perhaps unfamiliar and esoteric. Many of these you'll find briefly defined in the Glossary (*see pages 290–95*) and most will be expanded upon as we continue my story.)

More than anything else, it was the remnant people remaining close to the earthplane through millennia of time, who drew me forth to ancient Egypt. Known as the Brother–Sisterhood of White Light, they have carried Shekinah/Sophia's (the Divine Mother, the intelligence behind all things) torch of wisdom that reveals the Logos/Gnosis' (The Word of Creation) hidden face. These are ones that remember from life to life, through the veils of flesh, their origins in that life eternal far beyond Earth's gravitational pull. These were my teachers, who cultivated my soul and awakened my mind to remember the Law of One.

The ascended masters – mighty Thoth and his consort, Seshat, embodied in form – were my most revered teachers. Serapis Bey, resplendent of countenance, was like a diamond of purity and power. There were also others, male and female, who towered before me in their bodies of radiant light and had mastered the physical plane. Ancient ones whose names do not matter, some recorded in history, and many others who choose anonymity. With these, I mingled both night and day. Then there were my spiritually impoverished brothers and sisters who walked as if asleep on the surface sands. The humble of the land were also my teachers as I occasionally walked among them, my mantle of compassion touching those who would be free.

Having come to Egypt, pulled here by the request of my soul and the Brother–Sisterhood of Light, I was as one ancient in the ways of wisdom, yet inexperienced in the flesh of my current incarnation. Focusing my energies, I pressed through the rigours of much training and discipline, which prepared me to move freely through the labyrinthine passages of our underground city. I was able to pass as a thief in the night through the outer temples of the city of On and the surrounding plateau, unseen by those who would take me hostage. So it was that I learned to live and work in a secret world, hidden from the eyes of those who would deride and cast into darkness the sacred truths of the One God.

Knowledge of passwords, frequency signatures, secret handshakes, symbols, and emblems were required to move freely within this cloistered world. These occult signs had come from a time so ancient that most had forgotten their actual origins. I became privy to such knowledge because of my lineage, because of my intense desire to know, understand, and practice esoteric wisdom. And most of all, I came because of the undeniable commitment within my heart to accomplish a Great Work that was hidden from my mind but felt as a fountain of living water sustaining my soul. Once I had adjusted to this new way of life, I laboured both day and night as one who required little sleep or the light of the solar sun.

Within the hidden vaults where I laboured were treasured scrolls of papyrus and parchment, and tablets of metal and stone. Some of the tablets were of gold, copper, bronze, and electrum. Some were of unknown elements said to have been brought by peoples who carried them to Earth from the stars. It was those treasures of wisdom whose mystery I desired to unravel that most intrigued and stirred my soul. I pursued the wisdom teachings as if they were fleeting birds, butterflies, and rainbows. These most ancient works held a magnetic attraction, etched by hands unknown yet known, which drew me irresistibly to Egypt and her libraries hidden beneath veils of stone.

The focus of my attention was upon the translation of records of the stars and of Earth's most ancient peoples into the Egyptian, Greek, Hebrew, and Aramaic languages. Other scribes had the task of bringing other languages, such as Sanskrit and Sumerian, to papyri, parchment, stones of clay, and thin metal tablets and scrolls. Our records were preserved in archival vaults. Most of my work was carefully etched with a stylus into sheets of damp clay before being brought to the attention of a council of scholars, who would then come to a consensus regarding the accuracy of my translation. When all was in agreement, I then transferred the letters and hieroglyphic patterns to documents of more fragile, yet more transportable, 'paper'.

Many labourers were employed in the making of papyri from the lotus plants that grew along the Nile. After weaving the dried, pressed fibres into lengthy sheets, one who was a member of our

Brother–Sisterhood carefully stacked the papyrus in a corner of my cell within the dormitory of the scribes. Here, below the sands of the desert, I took of the records hidden from the profane and made copies that could be taken back to Mount Carmel, the mystery school of the Essenes.

There was light sufficient for my seeing supplied by oil lamps and shining stones, which were anointed by those empowered Atlantean priests and priestesses who knew how to bring down the light of the sun god Ra. These were my teachers who still retained the secrets of light, sound, and colour. Through the use of concentrated thought and frequencies of sound, they directed the inner eye to its focused purpose. With charged hands they held amplifying rods and staffs as extensions of their minds and bodies to carve and lift mighty stones into their perfect places. It was in this way that ancient monuments such as the Sphinx and Great Pyramid were created, which your archaeologists attribute to slave labour. However, after many of the telekinetic powers had been lost, indeed, many slaves were used to build pharaohs' palaces, tombs, and temples.

There was adequate air in my underground chamber, which was supplied and circulated through ducts tunnelled ingeniously in stone from portals above to vast caverns below. In our initiations, we remembered how to breathe in such a way as to access the God force permeating all creation, thus not depending only on oxygen to maintain our being. Underground streams and aqueducts filled cisterns and quenched our thirst. Food was simple, supplied by those who tilled the diluvial soil of the fertile Nile. There were those of the Brother–Sisterhood who husbanded gardens and flocks. They took delight in serving those of us who sequestered ourselves away from the burning sun and the Nile's fresh breezes, which scattered rays of light into shimmering diamonds upon the flowing, blue waters above. Thus, our basic requirements were met.

Every other night I arose and went forth to the outer temples through doorways that were opened by the power of my voice. This I did to meet with companions and perform rituals known as the High Alchemy of Horus and the Magic of Isis – until the sun returned at dawn. The purpose of our coming together was to keep our bodies strong and to celebrate the cyclic seasons of Earth, Moon, Stars, and Sun. Through meditations upon the Sun and Moon we balanced our internal polarities and illumined our minds and bodies. We performed mystical practices that took us into the archetypal Garden of Paradise in which the 'Tree of Life' was revealed. Here we learned how to erect and climb the 'Ladder of Light' in order to harvest eternal, golden fruit. In this way and because of our internal illumination, we were able to live below the Earth's surface in relative comfort and security. Our physical lives, if we chose, could extend into many centuries so that we could render great service during one lifetime.

Eventually, I joined the very ancient Brotherhood of Tat, which gathered its members on the nights of every full and new moon. Also during the solar cycles and galactic portal days, we came together from many lands throughout the world. Some of us were immortal, having lived upon the Earth for thousands of years. Some were as I, freshly returned, growing in the remembrance of our Way, which illustrates Osiris' resurrection, Isis' immaculate conception, and Horus' archetypal journey into full enlightenment. We shared our wisdom with those of earthly flesh who desired to awaken and who prove by their progress that they could withstand the rigours of sustained discipline.

We brought ourselves into circles, mingling with upright stones that carried the inscriptions and frequencies of those worlds and stars beyond Earth's present season. We brought our records, data we had gathered as we traversed the Earth, and shared in our meetings the nature of humanity's evolution, conditions, concerns, and resolutions.

In some of your mystical literature, you have heard of the Dweller who resides deep within the Halls of Amenti. This one was our primary spokesperson, being neither male nor female. It was indeed an androgynous energy field that facilitated interdimensional communication. There were chambers of initiation where we would go from time to time to meet with the Dweller and remember who we were through space and time. Then, we would go forth to fulfil our various assignments and duties. Some arose and returned to light craft to observe and influence the affairs of Earth as decreed by Universal Law. Some walked among the populace of the lands of Earth as seemingly ordinary men and women. Others stayed obscure, hidden below. Such a one was I, until I had completed certain initiations, which would make me capable of playing my part by moving freely among the surface tribes of Earth to fulfil my destined part.

There was much to learn and much to remember. Fortunately, there were the records others and myself had kept during earlier eras. And there was always the true Self, who holds the mysteries whole and pure within the inner temple. I learned how to access this Self through stilling my mind and opening the seven seals or rings of power. These are known as the subtle energy centres yogis call chakras. There were methods for erecting the internal etheric rod of light, raising life force through the spine's three channels, and circulating cosmic energy through the physical body's staff of life or endocrine glands. I remembered who I was before the rising of Lemuria and Atlantis when I served the cup, the Holy Grail. And I remembered my promise to remain on Earth until all are lifted up.

Once I had gained a greater mastery of physical laws, I began taking my advanced initiations within the many temples that had been created by the ancient ones along the lower and upper Nile, some gracing oases and mountains on either side. I travelled deep into Nubia and beheld the spectacle of Ramses' tomb and the monument to my lineage you call Hathor. As I enacted the lion-headed Sekhmet's and Hathor's ancient creation rituals, I sang the Great Mother's praise, chanted mantras, and danced with timbrel, frame drum, and sistrum.

The Divine Mother's rites had become corrupted and her voice suppressed by the politics of priests and pharaohs who held to untransmuted lust, greed, and blind patriarchal dogma. Nevertheless, there were those of us who kept the way pure and untainted, though to be sure, even we were pressed to remember and pass on the energies in complete fidelity. Having access to reality that is beyond the human senses, we could see those who were invisible to untrained eyes. Yet, it must be acknowledged that, in our fervour to preserve the power of internal high alchemy through the darkened ages, we inadvertently created initiatory processes that hardened into secret rituals, cryptic codes, and elitist hierarchies, which made direct experience a most circuitous route. Many lost their way and confused the outer practices with that for which they sought. Few fully quenched their thirst by drinking the living waters poured directly from the Goddess' internal revelatory cup.

Forty years after my arrival in Egypt I completed my advanced initiations and began serving the Great Mother as a priestess of Isis, Hathor and Sekhmet, in addition to continuing my work as a scribe.

I developed the capacity to be conscious of many different dimensions and realities through astral travel (conscious 'out-of-body' travel), bilocation (splitting and projecting one's conscious awareness to another location, time-line, or dimension), and teleportation (destructurizing one's body into a more subtle form and projecting it to another location where it is physically reassembled). Through Isis' mysteries of resurrection, known as the Rite of the Sepulchre, I continued to regenerate the cells of my body as one of immortal youth. As the years went by, I became known as one who excelled in the mysterious arts and sciences of high alchemy.

Although I demonstrated wondrous spiritual powers, psychic gifts were not my primary focus. They were the means to an end and the natural by-products of my devoted discipline and love, by which I sought to serve the Creator and uplift the whole of life. Throughout my journey I became intimate with the full spectrum of the Great Mother's many faces and her creative powers. The attributes of the Goddess were expressed through me all my days, until my sojourn as the one called Anna was finished. My soul has served Her Grace through all my incarnations.

I became known as a high priestess of the Great Mother and received many initiates whom I taught how to cultivate the energies for which they were prepared to incarnate. I assessed their learning and capacity to hold high frequency light patterns coherent within their bodies, minds, and lives. I was, as it were, a psycho-spiritual counsellor. Eventually, my work took the form of assisting initiates to prepare themselves for the resurrection sepulchre in which they overcame the illusion of death. Thus, I laboured within the temple mystery schools assisting everyone, whether male or female, who chose to transmute his or her mortal soul's base dross into the gold of immortal enlightenment.

I share my Egyptian experiences with you as a way to assist your own evolution and empowerment. *Your life on planet Earth is your initiatory temple!* Christ consciousness is expanding exponentially everyday. My dear friend have you noticed that time is accelerating or that extreme polarities are becoming more obvious? Perhaps you are experiencing or know people who are having extraordinary, metaphysical (beyond physical) experiences. Have you seen in the media how science is validating realms of consciousness that just a few years ago were not considered possible or even relevant?

Once one begins to have the experiences of extrasensory phenomena as I did, the mystery dissolves and the realization comes that superconsciousness is the birthright of humanity. You do not need me in order to accomplish your heart's deepest desire to attain the enlightenment of a Christ. However, as a catalyst, through reflection and compassion, I am here to assist you into a greater awareness of ultimate freedom and union.

Because of the lofty nature of what I have been and will be sharing with you about my initiatory accomplishments, you might think of me as much more advanced than you and that the Great Work is beyond your capabilities. But I am here to reassure you that you would not be taking this journey with me and others, if you were not already well prepared. The essence of what we will accomplish together is more a remembrance than a learning of something new.

What I ask of you is to allow your awareness of the planetary awakening that is presently underway to increase day by day. With every step you take, the seen and unseen realms will support the comforting and encouraging realization that you are not alone. To help you with this, I encourage you to think of me as being very much like yourself. Indeed, if you were to see me in 'real' life, I would seem so ordinary that you might miss the chance of walking with me if you were looking for someone you thought to be 'spiritual'.

My job is to take you to the mountaintop where I will show you expanded vistas of your potential. Then, our real journey begins when we come down from the spiritual mountain and enter the valley of ordinariness and personal application. My beloved friend, please understand that those of us who demonstrate Christ consciousness support your choices to increase in wisdom so that you may also be of service to others as a model through your presence and actions.

～

Chapter 5

Alexandria

After completing my Egyptian initiations, a number of my fellow Essenes and I came together to counsel with one another in Heliopolis. We knew we would be soon returning to Palestine, and we agreed that it would be advantageous for us to move to Alexander's great seaport city, which had taken his name. So it was that I concluded my last thirty or so years in Egypt within this cosmopolitan Greek city situated at the mouth of the Nile delta.

Some of us entered into the rather extensive subterranean caverns under Alexandria because we were more comfortable in our familiar habitat below the Earth's surface. It was here that I again went underground. I spent my first nine years at Alexandria within a complex of hidden chambers, where I and my Essene brothers and sisters worked diligently to copy ancient and more current texts. We had brought many records from On, or Heliopolis as it was now called, of which we had made copies to give to Alexander's library in exchange for our sanctuary status. And more importantly, our willingness to barter our expertise as scribes gave us access to the ever-expanding treasure of sacred, philosophical, and historical works that were pouring into the massive library Alexander had built to impressively reflect his empire and his Hellenistic ideals.

There were those of us who worked above ground as liaisons, to secure our operations below and within the external library. Some of our community departed Egypt to return to Palestine early on and others lingered. I chose to continue my studies and the work of copying texts for the next twenty years. Needless to say, I had become very accustomed to my incognito identity and cloistered lifestyle. Yet, I knew it was time to begin preparing to rejoin my Essene community at Mount Carmel. This choice required me to gradually reacclimatize to the life of surface dwellers.

In order to deal with the harshness of the outer world, I began making expeditions into the great library and openly visited the nearby temple that was dedicated to Isis. I braved going into the marketplace. I had already made many secret visits to the temple and had become quite well known over the years to a number of high priestesses who served our Lady, as we called Isis. At last, when I felt at ease with the external chaos all around me, I agreed to take up my high priestess friends' invitation to live permanently in the priestesses quarters within the temple complex. Although I was still cloistered, I had successfully made the transition to being a surface dweller again.

I will also share with you that during my last hundred years spent primarily in Egypt, I also began to make voyages with others of my fellows to Britain, Greece, southern Gaul, and various Mediterranean islands. Most of these journeys occurred during my last years in Alexandria. I found my foreign adventures grandly uplifting and expanding for my soul. I especially enjoyed my sojourn in Britain, which I felt was like an extraordinary homecoming. While I was there I was adopted by a Celtic chieftain and became one of his daughters, although I was many years his senior. As I gazed into the probable future, I knew I would someday return to Britain's verdant hills and plains. Many years hence, I could see myself making preparations for my physical body to take its eventual rest on Avalon's fair isle. That, however, is for another telling.

Let us return to Alexandria and a brief biography of her namesake – Alexander the Great. Alexander of Macedonia was a student of Aristotle, who took his initiations in Egypt within the most sacred chambers hidden away from those blind to inner seeing. He was indeed a wise serpent, as initiates of the mysteries were often called, who knew how to lift the fiery serpentine energy up his spine and how to decipher the cryptic codes of the occult world.

Alexander supported and gathered to himself the Elect, the Magi, the Soothsayers, the Magicians, and the Doctors of body, mind, and soul. Long before leaving Egypt for my return to Mount Carmel, I chanced to meet Alexander in a secret council meeting when he was but a youth. Therefore, I looked upon him as a brother, though he was eccentric and was eventually seduced by the glamours of power in later years, when corruption entered his mind through a sickness that is common to those who compromise their souls. Though his years were short, his influence left a mighty legacy.

One day as I was making an excursion into the inner city, I looked up and saw Alexander's conquering banner waving above the monumental tomb that had recently been erected in his memory after he had died at the age of 33. All the peoples of Alexandria and the Nile's templed cities had felt heavily oppressed by the inept governance of the Ptolemaic Macedonian dynastic families. A teeming throng of humanity, to be sure, called Alexandria their home. Here was a large cosmopolitan city of such grandeur that I could not compare it to Jerusalem, except to say that Alexandria held far more wonder for my inquisitive soul.

Long it had been since I left Jerusalem and her defilement. From messengers who traversed the lands, I received word that Jerusalem had now become so corrupt and the ways of the Lord so distorted by politics and dissension that I found it a grievous sore upon my heart to think of returning to be within her towering walls. But, ah, to be in Alexandria, even with all her intrigue, violence, and suffering was a relief and a solace. In her port were harboured the boats of many distant lands, and among her narrow streets and wide boulevards were peoples of all colours, beliefs, and customs.

There was a facet of myself that took delight in the clamour, excitement and adventure of so much stimulation to my mind and senses. Yet, there was also another side of me that preferred the silence, the inner contemplative life, and the rejuvenating balm of nature. Thank God, I could enjoy both aspects here in newly born Alexandria, built over a remnant outpost of the Brother–Sisterhood of Light that came from Atlantis. Here, in the form of marbled halls and temples and great fortresses of granite and sandstone, were the monuments to humankind's evolution through time. Sequestered deep beneath the outer vaults was also a hidden city, as I have already revealed, not known by those who rioted, caroused, and numbed their souls. It was to this boon of ancient wisdom that I was drawn like a moth to an eternal flame, to be lifted up into the light of direct revelation.

From its very inception, Alexandria was destined to become an international melting pot. And it did, indeed, facilitate the merging of many different cultures: Atlantean, Egyptian, Cretan, Phoenician, Hebrew, Assyrian, Babylonian, Persian, Greek, Macedonian, and Roman. Yet, the predominant culture was Greek rather than Egyptian, so that, for all intents and purposes, it became a Greek outpost in Egypt that was essentially devoted to the cultivation of Hellenistic culture.

Those of Egyptian descent who were of the priestly line or the pharaonic lineage had temporary residences in Alexandria, where they were entertained. However, their primary residences were at Heliopolis, Thebes, and other cities along the Nile. Thus, their presence was honoured, but they had little influence upon the political and social environment of Alexandria until the incursion of Rome brought an end to the Ptolemaic dynasty. Cleopatra, who was of Macedonian descent, was allowed to reign as Queen of Egypt from 51 to 30 BC. On the other hand, those Egyptians of the working classes within Alexandria were held in subservience and had little opportunity to raise their social status through intermarriage.

The Hebrew population was especially welcomed for a number of years, during which they were accorded privileges comparable to those enjoyed by Greek subjects. However, this policy resulted in such a rapid increase of the Jewish population that they had aroused considerable resentment by the time I made my departure in 207 BC.

So it was, that during the months before my departure, I began in earnest to finish my library assignments and temple service, and make my farewells. Through the remainder of my days I would continue to feel Egypt's influence and in a future time my story will return to her ancient monuments.

When we meet again, my dear friend, we will take up the accumulated treasure of wisdom gathered in Egypt and make our way to my beloved Mount Carmel by the sea.

ᔐ

↪ Chapter 6 ↩
Anna's Return to Mount Carmel

B riefly now, let me share with you, my friend, the circumstances surrounding my departure back to the land of my parentage. That is, the parentage of my physical body; for indeed, my true parentage was the Father/Mother, Cosmic Birther of All Life. Now, in those last days, there was much preparation to be done before we could leave Alexandria. There was a company of us who would travel together, some going to Mount Carmel, others to Jerusalem and the recently redeveloped Essene community of Qumran near the Salt Sea. Fifteen of us would be departing together during the season of Atonement. Indeed, for us, this return to Palestine was a new beginning! The year was 207 BC, according to your Roman calendar.

We had engaged a sailing vessel owned by a Greek seaman who knew something of the Brother–Sisterhood, though he was not one of us. There were five women and ten men who would set sail. Some, like myself, were returning to Palestine. Several had been born in Egypt through the physical birth canal, while two were physical immortals like myself. These came along on the journey so as to enter into Palestine as members of our party, not calling undue attention to themselves. Mark and Thomas were the aliases they used, and their initial destination was Persia. Then, they would go on to India and the Himalayas to meet at the conclaves of adepts and masters. There, they would deliver manuscripts, give reports, and receive instructions and materials to be brought back to the mystery schools along the way. All of us were adepts of a high order, with specific work to do to prepare the way for the coming of the Teacher of Righteousness, He who was prophesied as the Messiah.

We gathered the records we had translated, which had been one of our primary purposes for coming to Egypt. These were placed in cedar boxes, glazed earthen jars, and hermetically sealed metal containers. Our activity was almost feverish, in the sense that we felt compelled to bring these records out of the underground vaults in as short a time and as inconspicuously as possible to the surface dwellers of Alexandria. There was much unrest among the populace, and those who were of Hebrew blood were suspect. We desired few, if any, to observe our departure with our treasure.

As I have already explained, long before the city of Alexandria was built over and around it, the seaside village of Rhakotis, overlooking the Isle of Pharos, had been used as a port through which the Brother–Sisterhood had passed to and from distant lands across the Great Sea. Fortunately, we had access to ancient underground passages that took us directly to the wharf. And so, within several days, we brought many freight boxes to the storehouse, from which they were then loaded onto our hired ship, along with our provisions. Our plan was to set sail on the night of the full moon, when the city was in slumber.

I had already said my farewells to my beloved friends and relatives, knowing well that I would return to Egypt whenever necessary, through the power of my will to bilocate, to carry on my esoteric work. Most difficult it was to say goodbye to the descendants of my beloved daughter, Aurianna; she who had been born when first I merged with Hannah long ago. This remnant of my family, many of whom had taken initiation and become adept in the mysteries, would remain in Alexandria, Heliopolis, and Thebes to play their parts by welcoming Him who would fulfil the prophecy that, 'out of Egypt, I called My Son.' Only one of these, my great-granddaughter Hismariam, came with me. She was one of the first of my many descendants to be born in Egypt. And of these, she was one of the few who had eventually mastered the secret of perpetual youth. Of her, I shall have more to say later on.

The destined hour of our departure finally arrived. The great Pharos Lighthouse cast forth its golden rays through thin veils of fog, and the full moon lit our way as we watched Alexandria's beacon slip into the mists. Our passage was unhindered, as the winds and natural current provided adequate thrust to our movement across the Great Sea. One of the brothers who came with us was called Philoas, and he was one whom I had known from time to time in my temple activities at Heliopolis, Memphis, Abydos, and Denderah. He had been a disciple of Socrates and had witnessed his trial and execution in 399 BC. For those who would know the truth, Socrates passed through that dark night to become one who was available to initiates on higher planes. He knew the way to resurrection and had passed the test.

Philoas warmed my heart with his robust presence and uncanny knack of foreknowing. He played the flute and lyre, lifting our spirits as we sailed. Indeed, I felt a deep connection with this brother, though there was no desire to consummate our heartfelt longing through our loins. To be close, hand in hand, was enough celebration of the life force to fulfil us. It had been a very long time since last I was taken to a man's warm bed.

Being with this one stirred memories laid aside while mastering the Shekem (life force) and claiming the rewards of celibate discipline involved in mastering the high alchemy of Horus. Occasionally, I had participated as a high priestess in the enactment of the Light Conception of Horus in order to learn the sexual energy practices of Isis with a partner. Although that expression was very rare, it was as if I were back in the priestess role serving Isis, suddenly feeling the intense rising of my sexuality, as the days passed in Philoas' company.

Surely, Philoas was opening me to look into my as yet unknown future. Perhaps a mate was forthcoming? Reading my thoughts, Philoas, chose to remain silent and became somewhat aloof. Alas, as my life's path unfolded, it would be many more years before I was called to stand with another beneath the canopy of marriage.

So you see, my friend, I, like you, have sexual urges and the desire for companionship. I, too, know well the stirrings within flesh to open myself to love's full tide and to fill my womb with the seed of man, remove the sting of barrenness, and bring forth the fruit of progeny.

We landed at the port of Ptolemais, just ten miles north of Mount Carmel. In ancient Phoenicia, this port had been known as Akko, and in your present land of Israel it is once again known by its original name. Awaiting us were a group of Ptolemy's soldiers and a tax collector. Also there to meet us was a welcoming party from Mount Carmel, including a young initiate and priest by the name of Matthias, about whom I shall have more to say later on.

Fortunately for us, we had papers from the governor of Alexandria, sealed by his own hand. One look, and with the convincing words of Matthias, all our goods passed inspection without being profanely opened to curious eyes. We gladly paid

Ptolemy his tax. Our preparation was paying off, not that a bribe was involved. It was a time when knowing how to ingratiate oneself with the powers of the land was necessary to accomplish our work among humanity. At times such as this, those who knew how to wield influence through wit, logic, and Hellenistic connections could overcome political obstacles. To meet any circumstance that required diplomacy, members of the Brother–Sisterhood were specifically trained to open doors that would otherwise remain shut.

From Carmel, Matthias had brought wagons pulled by oxen and donkeys. Our entourage and precious freight trekked slowly southward from Ptolemais, past tilled sod to the rocky precipice lovingly called Mount Carmel or fruitful garden. Moving inland, we made our way across the cultivated land that you presently call Haifa. Then, pitching and lurching, we wound our way ever upward over the rough-hewn, stone-paved highway. How my heart took flight as the winds bore the scent of cedar and pine! Thank God to be returned to this sanctuary that I loved above all others! Weariness fled as we approached the small pinery. I alighted from the wagon and ran ahead on foot. Though the grasses were parched and the air cold in comparison to the desert from whence I had come, ah, here was home, and I gratefully received her welcoming scented gifts, wafting in the autumn breeze.

Bells rang out, and the joyous clamour of children greeted us, as we were hailed by the community of the Essene Fellowship. Out to meet us came old and young. A high day it was for all, as we ran into each other's arms, singing and laughing. Then, after giving each beloved one an embrace and kisses on both cheeks, I ran up Carmel's thinly forested mount with winged heart and feet. Enraptured was I to greet each familiar tree. Now many were towering above me, where long ago I had known them as saplings. I threw my arms around these beloved friends, some ancient, having stood silently through the ages. Some had departed, taken to build edifices far away or to add to the monastery. I released them to their mutually agreed purpose to assist humanity.

Children pulled at my skirt while I was thus engaged in my reverie, returning me to the path that led to Samuel's sanctuary and my old room within the quarters of the scribes.

So it was that I, Anna, returned to my beloved Carmel in the year 207 BC after my 303-year-long sojourn in Egypt. How oft I had reminisced of her beauty and wide-open spaces, her towering trees, fresh breezes, and those precious beings who lived within her sanctuary of peace. Long had been the time since bringing all my focused energy and presence here to this sacred place. Now that I had returned, what lay ahead? To be sure, it was a mystery. Yet, there was also a knowing that the drama to unfold, for which I had prepared my soul for millennia, was at hand. Coming to myself, I ordered the affairs of my life to bend to the will of my higher mind. And so it was that I began the next phase of my long life to fulfil the great desire of my heart, which was to bring forth those characters who would support the coming of the High King, born of the lineage of David.

There were wondrous ones gathered at the Mount of Carmel, whom I would have you know. I shall begin by introducing you to those who still remained, even ones who were there when I took my departure to Egypt in 510 BC. First, there was Solomon, a worthy soul, head of the Essene order, who took the name of his forefather, Solomon the Wise. He was approaching nigh 500 years lived within his body. His days were soon to be accomplished, and he was preparing now for his transition to higher planes. I was deeply honoured to be with him as he took his journey back to his Creator Source, several years after my return.

Then, there was Timothy, as bright and jovial as when he was a lad beginning his initiations into the Essene Order, at the time I was preparing to leave for Egypt. He had come to Egypt at my invitation, and there I had prepared him for his work as a scribe and teacher of the Way. He had then returned to assume his duties over the Carmel library and the teaching of the young boys. His presence would continue to bless Carmel for yet some time. And later on, his great wisdom and devotion would be of great assistance in laying the foundation for the library at Qumran.

There was also Micah, who had spent his early years in the Temple complex at Jerusalem. He was one who knew the Mosaic Law forward and backward, as the different sects of Jewry understood it. He was also well versed in a portion of the original records that dated back to Moses and Akhenaten, which were secreted away in the vaults below the Temple of Solomon, where a remnant of the Brother–Sisterhood remained as its secret custodians. He observed and bore witness to the truth within the higher law whenever the opportunity arose to share his wisdom. He was grateful to be free from the intrigue and turmoil of Jerusalem in exchange for the simple, carefree life upon Mount Carmel. Micah had escaped, with several of his Essene brothers, when Jerusalem was besieged in 587 BC, during the reign of Zedekiah.

Memories continued to weigh heavily upon Micah's shoulders over the loss of lives and the imprisonment and torture of many of his family and brothers of the secret order. Nebuchadnezzar's hordes had eventually overrun Jerusalem's walls, and the entire city had been sacked and burned. Micah, too, had suffered injury. His limbs were broken and brutally crushed. Consequently, though he was an adept who had the power to heal, he walked with the aid of crutches through his many years. It seemed as though his soul gave him this reminder so that he might continue to choose compassion for those his mind would judge. Now, Micah, too, would soon take leave of his earthly duties of teaching and calling the congregation to prayer and ceremony. With this one, I would again be honoured to hold a beloved brother's ancient form within the shroud of white light as his soul slipped away one cold winter night.

Over the next two centuries I joyfully settled into my routine of sharing the wisdom teachings, initiating the mysteries, cultivating and gathering medicinal herbs, and giving my time and energy to our little community as it gradually expanded. Many new initiates came to Carmel to be taught and prepared to enter into the mysteries of the Way. Some of these initiates I had met while in Egypt. Most were yet to be born.

Remember, my friend, because I knew the way of cellular regeneration, I continued to extend my physical expression for quite some time. Every month I expanded my consciousness into my subtle light bodies. In doing so, I activated the Grail or Christ codes within my physical body as though I were pouring eternal life's liquid light elixir into every thirsty cell. This I had begun to do before my many years in Egypt. Having developed this ability to renew my body, I was indeed able to pass through the halls of time for century after century. It was as if the spindle of time had unwound itself according to my word and decree so that I appeared as one who did not age. I will have more to say about this later.

Records which have been unearthed, and those yet to be found, shall testify to the truth of my words describing my longevity. Yet, believe according to your capacity, my friend. For I tell you that what I have done, you may also do; and even more may you do in your day. So it is that I have come forward through these pages to bring the glad tidings of life everlasting, regardless of how long the soul is housed within a physical body. Thus, I invite you to partake of my words as though they were food and drink, allowing the essence of my words to stir the Holy Grail within you, so that you may fulfil your soul's destiny.

In pages yet to come, I shall share more fully the design of immortality and those rites of passage that facilitate consciousness to awaken the matrices of the physical and subtle bodies to receive ever-expanding cosmic energies.

❧ Chapter 7 ❧

Hismariam's Ascension

There was one in our community who had been with me in Egypt and who had accompanied me on the boat during my return to Mount Carmel from Alexandria. Her name was Hismariam, and as I have already said, through my daughter Aurianna, she was one of my descendants who had succeeded in mastering the secrets of cellular regeneration.

During previous lifetimes, her soul had been prepared by the Brother–Sisterhood to teach and exemplify virgin birth and physical immortality. In ancient Lemuria, she had graduated from the Naacal Mystery School. And in more recent times, she had incarnated as Tiye (pronounced tie-ee) the daughter of Joseph the Israelite, who was sold into Egypt. Although her identity has been concealed in your Bible, Tiye became the queen of Amenhotep III. Queen Tiye further merged the royal bloodlines of Egypt with those of the ancient Hebrews by giving birth to a number of children including Amenhotep IV, who took the name Akhenaten.

Queen Tiye was known for her ability to synthesize the Egyptian pantheon of gods and goddesses under the umbrella of 'One God'. Thus it was that through his mother's influence Akhenaten brought forth monotheism to the resistant Egyptian priesthood, who called him the 'heretic king' and later attempted to eradicate any trace of his revolutionary reign. Although unrecognized by many, it was also Tiye who was instrumental in her son's mystery school teachings of immortality and ascension.

Now, of Hismariam, I shall say further that she carried the energy that was later destined to come forth once again as a fully incarnated representation of what you term the Divine Mother. Through her choices to complete her initiations in this life, this one was prepared to play the role of Mary, whom your churches call the Virgin Mother.

I had always known Hismariam to be tireless and one so devoted to the ascent of humankind that there was nothing that could deter her from her focused purpose. She was illumined of mind and body. Indeed, I would not be exaggerating to say that she was the Mother Godhead incarnated in flesh. Yet, she was humble and completely unassuming, always asking what she could do for others. Simple in her ways and completely empathic, she was aware of every nuance of energy as it passed through and around her.

So it was that Hismariam and I prayed, talked and walked together within the sanctuary and upon the grassy hillsides of Carmel. During the course of our meditations, the specific details of the Divine Plan were gradually revealed to us. As a consequence, she and I agreed to allow her essence to gather within my womb in the appropriate timing. At that time I would be her mother again, as I had so often been through the cycles of time. We had played these roles of mother and daughter, holding the Grail Cup of the Divine Mother as our stewardship for humanity. The time was not yet, however; for there was still much preparation to be done to pave the way for her return in flesh.

Both Hismariam and I were high priestesses of our sacred order and were well acquainted with the processes of physical immortality. Thus, when it came time for me to assume my duties as one of the primary overseers of our Essene community and mystery school, it was well understood by everyone that she would become one of my chief assistants. She was, indeed, my dearest friend and companion, and over the many years that we served together in Mount Carmel, our relationship continued to deepen.

As the years progressed, Hismariam and I discussed how her transition from the earthplane would be accomplished. For many years we had been practicing internal alchemy so that our conscious awareness of our subtle energy bodies was greatly strengthened. We knew that consciousness could survive the dissolution of the physical body and that all our memory of our earthplane experiences would pass unhindered into the spiritual planes. The difference between most people who pass through death and initiates such as Hismariam and me is that we knew how to remain conscious while dying instead of 'falling asleep'. We also knew processes that gave us the option of choosing to either 'lay our gross physical body down' or ascend our physical bodies into a higher dimension.

Either way, we were in service to life. If the choice was to consciously slip our light body out of the physical focus, the physical elements that were 'left behind' were charged with higher states of ascended consciousness. Our interred bodies would continue to radiate benevolent blessings into the Earth Mother to assist her eventual ascension. If the choice was to ascend our physical bodies we could increase the frequency of the physical elements in such a way that we disappeared from the earthplane, thus ascending the physical elements of the Earth to the 'other side of the veil'.

The idea of consciously passing through death was not to remain identified with a body. We knew we were much more than a body. Our desire was to expand consciousness in such a way as to exemplify to humanity that life is eternal and that all who choose to reclaim union in God can rise beyond the limiting belief of being imprisoned in flesh. Our hope was that by evolving and mastering our own souls we could liberate collective consciousness from the fear of being lost in a wilderness of separate bodies and minds.

Hismariam's choice was to ascend her physical body into the light realms and when the time came for her to slip out of her earthly body's focus, we were ready. I remember well that peaceful evening when Hismariam confided in me that she had been directed to take her leave just before the dawning of the day that proceeded the Sabbath sunset. We both knew that it was time for her to reconnect in the higher realms of light with the One who would come through her loins after she returned to the earthplane as my daughter.

Hismariam had received guidance to take herself to that place near the top of Mount Carmel where, many centuries earlier, Elijah the Prophet had bowed his head to the ground after building his altar of twelve stones in the name of the Lord. She confidentially invited Judith, Josie Mary, and me to accompany her. Late that night, we quietly left the sanctuary and made our way up the mount to the top, bathed in the light of a setting full moon. Hismariam bade us sit on the benches, which were made from the plentiful flat stones along the meandering path. Judith took her position on a lower bench and Josie Mary found her place a little further on. Then, not far from the crest of the Mount, I was invited to sit and pray.

I continued to watch Hismariam as she made her way to the very top. The wind gathered her skirts and shawl and whipped them around her small, slender body. As she disappeared from my view, tendrils of her long, black hair caught the breeze, and the fragrance of roses and lilies permeated the air. Although my outer eyes did not see her glorious ascension, my inner eyes beheld an expanding globe of brilliant white light move out from her heart centre. I felt the very molecules of her body quicken and restructure into a much more refined form as she merged with a spiralling light. Then, as if the wind suddenly exploded with a whoosh through a vacuum, she was lifted up.

The three of us remained in our places until the first glimmer of easterly light began to gather. Then, hearing an inner signal, we all stood up simultaneously and walked to the place where Hismariam had taken her ascension. There, we wept in joyous exaltation, praising the Father–Mother of all life. Deep within our hearts, we knew that we had not lost our beloved sister, but had gained a witness to the highest truth that, no matter what we are called upon to do on this earthplane, life is eternal. And we also knew that when our time came, we each in our own way would follow the ascending footsteps of our beloved friend.

Then, the Spirit of Shekinah enveloped us, and we received that peace which passes understanding, each according to our allowing. Thus, the witness of the Holy Spirit penetrated us with deep peace and direct revelation so that we could understand the roles that we had agreed with the Councils of Light to play before we were born. Thus, we further conceived in our breasts the light of Christ, which prepared us to receive Hismariam when she would later return to be the mother of the Son of Man.

The sun had risen well above the horizon as we gently gathered up Hismariam's white, handspun linen robes that lay neatly folded where she had sat. After silently embracing each other, we took ourselves to the sanctuary and to the rituals that precede the Sabbath. It was not until the following day that our mouths were unstopped so that we could explain the circumstances that caused Hismariam's absence and comfort those who sorely missed her.

Not everyone in our community was able to understand her sudden departure. Some were grieved by her disappearance, thinking that perhaps soldiers who patrolled Carmel from time to time had taken her by force. However, there were high initiates in our community who knew the purpose for which Hismariam had passed through the physical veil. For the benefit of our youth and novices, her unannounced departure was used as a lesson to better understand the purpose of their initiations. Thus, our community began the process of preparing for the advent of the Messiah. I knew in my heart this was only the first of many signs that would help our people gradually wake up to a growing internal awareness that the time of His coming was nigh.

And what was the experience of those rejoicing beings on the other side of the veil welcoming Hismariam's return into the light? As I looked with my inner eyes, I saw legions of angels gathering her into their arms. Ever so gently they touched her with their healing energy as she continued to joyfully spiral upward through dimensional corridors. Pausing along the way to greet many hosts of beings, Hismariam joined a triumphal chorus until she stood face to face with the Radiant One who would be born into the earthplane through her loins.

I saw these two embrace one another and then they passed through a portal of great light. Although their humanoid forms did not pass across the threshold, I knew from my own experiences, that their consciousness was still intact. As I inwardly experienced them 'standing' before Councils of Light to give their report, to receive counsel, and to begin the next level of preparation for the coming enactment of the Christ mysteries, I also felt that a greater aspect of my consciousness was joining them in the meeting. Once again there would be an opportunity for us to gather our wisdom across all time and to bring our energy together to assist humanity and planet Earth to have the same experience Hismariam had so magnificently demonstrated.

Now that you have read my account of Hismariam's ascension, I would invite you to turn inward and contemplate your own life lest you believe that the ascension into Christ consciousness is only for ones such as Hismariam. Have you not noticed that the time it takes between your thinking something and its manifestation is far less than it used to be? Are you also witnessing that when your thoughts are accompanied by deep feeling, how much faster your desires or fears come into your physical reality? Have you not noticed increased synchronicities, déjà vu's, meeting people who feel very familiar, and the intensified emotional roller-coaster experiences that are occurring in your life? All of these events are benchmarks of awakening and ascending consciousness.

When you choose to be awake, aware, and feeling appreciation of all your experiences in every moment, while knowing that you are already enlightened and ascended, so it is. Coming to know that you are the path and the destination you seek is greatly assisted by meditation and internal energy practices. But know this, my beloved friend, ascension is not a destination at the end of a path that eludes you in a distant future. The only time union in God may be realized is NOW!

You are already, in this present breath, in the midst of your personal and planetary ascension into Christ consciousness! What remains is for you to simply choose union and to allow your Creator to express through you, just as you are. And know this, in the same way that Hismariam asked her closest friends to 'hold the space' for her, so may your ascending path be supported and accelerated when two or more gather together. When a group of souls are focused in the present moment with the aligned intent to know that the desired outcome is already so, miracles occur easily and effortlessly. And so it is that the consciousness of Hismariam, as the one you know as Mother Mary, is now joining with you and is being born into conscious expression through every diverse form and ascending heart!

૭

✍ *Chapter 8* ✍
Anna Reveals the Resurrection Mysteries

During the 150 years that bridged my return to Mount Carmel from Egypt and the beginning of the phase of my life in which I began to give birth to my numerous children, there were many changes made upon the political face of Palestine.

After Alexander the Great died of a fever in 323 BC at the age of 33, his Macedonian generals divided up the spoils among themselves. Although they had been skilled at war, they were, in most cases, inexcusably inept when it came to political governance and social reform. It was only a matter of time before their descendants began to do battle with one another for control of the lands that they had inherited. Shortly after my return to Mount Carmel, the storm clouds began to gather again.

When Hellenistic culture was enforced upon the Jews, the resulting political tension gradually increased until finally in 167 BC it culminated in the Maccabean revolt. Eventually an independent Jewish state was established in 142 BC, governed by the Hasmonian dynasty. One of the descendants of this dynasty was King Herod, who is known in your New Testament account. Much of the impetus that later created the Jewish Zealots and spurred the conservative fundamentalism of the Qumran Essenes derived from this divisive revolt, which was further amplified by the presence of conquering Roman soldiers and governors. It was within this context of political ferment that I settled into my life's daily routine in Carmel.

This was our situation in those troubled days that I began to go out from Mount Carmel to tread the fertile hillsides of Palestine with others of our Essene Order. First we went to the nearby villages in Galilee and then to the towns and cities of Samaria and Judea in the south. I often journeyed to Capernaum on the Sea of Galilee and Qumran on the Salt Sea, or the Dead Sea as it has come to be known. Along the coast of the Great Sea, which you now call the Mediterranean, I made my way by boat from Ptolemais to Tyre in the north and to Joppa in the south. The Plain of Sharon, which extends along the coast all the way from Mount Carmel to Joppa, was well known to me.

I also trekked northwards, following the River Jordan beyond the Sea of Galilee to its source, and upwards I climbed to an ancient sanctuary near the top of Mount Hermon. I made a pilgrimage to an even more ancient sanctuary high on the slopes of Mount Ararat. No further during those years, by land or boat, did I travel in my body of flesh as do most pilgrims; however, I teleported and bilocated to any number of places and across many timelines.

As a high priestess of the Order of Essenes, I now had a sacred responsibility to reach out to our people. Yet, we who were from Mount Carmel were neither zealous nor fanatical in our evangelism, as some might think. Rather, our work was quiet. To those with ears to hear, we brought the Way of the Teacher of Righteousness (the wisdom teachings that reveal the right use of energy). However, only those who were receptive to our message did we invite to join our Order.

My reasons for making my pilgrimages were twofold. The first I have already explained; however, the second reason is much more hidden. I will now introduce you to some of the little understood resurrection processes I used as a Teacher of Righteousness to maintain my physical body from generation to generation.

In addition to deep, daily meditation, in which I disengaged from the tribal consciousness belief in suffering, disease, and unconscious dying, I also took myself for extended periods into sequestered silence away from any possible distraction. As you may recall, I said that I had mastered the Rite of the Sepulchre in Egypt. Therefore, it was possible for me to go into states of consciousness that the Hindus call samadhi or union in God, during which time my physical vital signs were indiscernible, and in some cases, nonexistent. Yet, my body remained sweet and vital. Because I chose to continue to abide on the earthplane in order to extend my days of service, I did not master the higher states of samadhi that would have caused me to become completely absorbed in God. Thus, in order to attain my purpose on the earthplane, there were times when it was required of me to enter the lesser states of samadhi, not only for a few weeks of rejuvenation and rest, but to remain in suspended states of animation for many years.

Indeed, there were periods in which my physical body abided in such states for a generation or more, so that when I resumed my walk upon the Earth, ordinary society around me thought of me as one of them without raising questions or fear. Those of our Essene Fellowship who knew the Way of the Teacher of Righteousness kept its practices strictly guarded, supported each other's bodies during our 'vacations', staged funerals, provided aliases, and offered understandable explanations for our rather mysterious comings and goings.

I'm sure if you were to stop and imagine yourself chronologically older than everyone around you; you might begin to understand the rather delicate situation that a physical immortal experiences. After all, how would you explain to someone who didn't understand physical immortality how you could live for hundreds of years? Although you might look like a youthful adult, would you openly admit that you were the ancestor of hundreds of descendants, most of whom had died, and some of whom are presently living and appear older than you?

Often when I took myself out into the surrounding countryside to serve our Essene communities and to visit my descendants in their various villages, I would go to the secret places that supported rest and regeneration. These places are known to the Brother–Sisterhood of Light and have been preserved through the rises of civilization. They are always protected from the uninitiated, the naïve curiosity seeker, or plundering thieves. There were three primary sanctuaries that supported my cellular regeneration. The one I most frequented was within a cave at Mount Carmel. The other two were in caves near Qumran and Mount Hermon. These three caves acted as a focus of triangulated energy that was held constant by the priests and priestesses who facilitated the caves' maintenance and served the adepts who came there.

Within these caves were stone sepulchres carved to precise dimensions, inscribed with magical prescriptions and life-sustaining antidotes, and filled with a peculiar kind of living plasma that had the consistency of amniotic fluid. Anytime I desired to rest and regenerate, I always went through a period of purification and an extended fast, accompanied by deep meditation. If it was time for me to be 'away' for a while, I was prepared for the full Rite of the Sepulchre.

You might well ask, 'Why would a soul as evolved as mine choose to undergo the rigours of the Rite of the Sepulchre and the potential dangers of lying in suspended animation?' My reasons for doing so were multifold. First of all, I was deeply guided from within to remember how to preserve and resurrect a physical body for short and extended periods, which I later came to understand was a preparation for me to teach my grandson, whom you call Jesus, how to resurrect his body. Secondly, I personally preferred to maintain my physical body, as long as it served my soul's purposes, instead of passing through the rigours of the birth canal and infancy or 'walking into' a body again.

My desire was to master the laws of the physical plane and spiritual immortality, remain in service to humanity as one who appeared quite ordinary, and then when my soul had accomplished all that I had come to do, eventually take my ascension. My few experiences with ascended beings informed me that their visitations into the density of the earthplane were infrequent and that when they came to assist humanity it was for short periods of time. At some point, 'popping in and out' as an ascended master would also be my choice, but for now I was content to linger close to humanity and Mother Earth as long as I was guided to do so.

After going through the appropriate Rite of the Sepulchre purification rituals, I then proceeded into a deeply altered brain state. When I reached the desired state in which my body was asleep, and my consciousness was identified completely with my higher light bodies, my anointed physical body, or Khat, was wrapped in swaddling clothes. These are similar to the cotton and linen shrouds that are used in mummification. The cloths were saturated with essential oils known to preserve and regenerate tissue. If I were to go through a relatively brief regenerative process, my swaddled body was placed on top of the sepulchre or inside without the lid put in place. In such circumstances my face was exposed, except for a napkin that fluttered with my returning breath, signalling to the attending priest or priestess that my body was becoming animated.

If I were to be 'away' for several months or for an extended period of many years, my entire body was carefully wrapped and placed inside the sepulchre where a nurturing 'amniotic-like fluid' or 'molecularly restructured water' had been poured, facilitating a state of suspension or antigravity. Attending priests and priestesses then hermetically sealed the lid of the sarcophagus once it was levitated into its precise position. So it was that all the elements of the Rite of the Sepulchre acted in complete synergy.

At times, appearing in my Ka (etheric twin), I returned to the cave and hovered near my physical or Khat body to support its regeneration. At such times I was quite visible to those who were guarding the sepulchre, and we communed together and gave my physical body the appropriate healing energy that it might require. Most of the time my consciousness was elsewhere, even visiting other planets. I especially enjoyed going to the Hathor healing temples on Venus and continuing my studies at the higher spiritual universities located in the Pleiades and Sirius B. There, I was prepared for my role to be the mother of Mary and the grandmother of Him who would publicly demonstrate the Way of the Teacher of Righteousness – the way of a Christ.

When it was time for my return to the earthplane, I made my presence known to an overseeing priest or priestess, who supported me in my full reentry into my physical body. The silver cord or secret channel that always remained connected to all my bodies was charged with life force and then I spiralled back in much the same way as I had spiralled out. The lid was unsealed and I was lifted out of the sepulchre, unwrapped, bathed, and given liquids to drink. It usually took a number of days, sometimes weeks for me to fully regain my physical faculties. All of these experiences assisted my soul to evolve and to prepare for my coming work on the earthplane.

You may think I am fabricating a fairy tale, or at best, science fiction. Yet, I assure you, my friend, that as the approaching Golden Age reveals this ancient science of physical and spiritual immortality, you may awaken to super-consciousness and remember what we called The Way of the Teacher of Righteousness, the Grail Codes of Light. These presently lie dormant within the sepulchre you call your body and the larger sepulchre that is the unconscious material world, and they are rising in resurrected consciousness. Although you may think that my life was more significant than yours and my level of self-mastery greater than you can attain, I am compelled to emphasize once again, that you, too, are remembering your soul's past and future lifetimes of mastery, which are now culminating in your everyday life. You may make different choices to serve others through your self-mastery than I demonstrated. Yet, regardless how you express your full divinity, I am here to catalyse you into resurrecting the indwelling Christ, your true Self, who always knows the way.

Thus, you can see that I knew well the initiatory process of 'crucifying' my separate identity as a physical body and ego, laying that small self to rest, and resurrecting my vaster consciousness that is always in union with my Creator. The crucifixion initiation, as it has been taught by those who attempt to control the masses through fear, would have you believe that atonement – to be at one with God – is accomplished through suffering and blood sacrifice. I reassure you that suffering is the consequence only when the 'separate self' resists being at one with God. When God–Goddess is realized as the source of love, the only sacrifice required is the willingness to offer up one's arrogant sense of separation, so that love can claim its own.

Over a long span of years, I continued to participate in the ritual of the Rite of the Sepulchre. As time passed and my mastery increased, I had the opportunity of initiating others into the mysteries of the crucifixion and resurrection initiations. With the continuing passage of time, I gradually arrived at a clearer understanding of the nature of my assignment to prepare the way for Him who was soon to come. I also realized how it was that all my experiences would serve a greater part. But first a cast of characters who had agreed to play our supportive roles had to be provided with opportunities to enter upon the stage. And so it was that I passed across the threshold of celibacy in order to experience a more expanded compassionate love that can come through conscious, sacred relationship and childbearing.

ᔕᓂ

∽ Chapter 9 ∽

Matthias and Joseph of Arimathea

Now, I will remind you that there were wise ones who travelled a far wider range than did I during those years when I awaited my calling to bring forth the children who would be the Radiant One's support team. These were of a very ancient fellowship called the Order of the Magi. Some came from the Fertile Crescent and the Far East, while others came from Britain, Egypt, and Greece. For centuries, they had come to Mount Carmel to partake of our library and to exchange with us the most ancient wisdom that was preserved within their respective traditions.

To be an Essene, as most of us at Mount Carmel chose to practise our understanding, was truly to be one who was receptive to a full spectrum of light. You could say that we were cross-pollinated by the many wisdom teachings that were disseminated by the wise ones who came and went like the wind. Ours was more a way of life than what you would call a religion. Thus, we were as knowledgeable about Gautama Buddha and Zarathustra in more recent times as we were about Akhenaten and Moses in olden times and Krishna, Isis and Osiris in ancient times.

Our eclectic and ecumenical tradition allowed us to honour all perspectives, thereby enabling us to appreciate all the various names that the One God–Goddess had acquired in many different cultures and languages. Our teachings were transmitted primarily by oral rendition and by our living example. However, we also kept written records. Some of us were gifted scribes, and many of us knew a multitude of tongues. Yet, all in all, we were primarily of Hebrew descent and our communal language was Aramaic.

In all the ways that I have shared with you, my friend, I engaged myself for over four hundred years. Now the time has come in the telling of my story in which I desire you to know me as a woman with human emotions much like those you experience when it comes to intimate relationships. Indeed, as I came to embrace life more fully and prepared myself to bring forth Hismariam again as my daughter, I drew to me a mate, a divine mirror. Thus, I came to know my Self in ways not known during my previous long years.

As the days passed, I began to feel a flow of energy that I had not experienced for quite some time. A desire for joining with another grew stronger and stronger. I knew this was my internal guidance preparing me to take the necessary action to fulfil my part in bringing forth the host of characters who would co-create and enact the Christ resurrection drama as it was secretly taught and portrayed in the mystery schools. As I felt irresistibly pulled to the canopy of marriage, I made myself known as one eligible for the nuptial rites.

There were several brothers among our Carmel community who felt drawn to me. One of these was Matthias. He was the son of Matthias, a Levite high priest, and the grandson of Matthias the Elder who had come to the port of Ptolemais when I returned to Mount Carmel from Egypt in 207 BC. Another was Timothy, who kept the library. Matthias, in contrast to Timothy, was much younger in years and had not accomplished full mastery of all the initiations available at Carmel. I understood that either of these high initiates would be appropriate.

My heart was drawn to Matthias. His love of nature and his ability to grow the most beauteous flowers and the most nurturing of produce was a delight to my soul. This, together with his genuine interest in the welfare of our community and his devotion to God, made him my favoured candidate. And, I confess I also honoured the Hannah aspect of my human nature that was attracted to Matthias because his soul had previously incarnated as Tomas. You recall that Tomas was Hannah's betrothed sweetheart who had been captured and taken away to Babylon before I 'walked into' Hannah's body. From some deep place within my heart, a desire arose to somehow fulfil Hannah's unrequited love.

We allowed a period of courtship, which took us away from our usual occupations for short periods of time so that we might draw our soul essence together, as well as our personas, into a more intimate understanding of one another. We found compatibility and soon, within weeks, we were betrothed. Our betrothal took place in the fall of 58 BC after the harvest. A wondrous feast was prepared for us. The whole community of Carmel was in celebration. Much merrymaking lifted everyone's spirits, for they had known us as ascetic celibates for more time than most could remember. Much laughter and sincere well-wishing turned our feast-day into a high day for Mount Carmel.

Near the time of winter solstice, Matthias and I met beneath the canopy to exchange our rings and speak our vows. And on the eve of the year's longest night, I found myself with child. Now, let me say further that this child's conception was overseen by the Brother–Sisterhood of Light. Into my womb was placed the very essence of this one's great soul, and the seed of Matthias also received high frequencies of light that would allow this child to grow in awareness beyond earthly limitation. I will always be grateful to my husband, Matthias, for so profoundly opening me to the wonders of nuptial bliss and Light Conception.

I initiated Matthias, who had always been celibate, into the mysteries of Isis. Remembering my experiences in her temples, I guided Matthias in the ways of her sexual energy practices in which the sexual energy is lifted upwards and the consciousness of the couple is resurrected into unity until they mutually attain states of bliss. It was into this high state of love that our child's soul was invited to enter the physical plane. And so did we consciously nurture him with our love through the months that he was in my womb.

Intimate relationship with a man and the bringing forth of children was a gift of such deepening awareness I wondered why I had not allowed it before. Yet, as I have contemplated the price of the deepening, I have realized that the opening came through the breaking of my heart, which I had avoided. The recalcitrant pain that had lodged in Hannah's wounded heart, gave me every reason to postpone marriage. As an initiate, I had transmuted much discordant emotion. Yet, I realized that I had, nevertheless, avoided the intimacy of love by justifying my prolonged celibacy as the path of least distraction, as I bent my personal will to that of Spirit's.

How comforting it was to feel Matthias' gentle touch and how awesome to celebrate life within my ancient, yet youthful body! My daughter, Aurianna, had passed on over four hundred years ago. So at this point her descendants were many. Most of these still lived in Egypt. Some were at Carmel and others were in the surrounding communities of Galilee and Judea. Thus, when my time for delivery arrived, there was a great gathering of my descendants who came for the circumcision and naming of our first son.

Our son was born on the cusp of Virgo and Libra in the year 57 BC, according to your Gregorian calendar. Because he was of the lineage of Joseph the Israelite, who had been sold into Egypt, we chose to name him after his forefather. As Joseph, our son was known by all.

This gifted child was reared with great love and devotion. At a most tender age, I took him to my knee and spoke to him of the lineage of our people Israel, or Isis Ra Elohim, as I liked to say. I recited wondrous stories of ancient Egypt and other places I had travelled. I told him, as well, how I had spent time in Britain and had been adopted into a royal Celtic family who initiated me as a Druid priestess. His mind was like a sponge, absorbing all that I could give him. And still he thirsted for more.

It was a year and a half after Joseph's birth, while our love was still strong for each other, that Matthias and I conceived a girl child. We called her Martha. She was steady and resolute, gifted with wisdom of the hearth and a talent for managing details. She, like Joseph, would play her part in our unfolding story.

Now I will share more fully about Joseph whose life would continue to play a key part in the divine plan. Because Joseph eagerly took to linguistics, we taught him our native Aramaic language between the ages of one and two. Then, between the ages of two and three, I introduced him to the Hebrew tongue and fiery letters. During the following years some of the Celtic language that I remembered became the focus of our attention because of its basic affinity with Hebrew. At the age of six he was introduced to the Persian and Sanskrit languages. Greek came next, followed by Egyptian. Latin, the formal language of the Romans, was somewhat reluctantly introduced into Joseph's curriculum when he was eleven.

The reason for our procrastinating the introduction of the Roman language was because of the bitter taste that still lingered over Pompey's Roman Legions invasion of Palestine in 63 BC. The political strife between the aristocratic Sadducees and the orthodox Pharisees had caused Rome to intervene. Jerusalem had been besieged and nearly 12,000 Jews had been slaughtered. By the end of 63 BC, all of Palestine had been incorporated into the Roman province of Syria and made a tributary of Rome. And, to make the situation even bitterer to my taste, Rome had reintroduced crucifixion as punishment for any form of resistance, in order to control the people. The emotional shock was profound when I happened to pass along the roads lined with crosses. It seemed that I could never close my heart to the suffering of the people. Would humanity ever learn the true meaning of the cross as the symbol of spirit joining matter?

Matthias adored his son, yet he could not offer Joseph the same learning as I could. Consequently, there began to be a tension that arose between us with regard to Joseph's upbringing. A shadow of jealousy and self-criticism eroded Matthias' mind. Though Joseph loved to go with his father out into the fields and gardens and to walk hand in hand beneath the canopy of stars, his preference was to come with me and spend endless hours researching the ancient scrolls within the library. Thus, Matthias felt that he had lost his son, and, blaming me for the intense loss that he felt, he began to distance himself from me. Our bed became one filled with thorns instead of sweet-smelling roses.

As the months passed, Matthias drew a cold blanket of distance around himself. His many years of celibacy began to invite him back into a 'safer', more ascetic life, which protected him from feeling the emotional undercurrents that disturbed our family setting. My heart was sore, and I felt remorse over the loss of my husband. Yet, what could I do? Joseph was as he was, and Martha preferred to be with the women. Knowing that there is a divine purpose behind everything that occurs, I simply placed my trust in God and did my best to accept our situation.

Several months after Joseph's fourth birthday, Matthias decided that it would be best for all concerned if he moved to the Essene community at Qumran, which was located near the Salt Sea, about 80 miles to the southeast of Carmel. He approached this as an experiment, thinking that perhaps it would be only a temporary separation; however, I knew in my heart that our marriage was no more. Every few months, he made brief visits to Carmel to be with his children. But, with me, he felt a wounding and would not suffer himself to take me to his bed. So we took our case to a council of Elders within our community and petitioned for an annulment of our vows, even though we did not find in one another any grievance of sin. It was an unusual request, yet the council granted our petition. And thus, Matthias was free to express his exceptional gifts and extraordinary devotion within the gardens of Qumran.

Matthias enjoyed peace and contentment at Qumran until 37 BC when he died of wounds suffered when he resisted Antony's Roman

Legions at the time they burned Qumran to the ground on the orders
of King Herod the Edomite.

Following Matthias' departure from Mount Carmel, much of my
attention was devoted to preparing my son for the role that I knew
he was to play in the sacred drama, which even now was unfolding.
So, Joseph grew in stature. His capacity to learn far exceeded mine.
He read and expounded the Mosaic Law and the ancient records
with anyone willing to engage with him. He especially loved the
magi who came from afar. His soul took flight while listening to their
stories. At the age of twelve, he was drawn to travel with these wise
ones. It was not easy to let him go, yet I knew I must.

Joseph was taken to Alexandria's great library to study and
then he took initiations in the temples of the Nile. Next he travelled
through Parthia into India. He became well versed in the teachings
of Zarathustra, Buddha, and Krishna. High into the Himalayas he
trekked without purse or scrip. For several years, he lived among
the saints and masters. Some of these were physical immortals,
such as the one called Babaji, whom you know in your day as the
revered father of the Kriya Yoga lineage. It was this beloved master
who would also be a guru to the Son of Peace, although some stories
say that Babaji was my grandson's disciple. Although it creates
confusion for those who do not experience life in unity, in truth it
matters not who be guru or disciple when avatars (those who fully
incarnate God consciousness from their youth) meet one another.
They clearly reflect divinity in the mirror of Oneness.

When Joseph returned to Carmel as a young man in his early
twenties, he joined his acquired learning into that of our community,
thus enriching us all. He was indeed a bright light. For the next few
years, Joseph created home bases at Mount Carmel and Qumran.
He translated the scrolls that he brought from Tibet, India, and
Mesopotamia. During this time he delivered as many of these
records as possible to our Essene community at Qumran. There
he assisted the Brethren to place strong energy barriers around the
chambers in which the records were placed.

We had come to feel great concern for our library at Carmel, not
knowing if or when the Roman Legions might turn on us, as they had
upon Qumran in 37 BC at the insane insistence of King Herod, who
was incensed that the zealous Essenes at Qumran were unalterably
opposed to his rule. The conservative and rather militant Qumram

community considered him not only unfit to govern because of his corrupt morality but also because he was a descendant of Esau rather than Jacob.

Qumran, in spite of Herod's hatred, was now beginning to revive, albeit with an increased sense of caution among the two new sects among the Jewish people: the Zealots, who militantly opposed Herod's corrupt rule, and the Herodians, who actively supported it. Nevertheless, because of Mount Carmel's vulnerable position, Qumran seemed the better place to keep our precious records during this time of great uncertainty. Later in AD31, after Qumran was the epicentre of a massive earthquake, Joseph conceived a plan for disseminating much of the Qumran and Carmel library to scattered Essene communities throughout the greater region of the Mediterranean and the British Isles, especially the larger isle called Albion.

In 32 BC, a member of the Order of the Magi who was visiting Mount Carmel invited Joseph to come to Britain and enter into the initiations understood by the Council of Druids. Joseph had already met some of the Druid magi while in Egypt. The Druids were a remnant that preserved the wisdom of ancient Atlantis (and even more ancient Pangaia) upon the British Isles.

Even before Moses took the Hebrews out of Egypt, he sent representatives of all Twelve Tribes of Israel to establish colonies in Albion. Britain had also received some of the 'lost' tribes of Israel during the Assyrian and Babylonian captivities. Through intermarriage the Hebrews had emerged as the Celts during the many years they moved from the Middle East across Europe. As these migratory waves mingled, the isle of Albion became known as 'Brith-ain', which is a Hebrew word that means 'The Covenant Land'.

So it was that in the spring my son made the first of many trips to Britain including journeys to what you call Ireland, Scotland, and the lands surrounding the northern shore of the Great Sea. In Britain, Joseph began the long initiatory process that eventually saw him an Arch Druid in his old age.

Shortly after returning to Palestine from his first pilgrimage to Britain, my son conceived the idea of owning and operating a fleet of freighting boats that primarily carried tin and lead ore. Also, having acquired partial ownership of two mines in Britain, he was now qualified to become a minister of mines in the Roman Empire. These credentials and resources provided him with a perfect cover for secretly transporting initiates and documents to Britain and to other Essene libraries located throughout the mountainous regions surrounding the Great Sea.

So it was that Joseph developed his entrepreneurial and diplomatic skills. Over the next ten years with the aid of the Druid councils he purchased and amassed a fleet of twelve boats. From that point on, it became his practice to make at least one trip to Britain every year.

Now that his wealth and influence were becoming quite noticeable within the administrative structure of the Roman Empire in Jerusalem, he began to come to the attention of a wealthy Hasmonean prince. Arimathea was his name and he was a member of the Jewish high judicial and legislative body called the Sanhedrin. He had inherited lands in Samaria from his Macedonian forebears. This large estate was located in southern Samaria on the caravan route between Galilee and Judea. Arimathea took a strong liking to my son, and he offered his eligible daughter named Eunice Salome in marriage. This arrangement would further their ambitious visions. Consequently, the marriage was arranged and celebrated in Jerusalem in the summer of 29 BC.

Arimathea saw in Joseph a prodigy who could set aright the corruption that currently was sowing so much strife in Jerusalem. After marrying into the Arimathea family, my son began to study the law of mediation with his father-in-law who took Joseph to his bosom, not only as his son-in-law, but also as his adopted son.

It was at this time that Joseph became an adjunctive representative from Galilee and Samaria to Jerusalem's Sanhedrin. Shortly thereafter, he moved to Jerusalem to make his home among the wealthy and the learned. There, he served for many years as an influential advisor. Thus, Joseph acted as a liaison between the many factions and sects that were often in conflict. His mastery of languages and his knowledge of human nature made him respected by all. Though he could at times be cool and reserved, he was always available to those in need and to those of the Brother–Sisterhood who knew him as an adept. His three residential properties in Jerusalem were strategically placed so that he had access to underground passages known by the Brethren of Solomon's secret orders. The descendants of these secret orders became known as the Cathars, Templars and many of the ruling families of Europe.

Joseph continued through his long life to practice the sciences of longevity for which the Essenes were publicly known, as well as the esoteric science of physical immortality, which very few understood or dared to practice. Thus it was that Joseph made himself available to many people. While he served the masses outwardly, he quietly and freely gave his unusual talents and example of devotion to the hidden orders of the Brother–Sisterhood of Light.

Although I have got ahead of my story, I desire to lay a foundation for what is to come by telling you about the early years of my first-born son, Joseph of Arimathea.

᭡

◈ Chapter 10 ◈
Anna's Light Conception Initiation

I have given you a rather lengthy overview of Joseph of Arimathea because he was to play a key role throughout most of the remainder of my life. Now let us go back to the time of Joseph's fifth birthday, shortly after his father, Matthias, moved from Carmel to Qumran in late 53 BC.

The rearing of Joseph and Martha was now my responsibility, and I devoted myself wholeheartedly to this task, knowing that I had the full support of the entire Essene community at Carmel. I welcomed these responsibilities with heartfelt gratitude and did not allow my feelings, for the most part, to become contaminated with grievance, when from time to time, I reflected upon the loss of my husband. Yet, my loins had been opened, and the flesh of my body given in marriage. Awakened in my soul was an intense desire, which I experienced as an unquenchable flame.

This passion I had known before, particularly in Egypt. There, I had learned how to channel this great energy up my spine and throughout my body. I consecrated my sexuality for cellular regeneration and spiritual enlightenment. So I had continued to use the life force of Sekhem through all my days. Even though I had been a handmaiden of Hathor and Isis, giving my energy to the enactment of mystical marriage with young initiates, both male and female, who came into the temples to be opened to high tantric alchemy, I was never married. I was married to the eternal Beloved, who is One with the source of my being – Yes! But, did I know a man to whom I fully gave my heart? No, the nuptial bed had not been my choice.

Yet, here I was now, as one adrift. For I had been opened to a world of feeling that before I had missed. I practised all the wisdom I had gathered. I circulated this great force, transmuting my emotions, which seemed to gather as a mighty storm. The cresting tides of emotion would be calmed only to gather once again into tidal waves breaking upon the shore of my heart and soul. Shaken indeed was I, as at few times in my long life. I asked to know the meaning of this great surge of the life force running rampant in every cell. How was I to deal with this intense energy and for what purpose?

Though I occupied myself with every moment given to the tasks at hand, the days seemed to stretch long, and the few hours of my sleep were restless and feverish. I seemed to be burning with a love energy that was taking me into realms of feeling within my body that I had not known possible before. A great compassion filled my soul for those who had come to me in the past, consumed by these flames. Then, I had dismissed the intensity of their experience and had sent them off to cool according to the ways I had known to accomplish quiescence in myself.

Could they have felt as I was feeling now? If so, then I had been amiss in serving them. Nothing that had once calmed the tide of emotion and the flames that burned my heart and loins seemed to work for me now. I knew no one in our compound I could go to for advice. However, in keeping this immense energy secret within myself, I became increasingly aloof and distant. These were the very behaviours I had found difficult in Matthias. Instead of my usual patience and stillness, I found myself an irritable shrew, a side of my nature I had glimpsed only occasionally before.

I continued to oversee the probationary initiates of Carmel. I instructed the young maidens to know how to receive their flowing of blood as an endowment of the Great Mother. I assisted the young men regarding the ways of honouring their manhood and the conservation of their seed. We observed sacred rituals and ceremonies that consecrated and graduated each novice to the status of a probationary initiate of the mysteries within our Essene Order. Now that sexual life force energy was running rampant within me, I understood with compassion the energies that ran through the young blood of our community's growing number of adolescents.

Then, one night, in a profound, life-transforming dream, Isis, Osiris, Hathor, and Horus took me to a receiving chamber where I had gone in the past to be initiated into the secrets of cellular regeneration. Here, they told me that it was time for my physical body to be strengthened and prepared for the entry of highly evolved souls through the process of Light Conception. I was shown that I would become the mother of a girl child to be called Mary who would give birth to the promised Messiah. I slowly began to realize that from my womb humanity would receive a great gift.

As I contemplated the gift of motherhood opening up to me, I felt the wondrous presence of Isis, a Mother of Mothers. As my dream continued, Isis, Osiris, Hathor, and Horus beckoned me to lie upon a massive altar of luminescent pink crystal that was in the centre of the chamber. It was carved round, and into the very centre was placed a six-pointed star, the Seal of Solomon, made of molten gold imbedded with polished emeralds, sapphires, garnets, topaz, rubies, and diamonds. As I lay on the altar, I became aware of twelve great beings of light – each stepping into the chamber through a separate door. Some I recognized; others were new to me. These gathered around the altar to form an outer circle. Their right arms were raised toward me while their left arms rested on the shoulder of their neighbour. This action focused their intent and soon a cool, milky white mist began to gather all around the altar where I lay. Out of the mist, a pillar of light began to manifest, enveloping me at its core.

At this point, Isis, Osiris, Hathor, and Horus took their positions around my body. Osiris stood at my head. Isis was at my feet. While Horus directed energy to my loins, Hathor placed her hands over my quickening heart. I was immediately immersed into an extraordinary geometric matrix of light, sound, and colour. The music of the spheres enveloped me in pulsating, palpable patterns of liquid light.

With light streaming from their hands and fingertips, the high frequency energy quickened my organs, molecules, and atoms, opening my DNA to remember the codes required for conceiving children through the process known as Light Conception. One by one, twelve beautiful light beings appeared and took their places in front of me. I recognized one of these to be Hismariam. To each soul I etherically turned, embracing into myself the primordial cellular encoding that would be activated when it was time for their future conception to occur. Thus, each soul was anchored vibrationally into my womb before ever they were birthed through me into physical life. I now understood that I would be the mother of all twelve. But how was I to do this without a man? I desired to understand.

Then a vision was opened to me, and I saw a man coming to the Mount of Carmel. I recognized him as one I had met in the high Himalayas when I had knelt before the lotus feet of my beloved teacher, the Lord Maitreya, while visiting on the inner planes. When he came plainly into view, there was a smile of recognition as we ran into each other's arms. In this way, I came to know who would be the father of our twelve children before ever we met on the physical plane.

As my vision ended, the supernal light withdrew into its own realm and I suddenly felt my body lying upon its pallet in my room. Sweat poured forth, exuding a sweet fragrance from every pore. I lay fully spent, with no energy to rise up to my morning prayers and ritual washing. Thus I chose to use this time to rest and integrate one of my life's most pivotal experiences. Unaware of the passing of time, my reverie ended when a soft knock at my cell door announced the concerned whisper of Judith, who had missed me. I aroused myself and bid her in. She looked upon me with eyes that were like great shining orbs. She, too, in a lucid dream, had witnessed what would become my profound role and increased responsibilities. Though she would not conceive children as I, she would be my conscious handmaiden to assist with the birth of all the children who would enter through me. So it was in those days that I was delivered into the hands of the Most High to accomplish that for which I had come and prepared.

Whether you have had children or not, you can share my wonder and awe as I began to realize what an extraordinary blessing and empowerment was underway. Whether a man or a woman, you are presently preparing the womb of your heart to immaculately conceive and birth the Christ, your indwelling Messiah.

I hope to encourage you to understand and embark with me into the mysteries of Light Conception, which are relevant in your life and coming destiny. I reassure you that you have chosen to be on Mother Earth at this pivotal time so that you can consciously assist every cell of your body and every atom of matter to receive the very high frequencies of light entering the Earth's atmosphere – a kind of spiritual insemination.

For some of you, this ascension process includes consciously conceiving highly evolved children in such a way that you, as mother or father, can resonate with their sensitive souls and assure a more harmonious entrance into the density of the earthplane. It is to assist you with this realization, that I share a portion of my understanding in order to catalyse your remembrance and to illuminate your possible choice to join with me by allowing this wondrous service to life.

Many of the children being light conceived are adepts and ascended masters who are returning to participate in an unprecedented way with the great work of global ascension. Many of the new souls coming forth have never incarnated on planet Earth and many of them have never experienced such physically dense bodies before. They are coming to serve as emissaries of pure love and many are bringing much required transformational technologies to bring forth the Golden Age. All of these children are calling forth a conscious support team, as did my grandson, Yeshua, 2,000 years ago. They, indeed, also reflect your own inner Golden Child who shall lead the way into a golden dawn.

Whether conceiving children in the light or allowing the alchemy of light to transmute your body, emotions, and mind, I wish you to understand that the ascension process you are passing through is a Light Conception. As you and Mother Earth are being impregnated with light, you are serving the Great Work of spiritualizing matter, which assists humanity's ignorant, warlike resistance to unity and harmony to shift. While this occurs, the earthplane can hold more and more coherent higher dimensional patterns of unity or Christ consciousness as you harmonize the accompanying chaotic birth pangs. In this moment you are simultaneously pregnant with the Christ light while giving its presence birth in your every action!

It may be that you choose to be a conscious parent, remembering how to literally conceive children in the highest frequencies of light. It may be that you are a conscious midwife, spouse, relative, or friend assisting coherent love energy to enfold mother and child during pregnancy, birth, and childhood. Whether you are participating in literal or figurative Light Conception, you are giving birth to the presence of the Christ in your self and you are assisting all life to remember the power of love. As you realize that you are the Christ and an emissary of love, you can co-create harmonious, supportive environments in which highly conscious children may easily express and manifest the love they are here to share and demonstrate.

Although Light Conception is a complex and often misunderstood topic, I deeply desire that you begin to appreciate and value your choice to facilitate the conception and birthing of Christ consciousness during the coming years. *I will remind you again, my dear friend, that it is primarily for the purpose of midwifing the birth of Christ or unity consciousness within all of life that I am sharing my story with you.* My immense love and support are freely offered as you choose to awaken and realize your highest destiny every moment of this present lifetime.

⌒

≈ Chapter 11 ≈
The Meeting of Anna and Joachim

My beloved friend, I know the desire of the human heart for true love. All too often the experience of love on the earthplane is frustrated, at best a shallow reflection of that for which one secretly yearns and knows is possible. I hear your soul's prayer for a mate with whom there is rapport on all levels, especially the spiritual in which the fulfilment of your soul is to uplift life through your committed example of wholeness and unconditional love. As your soul evolves, an intense desire emerges to join your life with someone with whom there can be deeply realized divine destiny.

Is such love possible? Yes, my dear friend. When all is in readiness, and most often when you least expect it, the Beloved comes forth in physical form to mirror Creator's divine love. As you come more and more into an ever-present, intimate relationship with your own eternal Beloved, as did I, you may also serve the evolution of life by attracting a soulmate with whom you perfectly mirror each other's internal mystical marriage of Divine Feminine and Masculine.

I will now share one of my most treasured memories of my experience when my beloved came into my life. As I recall, it was late in the summer season of the year 52 BC according to your calendar, when Virgo was the sign of the heavens. I was walking at dawn in the midst of the garden plot, within the cloister of the sanctuary. It was near the dormitory of the women that I paused to listen to an inner sound. This sound was as a soft, lilting trill of birdsong, and yet it was more like the sound of pipes. I wondered at its origin, for surely it was my inner ears that heard. I felt pulled by an irresistible urge to find the source of this haunting melody, which seemed to play upon the very strings of my heart. Quickly, I finished the gathering of fruits and vegetables and took them to our communal storehouse.

I kept the beckoning sounds to myself as I carefully washed the soil and sweat from my hands and face. I replaced the linens of my undergarments and prepared my body as if for the Sabbath. My heart continued to quicken while I placed the freshest of my robes upon my slender form. As I smoothed the finely woven Egyptian cotton over my breasts and hips, I felt an unusual awareness of my body. I carefully ran my Egyptian tortoise comb through my long, thick, chestnut-brown hair, which had bleached to a flaxen colour where it had been exposed to the summer sun's blistering rays. I took perfumed oil into the palms of my hands and lightly massaged it into my waist-length tresses, which I plaited into a braid to be wound around my head. Because it was so unlike me to give my appearance so much attention, I wondered with increasing curiosity what was calling me.

With one quick glance into my polished bronze mirror, I fled out of the cloister by way of the outermost gate. Through the pastures I ran. I darted like a doe among the small groves of nut, fruit, and shade trees and the few remaining pines and cedars. Upwards I climbed to the mount, my heart pounding as if to take flight from its cage within my chest. Finally, I stopped to gather myself. No one could I see, except the shepherd boys far below me, and faint hints of those who moved within the outer walls of Carmel. Seawards, there were those who were harvesting the wheat and flax upon the valley's lower hills. Warm, balmy wind currents rushed upwards from the Great Sea, cooling my steamy skin and dishevelling my carefully coifed hair. All I could do was laugh at my ardent passion for the Beloved, which brought me to the top of the mount empty-handed.

I sank into the tinder-dry grasses. Tears of longing mingled with laughter's sweet release. I lay down, my back against a smooth warm stone. Soft grasses cushioned my head as I gazed into the cobalt blue sky where swallows, hawks, grackles, and sea birds darted and soared. The sun waxed overhead, and still I heard the inner music, so haunting and familiar that I was transfixed. I continued to lie there engulfed by soothing waves of bliss, fed with effulgent nectar. Slowly, I dissolved in an ocean of flame. Such burning! I was too drunk to stand.

So the hours passed until I finally began to come to myself, still not knowing the purpose of my spontaneous excursion or the source of the heartfelt sound. When once I was able to rise to my feet, smoothing my skirts about me, I thought to myself, 'I must gather herbs, roots, and flowers. There must be some explanation for my going.' So I began to pluck stems, leaves, berries, rosehips, and petals. Roots I dug, until my outer skirt and shawl could hold no more. Then, there were wild roses and a handful of summer lilies which, last of all, were picked to place upon the altar.

I was so engaged in my labours that I did not notice when the inner song became the same as the song that wafted upon the breeze. It was only when I stood up, my cornucopia harvest gathered, that I realized the lovely sounds I heard were coming from across the crest of the hill beyond me. Carefully, I carried my treasure to the precipice and knelt amidst the boulders. Not far below, beneath the shade of a lonely cedar, was a robed minstrel. In turn, he played the lyre and pipes. So this was the music that had played upon my very heart, calling me to the mount. I gazed unashamedly while drinking in the melodies he sang and played. Then, as if sensing me, he turned his tanned, bearded face to scan the ridge above him. Our eyes locked in an eternal embrace.

Such joy! Here, at last, in physical form was the one I knew mirrored my soul in perfect wholeness! An unquenchable burning arose from somewhere deep within me to consume any remaining resistance that I might have had to fully dissolving into the vast arms of the Beloved on High. While fully aware of every sensation throbbing throughout my body, my soul again took free flight.

As if attracted by a magnet so strong that nothing could keep us apart, I let go of my precious harvest, except for my handful of the season's last roses and lilies, and ran to the path that led to the lone, ancient cedar below. Before I rounded the last outcrop of boulders, there he was running toward me. Catching ourselves just in time, we slowed to a measured gait, each eyeing the other, weighing feeling against reason, as we approached our moment of truth. Tears welled up from the tension of holding within our breasts eons of longing for the Beloved incarnate. Our eyes blazed with light. Out of our lips passed a suppressed sigh. Then, peals of laughter, quickened with deep recognition, lightened our steps until we stood before one another, face to face. I thrust the bouquet into his hand and, like a deer, almost bolted away, but he reached out and took me into his arms. Gently, he cupped my face, and stroked my cheeks, flushed and glistening with tears.

I hardly knew what to do with myself, feeling awkward and shy. Not knowing what to say, I silently allowed myself to be with this man, who announced that he was known as Heli to his Persian brothers and Joachim to his brothers of Galilee. The sun haloed his face. His curled, salt and pepper hair spun tendrils of midnight blue and silver. In that moment, he was a Greek sun god. It was as if Helios stood before me. For me, Joachim would never do. At that moment, in my heart, he became Heliochim. After I introduced him, the Carmel community began to call him Joachim, as I came to do.

My beloved towered above me, my head abreast of his heart. His shoulders were wide, his bearing strong. Lean was his form, contouring the bleached linen robe he wore. His long, densely tangled hair denoted a Nazirite Jew, a group of ascetic Essenes who wandered the lands much as the saddhus of India live by the Mother's grace. His hair was parted in the middle, as worn by those of Galilee, yet his olive complexioned skin and dark, almond-shaped, oriental eyes told me he was also Persian.

As we stood looking upon one another, reading our energy fields, I remembered the moment, several months ago, when I was lifted into the light realms with Isis and Osiris. My vision returned as I beheld before me the one who had knelt at the feet of the Christed master, Maitreya. Then, I knew who he was and realized that now was the time to bring the covenant of our one soul to fruition. At last when I could catch my breath, my winged heart content to rest, I introduced myself.

I noticed my voice, softer and lower in pitch than usual, as I explained who I was and my station at Carmel. As if catching up on a very long history, like children reciting our lessons, we informed one another's inquisitive minds, while all the time feeling the undeniable testimony of our hearts singing familiar, ancient rhythms. Our hands could not leave the other's clasp until we noticed the rays of the sun had passed behind the mount. The sound of a bell reverberated its call to the faithful to come to evening prayers and the communal supper table. Responsibility and a childlike eagerness to share the excitement of Joachim's arrival with my Carmel family moved us to gather our things we had laid aside during our rendezvous hour.

Down the uppermost slopes of Mount Carmel we descended, in joyful anticipation of Joachim's first meeting with Joseph and Martha. Those gathering around the long tables would soon see us washed and prepared for Joachim's formal introduction. So it was that my beloved and I entered the outer gate to bring our lives and destiny together within Carmel's sanctuary of peace.

Now that I have shared my story about my meeting with Joachim, who was my soulmate as well as my twin-soul and twin-flame, I will briefly explain the nature of soulmate relationships, a very popular and misunderstood topic. Every soul has numerous soulmates, both physical and spiritual. You might think of soulmates as a huge extended family that lives on the earthplane and also in the realms of light. However, before external relationships with soulmates can be understood, it is vital to become intimate with your internal soul with whom there is an eternal bonding.

Although I will elaborate on external relationships, I wish to emphasize the importance of establishing a loving and accepting relationship with your self – your physical, emotional, mental, and spiritual aspects integrated into a wholeness of being. Some individuals mistakenly put their lives 'on hold' thinking they can only carry out their divine purpose with a spiritual partner. Some miss their appropriate soulmate because they cannot accept the human element that disguises the soul essence of their beloved. If you find yourself single, or with a partner who is either spiritually asleep or awake, please know that your primary and most fulfilling soulmate relationship is with your beloved Self.

Soulmates, like divine complementary mirrors, perfectly reflect your consciousness in every moment. Sometimes the reflection may express as the opposite polarity from the one that you are consciously experiencing, but what you perceive is still mirroring your energy, which is expressing through the same resonance. You attract these experiences so that both of you can be conscious of your subconscious or shadow material. Then you have the opportunity to harmonize and balance the polarities within self as well as those that emerge within the chemistry of your combined relationship.

Soulmates are not limited to sexually intimate relationships. They can be relatives, teachers, friends, and even enemies. Always, they come into your life, and you into theirs, at the perfect time when your soul desires accelerated growth and healing of separation consciousness. Because there is so much love between you on a soul level, your souls agree before you incarnate that you will find one another and that you will play the most appropriate roles in your life's dramas.

These relationships prepare each of you for your highest empowerment and destiny. Sometimes those roles are very loving and harmonious. Sometimes there can be extreme suffering. Nevertheless, the ultimate purpose of soulmate relationships is to enter into a divine relationship in which the self is at first mirrored. Then once clarified through forgiveness and compassionate love, the Beloved who has always been present is revealed. Through self-knowledge and self-empowerment gained in a conscious relationship, each soul remembers how to be present for both self and the perceived other.

The giving and receiving of love through all kinds of relationships becomes the greatest of eternally expanding gifts. One way or the other, your soul comes to understand there are no victims, no tyrants, and truly there is nothing to forgive. Yet, forgiveness is the key that opens a wounded and callused heart to feeling the love that it has been missing and craving. Forgiving, compassionate love sees self and others in innocence. This love without limits is the open door that brings Heaven to Earth.

I could go on and on about the empowerment that comes through conscious, sacred relationship with the whole of life, which by the way, is constantly immersed in the free-flow of divine sexual expression. Indeed, I have come to celebrate all life as sexual! Human sexuality, when it is consciously and compassionately expressed through an awakened heart, becomes a powerful spiritual path in which you may come to know your Self as the Love, Lover, and the Beloved. Although this terrain of the heart – so often misunderstood – is near and dear to me, I will bring my discussion to a close.

Meanwhile, let us turn inward and feel the gentle presence of the Beloved with whom you are already eternally wed.

ف

◈ Chapter 12 ◈

Anna and Joachim's Children

So it was that I met my Beloved incarnate. How wondrous were those three months of courting and celebrating! The entire community of Carmel rejoiced for us and for the boon that Joachim's countenance was to everyone.

However, just three months after our betrothal Joachim began to inwardly hear the call of his master teacher, Lord Maitreya, requesting him to return to the Himalayas. The news lay heavy upon our hearts, for the thought of parting was not easy. Yet we knew that this insistent call was for a purpose beyond our personal desires. So, gathering several of the young men, Joachim departed in the early springtime to the Himalayan Mountains.

It would be well over a year before our reunion. In the meantime, I kept busy with the many duties of my station. And every evening, before slumber, I stilled my body and mind and projected myself into the ethers to bilocate in the high valley monastery, where I joined with my beloved Joachim. Together, we received further initiations from Maitreya, who imparted certain high frequency energies for our union and work together. I already had many of these light codes activated in my physical body, so it was not necessary for me to be physically present.

Now both of us were prepared for the advent of the twelve children who would come through us. In this way, we could be in complete alignment with the energies of each soul. And each soul's conception would be facilitated according to the design each had agreed to express on the earthplane.

It was in the late autumn of 49 BC when Joachim returned from his pilgrimage, two years after we met on the slopes of Mount Carmel. Within a month of his return, my beloved and I joined our hearts as one. In nuptial bliss, we gathered our essence and found in each other the mirror of divinity. Yes, to be sure, there were the human limitations that masked the inner radiance; and yet there had been such great transmutation during our earthly sojourn that we were not distracted by our personalities' foibles. Through the gift of our beloved I AM Presence, we stood before each other naked and transparent. Within the mirror of the other, we beheld the majesty and wonder of the celestial realms as well as the joy of being spirit incarnate. Long ago, we had transmuted the passions of flesh within the wine vat of spirit. Now, we cultivated the heightened flows of divine love, which pressed upon our loins and lifted up the wine of the Beloved to the crown of the 'Tree of Life'.

Never, in all my many years of devotional energy practices, did I find the rapture and ecstasy that I now experienced with my beloved Joachim. And, although Joachim practised the science of longevity and performed energy rituals that empowered his spiritual immortality, he had not chosen the path of physical immortality through the Rite of the Sepulchre, as I did. Because my beloved was already ripe in years, we knew our time together was limited. Therefore we chose to relish our every precious moment together. With a deep commitment to love one another unconditionally and to serve our Creator, we prepared ourselves for the conceptions of our twelve children.

I now will share with you a verse that was born of my heart at our first meeting. I give it to you as if you were my beloved; for indeed, in truth, you are. This poem I gave to Joachim after our nuptial rites, as we stood before the congregation, who witnessed our communion. Let me first say that the rose is the flower with which my soul is most aligned, her fragrance and soft petals, and also her thorns. Within this mystery, you may come to know me.

The verse goes like this:

Rosa Mystica

The season's last gift of roses beckon you and me
To stand beneath our nuptial bower canopy.
Golden sunset's brilliant star, our familial witness,
Cupped within a silver chalice, our beloved Venus.

Those roses that once were buds
When last, this way we came,
A cup of wholeness, now exclaim
Our rosy hearts to be the Holy Grail.

Let us breathe and be breathed:
Our kiss, the fragrance of the Rose.
Let us drink and be drunk:
The Beloved's Wine flows.

There is a rose of white and gold,
Within this heart of red,
That I would have you know.
Come, Beloved, enter my bridal bed.

Bring forth your risen flame,
Illumine this many-petaled chamber.
Sing with me the Song of Songs.
Let us renew Solomon's templed splendor.

Three-fold Flame of eternal love,
Transmute these fleshy stones,
Reveal the diamond Earth star
Risen above our merged hearts' altar.

Let us enter the Beloved's Garden
And find the twined Roses, silken and dewy.
Yours, Heaven's gold and sterling.
Mine, the Goddess' pearl and ruby.

Hidden within a garden of roses
Rests Christ's heart of petals and thorns.
The Mirror of the Rose reflects who we truly are –
God I AM... the ONE Beloved.

So we brought our faceted selves into love's furnace to be merged and refined until polished bright. We were found equal to the test of our soul's splendoured quest. Deeply we plunged into love's sweet well, as we mixed the fluids of our passion to bring forth the harvested seed, which bore forth our twelve children descended from the 'Tree of Jesse'. And thus through our loins we brought increase to those known through the Grail lore as the Shepherd Kings. We knew, likewise, the perils which time had wrought upon the household of David, those who preceded him and those who followed. The die was cast. Our destiny beckoned persistently as if a full moon's tide moved upon our soul's bright shore. How could we do other than what we had come to do or be? Ours was to bring glory to our Beloved Creator who sent us to prepare the way for David's heir!

Therefore, we looked to the heavens for the signs of the stars and planets to know the seasons of our nuptial unions when our intent was to conceive a child under a mantle of propitious light. We scanned the ancient tantric texts I had translated, we practised the ways of high sexual alchemy that we both had learned within the mystery school tradition. We enthusiastically prepared our bodies, minds, and souls to be in high resonance with the twelve who would gather around us and call us their parents.

Late one autumn afternoon in 49 BC, when the ember of the sun was setting upon the horizon, we were taken to our bed. With our inner vision opened, Archangel Gabriel could be seen standing before us. His countenance was of fiery white light, which activated Light Conception codes and imprinted perfected patterns of DNA directly into my fertile egg and Joachim's seed. Directly above us were the hosts of light who oversee humanity's evolution. Up, up I ascended an etheric spiralling crystal stairway, until into a chamber of light, I stood before the one who had agreed to enter the earthplane. She shone as a star, spinning gossamer rainbows. Swirling, we twined our souls until her soul's essence had entered into my womb. Her Seed of Light was grafted carefully into my fertile egg before my beloved's seed exploded like liquid light.

Then, I came to myself and looked deeply into Joachim's eyes, our foreheads touching and our soul stars converged as One. Our subtle bodies began to spin into a splendid pillar as we were caught up together into one merging. I was aware of Joachim's erection as a wand of light, which penetrated my womb's sacred temple door. Straightaway, his illumined seed was cast, filling not only my womb, but energetically lifting up my heart.

I breathed deeply and then my mind exploded. There was no more awareness of bodies as separate forms in space. Dissolved were we into the mystery of simply being. Just how long we floated in love's embrace, we knew not nor how long it took to return to body awareness. Yet, when we looked upon each other's glowing faces we felt a warm blanket of light covering our naked forms.

The waning sun cast pink light upon our chamber's wall as we realized that almost a whole day had come and gone. We lit the lamp and around each other's bodies we placed the robes that passion had cast off. Shivering and sweating in turn, we rubbed each others' hands, feet, and faces. All the while, our eyes shone with the immense wonder of Light Conception. Now, within my womb, I felt the warmth kindled by this beloved one's soul. Already, she had come into our embrace to be loved and cherished. We remembered she had announced her name was Ruth, and like Ruth of old she would tarry with us through our days until the Son of Man was returned to Earth.

And so Ruth grew, swelling my belly with her earthen body. Judith took time from her duties in the library to assist me during the last days before Ruth's delivery. There were three women, including Judith, who gathered the linens, water, oils, herbs, and fresh birthing pallet. When my labour began in earnest, they took me from my garden bench, where I loved to rest and meditate. In my chamber cell, they laid me upon the pallet filled with fresh grasses. Joachim was fetched from the fields, where he had taken his turn with the sheep. Running, he came to our door as the contractions caused sweat to break out upon my face. He waited outside, though from time to time I saw his shining face smiling through our small window. His eyes were wet with compassionate tears and his face shone with wonder at that which was upon us. This was his first child, though he knew in truth that she was of the light realms and he but an instrument to conduct her soul to Earth.

My loving attendants wiped my brow and encouraged me to breathe, as I took my awareness of my body's screams into a higher octave, which transmuted the pain. My labour lasted longer than most births I could remember having attended as a midwife. With strong yet gentle hands, Elizabeth reached in and turned the babe when she realized her body was in the breech position. Stabbing daggers of pain ripped through my spine; my entire nervous system shuddered. Yet, these women worked with me, encouraging me to remember what I had taught birthing mothers.

Contrary to dogmatic beliefs based in fear, women giving birth need not suffer. I turned the screaming sounds into a deep, guttural toning. I gave each tissue and bone an opportunity to sound its feeling, all the while lifting my body awareness into expanded consciousness. When at last, Ruth was born, her little body was somewhat bruised. Though her journey had been arduous, she was strong and healthy.

A moment later, she was in my arms, just as Martha came running from her duties in the communal kitchen. How excited she was to have a sister of her own! She poured a pitcher of fresh water into a cup and delicately placed a small wafer of flat bread into my hands. Such a blessing to be surrounded by such loving ones, especially my Martha, as she caressed Ruth's downy head, suckling at my breast.

Joachim could not restrain himself any longer. Though the women had not gathered up all the soiled linens, nor completed my anointing bath, he burst into our room and stood transfixed before our co-created nativity celebration. A great smile broke across his taut lips, and a sighed prayer of thanksgiving released all the tension that had been stored while he walked with me 'near the valley of death'. Laughter broke the silence. The walls of our small room dissolved into a growing light. Within our hearts, we knew the God of Hosts was well pleased with this soul's delivery as I held her gently in my arms and sang to her the Hathor lullaby that assists the soul to remember its highest calling. Thus were the days accomplished that the first of our twelve children was born.

Then Joachim and I proceeded with our assignment to bring forth twelve illumined souls who were choosing to make their entrance upon the stage at this time to help prepare the way for the coming of the Messiah. As was decreed from on High, we came together at those appointed hours when we were called by the heavenly hosts to bring our energies into the realms of light for the purpose of communing with the monadic I Am Presence of each soul. There, we met and merged according to each soul's destiny and ray purpose so that I could fulfil all my responsibilities the Lord God of my Being gave to me.

Now it was over a period of sixteen years, from 49 to 33 BC, that eleven of our twelve children were conceived and born. First came Ruth, followed by two sets of twins, Isaac and Andrew, and a year and a half later Mariamne and Jacob. Then in close succession came Josephus followed by twins, Nathan and Luke. After two miscarriages came Rebekah and Ezekial. My eleventh child was named Noah.

Even when these precious souls came forth to surround us, like stars of a brilliant constellation, we knew that there was still one more child to come. I had previously known this one as Hismariam, whose ascension had occurred many years earlier. We had been in continuous communion and I introduced her to Joachim during our meditations. We knew her time was nigh.

When Noah was still suckling at my breast, just before his weaning, I could hear Hismariam calling from the realms of light: 'My time is coming, my beloved Mother. Precious are you in my sight. Nigh unto us is the coming of Him long awaited. He and I have merged, and I am now prepared to come down. Forthwith, shall you hear the announcement of my coming to the earthplane. Therefore, prepare yourselves, my beloved Mother and Father.'

As we prepared for the Essene feast day of Moses' translation, in accordance with the promise of Enoch and Isaiah, Joachim and I awaited the tidings of Archangel Gabriel. As the stars gathered their light on the eve of the Feast of Tabernacles, we held to each other until the supernal light began to gather in our room. Lo, in the midst of our small chamber stood the Archangel Gabriel with whom we had developed a fond and intimate relationship. He had heralded each of the conceptions of the other eleven. Now, here he was again, according to his promise.

Thus did Gabriel speak to our hearts, 'Behold, born to you shall be She who reigns on the left hand of the God of your Fathers, even that one who represents the Divine Mother principle, the intelligence behind and within all that is. She shall represent to the world the very foundation of a New Covenant, and He shall come through her loins, even as She will come through you, who are favoured among women. And though her essence shall be imprinted upon Joachim, who represents the Father, his physical seed shall not enter your womb. But etherically, his seed shall enter in and his essence shall merge with yours and also Hers who is promised.

'Lo, it is not timely to come into the light chamber where Light Conception occurs for there is yet a further preparation. You, our beloved Anna, will be taken through seven more levels of initiation and insight so that the vast archangelic energy and other vast streams of consciousness that will be merging as a composite may come forth as your daughter who shall be called Mary Anna. Were this much energy to merge now within your womb, miscarriage would most likely occur. And for you, my beloved brother, you also shall pass across seven thresholds so that you can withstand the countenance of Her coming.

'And, I will tell you this: of the women of your family and Joachim's, there are those in whom the seed of man shall be implanted and those who shall know no man who will bring forth evolved souls. All of these shall support the going forth of your grandson who shall be known as a Christ to the peoples of the Earth. It is for you, beloved Anna, to prepare all things so that these maidens may bear wholesome fruit. All these ones in a time not distant shall rise up to call you blessed among women. I say, peace be with you both and Hosanna!'

We then knew from Archangel Gabriel's message that it would be a number of months before the promise would be fulfilled. In the meantime, our children waxed strong, as we laboured among our family and shared in common all our joys and sorrows with the community of Carmel. And even though Joachim and I had begun our work to teach a small group of women and maidens, as well as men, the mysteries of Light Conception, there were moments when I feared that I had lost favour with God. The months accumulated into years, and still the promise was not fulfilled in us. Nevertheless, we kept our faith strong in the knowing that there was a complex plot being co-created by many souls who were coming into the appropriate alignment and timing to play each divine part.

Also time was required for us to pass across the seven thresholds the angel Gabriel was gradually revealing to Joachim and me. With each initiation, I could evidence that we were growing in our capacity to be able to adequately hold the intense frequency patterns that were required for Mary Anna's conception. In addition, I was determined to provide a coherent place of habitation within my body for her full gestation.

Of these initiations I will now say little. In another timing, when many factors existing with humanity are ready, I shall reveal more. Please understand, my dear friend, that I am not intentionally withholding information that may be useful to your growth and the service you have come to give. Should you feel guidance to ask for an increased awareness, know that you can ask your Higher Self to reveal these seven insights. They will be given to you at time when you are certain to use the attending spiritual powers for a beneficial purpose.

Yes, my children were numerous and my days were filled to overflowing with the care of these sweet souls. Fortunately, within our Essene community there were many sisters of all ages who were delighted to assist me in any way they could. Some even wet-nursed my babies when I was taken ill during one of my two miscarriages. So, indeed, I have much compassion for mothers who give birth to many children during a short period of time. And for those who long to have a child and find their wombs empty, I also have much understanding. During my long life on the earthplane and since, I have often been present in the ethers to assist during conception, gestation, and childbirth.

So you see how it was, my dear friend that I fulfilled my agreement to bring forth those souls who entered through me.

‿ঌ *Chapter 13* ঌ‿
Mary Anna's Conception and Birth

It was in early summer 22 BC that Joachim and I were invited by my son, Joseph of Arimathea, to accompany him on his next trip to Britain. Joyfully, after consulting with Joseph on this matter, Joachim and I were able to take six of our children with us: Andrew, Mariamne, Josephus, Rebekah, Ezekial, and Noah. We would begin with a visit to Alexandria, where we would leave Ezekiel to pursue his musical studies with Pythagorean masters. Mariamne and Rebekah both desired to begin their Egyptian initiations, so it was arranged for relatives in Alexandria to escort them to Heliopolis. Then, Isaac, who had been living in Egypt since his eighteenth birthday, and was now ready to begin a new life, accompanied us from Alexandria to Massilia (Marseilles) on his way to visit Jacob, who was living at a remote Essene community in the foothills of the Pyrennes Mountains.

Ruth remained in Mount Carmel, Nathan had recently married and was living on his father-in-law's estate near Cana, and Luke was following his study of medicine in Jerusalem. Then, of course, there was my daughter, Martha, who was now living in a beautiful home in Bethany which had been built by her brother, Joseph of Arimathea, as a second residence.

To our surprise, Joseph's wife, Eunice Salome, decided at the last moment to join us. Her health had begun to wane after two difficult pregnancies and giving birth to their two daughters, Lois Salome and Susannah Mary. Sensing that her life on the earthplane was drawing short, she deeply desired to learn more about the other people who had been influential in her husband's life. Because of his frequent absences and lack of personal attention she wished to create an internal peace with him before her Earth experience was finished. It would be the first time that she had travelled abroad and she was determined to bring their daughters with them. However, Joseph and her concerned parents convinced her to leave them in their safekeeping.

By late summer all the necessary preparations had been made and we took our departure from the new harbour at Caesarea, which had recently been built by the Romans for King Herod, about halfway between Carmel and Joppa. Traveling together in one of Joseph's larger freighting boats, we set sail for Alexandria, where we were met by our son, Isaac, accompanied by the lovely young Egyptian woman who would soon become his bride.

We stayed in Egypt for almost two months. We met with several remnant members of the Brotherhood of Tat. These wise teachers introduced Ezekiel into the Pythagorean mysteries of music. We also renewed family bonds with those of my daughter Aurianna's many descendants who were currently living in Alexandria and Heliopolis. It was particularly satisfying to share Heliopolis and the ancient monuments of the Giza Plateau with Mariamne and Rebekah. Andrew, Josephus, and Noah were quite taken with Egypt, but they were more intrigued by the stories I had shared with them about Britain and they were eager to get there.

With my son, Isaac, and his beautiful, dark-skinned bride, Tabitha, whose wedding we celebrated shortly before departing from Egypt, we made our way, in a convoy of three freighting boats, across the Great Sea to Massilia (Marseilles) where Joseph took on freight. We followed the coastline westward, and then mooring the boats at a village wharf, we proceeded by land into the Languedoc region. We joined our son, Jacob, at a recently established Essene community in the foothills of the Pyrennes Mountains. We visited this beautiful region for several weeks where Isaac and Tabitha intended to stay and begin their new life together. Then we returned to our boats and continued on by sea.

After passing through the Straits of Gibraltar into the Atlantic Ocean, we made our way northward along the coast of the Iberian Peninsula, across the Bay of Biscay, and around the peninsula of Brittany to the little community on the Isle of Mont Saint-Michel. After receiving a hearty welcome, we stayed for a week in order to replenish supplies and to make minor repairs. Then we crossed the Channel, skirted around the southern tip of Britain known as Land's End, just ahead of gale force winds and torrential rains. How glad we were to reach the first of several small ports on the western coast of Cornwall where Joseph received the tin he traded. With God's good providence we were installed within warm shelter by the time the storm railed against the rugged cliffs.

When the seas were calm we proceeded onward to the flooded channel of the Severn River, which at that time was far more extensive than the inlet you now call the Bristol Channel. After transferring to a small, flat-bottomed boat, we made our way up the estuary of the Brue River to a cluster of islands about twelve miles inland from where the coastline is now located. We landed on the Isle of Avalon, meaning isle of apples, which formerly was also called Ynys Witrin (Mystic Isle) and is now known as Glastonbury or the Isle of Glass. Joseph led us through a beautiful orchard of apple trees to the top of the sacred Druid mound which is still known in your day as the Tor of Avalon. It had changed very little since the time of my first pilgrimage to Britain from Egypt around 300 BC. Indeed, even in your day, people from all over the world still make pilgrimages to this sacred site which, as we shall see, was soon to become a bastion that preserved the early teachings of mystical Christianity.

Westward of the summer isles of Avalon, there is a larger island off the coast of present-day Wales, which the ancient peoples also called Avalon or Mona. You know this highly esteemed sanctuary of the Druids as the Isle of Anglesey. After spending the remainder of the winter at Mona as honoured guests of the Celtic Druids, we next journeyed further inland to the great monuments of massive blue stone at Stonehenge. We also participated in ceremony at the serpentine grid composed of massive monolithic stones that you know as Avebury. There, we gathered for the Beltaine high feast with the local high priest and priestess of the Druids, to perform ritual ceremonies.

The Celtic tribe that had adopted me long ago had passed on a tradition by which I could be recognized upon my promised return. A small deep indigo tattoo in the form of a trident had been drawn at the hairline of my forehead, which though much faded over the years, confirmed my identity. So it was that I was remembered as one who had come from Egypt to Britain many years before. I was recognized as a Druid high priestess who knew of the lore and the energies of the Great Mother. Indeed, I was one who knew how to speak to the trees, stones, and waters. I joined circles of priests and priestesses worshipping at sacred groves and wells, bidding the opening of the Earth and spirit worlds to reveal the most ancient stories of the wise ones who had come this way and still lingered.

At Stonehenge, Avebury, and Avalon, I once again took upon myself the white robes of the Druid Order. I drew the mist around me to create veils of time and space through which I stepped to the other side. In Avalon, I met with nature spirits, fairies, little people, unicorns, and giants. These you read about in your children's fairy tale books. Yet, indeed, such ones do exist just on the other side of a very thin veil. And these still remain to teach humanity how to love the Mother, who provides all wealth and nurturing.

Our travels took us to many sacred sites that deepened my love for this ancient land. Everywhere we went, even to the northern isles and highlands, all rejoiced and gave me a solemn handshake, by which I knew that those who would come through me would be recognized and welcomed upon this land. I gathered high priestesses around me and told them all I knew about the coming forth of the incarnation of the Goddess who would birth the Son of Man. I anointed them according to their Order and opened hidden codes of the Matri-Christic Grail lineage. They, in turn, consecrated me to my destiny.

All the while, throughout our travels, Joachim was accepted as a brother. He was recognized as one from whom the Druid priests could learn while giving him the tokens of the Celtic arcanum. Although there were times we were apart, for we each had our own work to accomplish, we came together at the high days for ceremonial communion, meeting with those of leadership position at their board for supper. We continued many of our familiar Essene practices; yet, we were not unwilling to lay aside that which did not serve our higher purpose in joining as one with our Celtic brothers and sisters.

It was during one of our last days in Britain, while visiting stone circles on Mona, that Archangel Gabriel made one of his unexpected visits. Joachim and I had gone somewhat inland to an ancient holy spring where a monastic Druid Order trained priestesses. We were invited to take sanctuary with these wonderful sisters. The head of the Order was named Arianrhod, to whom we made known the wisdom and prophecy that the angel Gabriel had imparted to us. The Goddess, a living embodiment of the Divine Mother, would be coming forth very soon.

When I shared these glad tidings, Arianrhod and her priestesses took me aside to a special chamber where she brought forth drops of sacred oil and holy water from two flasks, which they used to anoint my entire body. Then they painted my body with pigmented clay, creating ancient spiralling patterns to anchor the Goddess' signature and blessing. Thus, I was consecrated unto my high calling. These beautiful sisters bowed to me, seeing Her presence all around me. Already there was a glow radiating from my womb. They called themselves blessed to touch the vessel that would bear the Daughter of the Sun, Earth, and Moon who would be called Mary Anna.

So it was that after we had made our way back to Cornwall, where Joseph had several more freighting boats being prepared for departure back to Palestine, we enjoyed two more weeks among the people and green hills that I so much loved.

Twenty-six year old Andrew, twenty-one year old Josephus, and Noah, who was twelve, were taken in to begin their initiations within the Order of Druids. All three of our sons then made the choice to remain near the isles of Glastonbury and Mona. After sharing reluctant farewells, it was time to depart the British Isles and make our way back to Palestine. We first returned to the Languedoc where we rendezvoused with Jacob, Isaac, and Tabitha, who was now with child. We passed almost a month at their newly constructed stone and thatched roof home. Then we proceeded to Ephesus, which lies on the eastern coast of the Aegean Sea.

Upon arriving in Ephesus, we were surprised to find a very stressed Judith and her new husband, Justinian, an Essene brother who was also a Roman citizen. We had thought they would be in Carmel. They reported the recent discord that was mounting throughout Palestine caused by King Herod's harsh edicts, immoral conduct, and insensitivity to the conditions of the Jewish people.

This increased unrest motivated the Carmel community to relocate much of its library and population. Ever since the attack by Mark Antony's soldiers in 37 BC and the massive earthquake of 31 BC, Qumran was no longer regarded as a safe refuge and repository. Thus, Judith had come to Ephesus to create a small library, which would be the foundation of another Essene community. It would also serve as the common storehouse and hub for the dispersal of goods and records to the Essene brothers at their various remote outposts in the nearby coastal regions.

After consulting with Joseph, Joachim and I made the choice to remain in Ephesus to assist with the dispersal of records, some of which were scrolls that I, myself, had scribed over the years. These we took to remote hillside conclaves of the Brethren. Into very inaccessible caves, we took these records and left them with monastic brothers to keep in their custody. Some of these communities were the foundation of later Christian monasteries, which you have come to know through your history of the New Testament.

Eunice Salome's weak condition had rallied while in Britain, but the journey had become increasingly taxing on her constitution by the time we reached Ephesus. Missing their daughters and concerned for their wellbeing, Joseph took his ailing wife and newly acquired freight to Caesarea and then on to her father's nearby estate at Arimathea where their daughters had relocated during their parents' absence. Gathering up his family, Joseph pressed on to Jerusalem. We were to learn later that Eunice Salome had died shortly after returning to her home. She had accomplished her purpose in going with Joseph, and with a great sense of peace, left her husband to carry on his important work.

It was twelve years later, while acquiring an estate near Magdala on the west shore of the Sea of Galilee, that Joseph met a woman of high birth, named Mary. As a young adolescent, she had rebelled against the strict discipline of her high priest father and married a Macedonian mercenary by the name of Phillip. With this husband, Mary of Magdala (as she became known) had three children – Thomas, Matthew, and Susannah. Phillip was often away from home and abusive when he was with his family. Several years after her husband abandoned her and their children, leaving them destitute, Mary of Magdala met Joseph in the marketplace. He asked her to become the primary housekeeper of his new home in Magdala. Soon thereafter, she became his mistress and intended bride.

It was in late December of the year 21 BC, one month after we first arrived in Ephesus, that Archangel Gabriel visited Joachim and me one night. He had a way of surprising us, even though his visit earlier in Cornwall made it clear that our beloved daughter's divine presence had already begun to enter.

We were both lifted up on High to meet with our beloved Hismariam, who now announced herself as Mary Anna, whose time had come. We took her to our bosoms and felt her presence descend into every cell of our bodies. Joachim also conceived the light which was this one's presence until he, too, was consumed by her being. We did not come together, as with the other eleven, in the penetration of my womb with his seed. Into my womb came Mary Anna, in totality, to fulfil the promise of virgin birth. And so it was that, in Ephesus, the Divine Mother, incarnate in Mary Anna, returned to the earthplane.

We stayed in Ephesus throughout my pregnancy. Only Judith remained with us until Rebekah and Ruth heard the glad tidings of my pregnancy and organized a small company of the Carmel community to be with me at Mary Anna's birth. Though my family seemed scattered to the winds, on the inner, I was with them and knew all was well. So it was that the monastic pattern that consecrated children at an early age continued to give me opportunities to realign my maternal instincts and heart-filled desires. Although I admit that there were sore times of grieving the loss of my children, I continually surrendered my human will to what I perceived was a greater purpose and design. Thankfully all my children had the support of communal family.

The days passed harmoniously. The presence of Shekinah blessed my every hour. So did Her supernal light increase in my being. It was an unusually blissful pregnancy. Not once was I ill nor did my body suffer pain. I was taken deeply inward. There, I beheld much of the divine plan, which would fulfil the prophecies of the 'chosen people', as the Jews liked to think of themselves.

Mary Anna grew very quickly within my womb, and it was less than the usual nine months when my time came for delivery during the sign of Virgo or the Virgin. The last three months, I was so taken inward that I chose not to speak. In silence, I bore witness to her grace. After Ruth and Rebekah arrived, our small community came to sit with me so that they could feel the Holy Shekinah's glow. As they sat, they would dissolve in bliss. Joachim also glowed with Mary Anna's presence. It was not the kind of experience most men were accustomed to when a woman was with child. During those last three months, Joachim remained by my side. He felt all that I felt and went into the silence with me.

At last, it was time for Mary Anna's full advent unto the Earth. The stars were unusually bright that night. A cluster of stars wove a web of ethereal light directly overhead. Sirius beamed through our east window and was bright enough to cast shadows upon our limestone walls. The moon's thin crescent had already set in the west. Judith, Ruth, and Rebekah had for many days rehearsed and prepared every needful thing. They were constantly hovering over me, plying me with their concerned, questioning faces. I would wave them on, trusting that when the time came, they would be at my side. So it was that when my water broke and my contractions began, Joachim went forth to Judith's apartment and bid her come to our small upper room.

My son, Joseph, had supplied every comfort, even a bed that was raised upon a platform. Specially consecrated urns, washing pans, soft sheets of Egyptian cotton, sweet and astringent herbs, healing essential oils, and candles were taken from their storage basket. Judith, Ruth, and Rebekah were like angels tending Mary Anna's completely pain-free birth. Joachim was invited to sit near my head. He, too, was feeling the force of the contractions as we both gave 'birth' to the Mother's return.

My soul took flight, just as the last contraction pushed Mary Anna's head to crown. My entire being exploded into light as Mary Anna's full presence descended through me and enveloped her small form. Her little body was received into Judith's gentle hands. Ah, what celestial music chorused through our hearts!

After the birth was completed and Mary Anna was put to my breast, those who had come from Carmel slowly entered into our little room and knelt as if before an altar. Here was the Mother of the New Covenant! With solemn rejoicing, each soul placed a gift beside my lap. Such a warm welcoming! Mary Anna's dark, auburn hair shone of molten gold highlights. Her skin was fair and her eyes were a deep blue-grey. All of the other children were dark-haired with light to deeply olive complexioned skin and brown eyes. Yet this beloved child was like polished alabaster touched by the rose's palest of pinks.

Joachim then brought forth the sounds of celestial music on his lyre, and I sang the Goddess Hathor's lullaby of highest destiny, welcoming our newborn into this world. Joyously, with a flood of love and gratitude flowing through our hearts, we rejoiced and celebrated her coming. All who were present knew who she was and vowed to hold her presence securely within our hearts. Thus, the way was prepared. We each covenanted to protect her and support her initiations until all was fulfilled.

We also knew that there were other women who had been and would yet be Light Conceived. These had come to Carmel to be instructed by me. There were other children, who would come forth to prepare with Mary Anna, so that all the souls who had agreed before their birth could play their destined parts. Some would be, as it were, waiting in the wings. Human nature and free agency were taken into consideration. Nothing was left to chance, as every possibility was rehearsed in the ethers. Should some turn away from the task at hand, overtaken by fear, then others would enter in. We knew that great strength, courage, and wisdom would be required to pass the tests soon to come upon us.

What comfort to our souls to feel the Divine Mother's love reassuring us that all was well!

Chapter 14

Mary Anna's Childhood

Now, as I listen to your heart, my beloved friend, I can imagine your desire to know more of the one who was destined to become the mother of Him who would fulfil the New Covenant. What were her joys and trials? Were there human foibles?

Let me answer those questions as I tell you briefly of Mary Anna's childhood in Ephesus and Mount Carmel. In doing so, I shall open the Book of Life in such a way that you may come to her as an expression of the Divine Mother, just as she now comes to you. Through satisfying your curiosity, may you open yourself to the Divine Mother's presence that is available to you every moment.

Mary Anna was a bright light. Brighter than your mind can imagine. To know her then and now, you must be still, centred, and open to the present moment, as is a child. Let us pause for a moment and allow that peaceful silence.

୭

When Mary Anna first came forth, she loved to bask in the light of the sun. She would stretch forth her little hands to the light coming through the window of our humble apartment in Ephesus and make sounds much like those of her dolphin brothers, who frolicked and leaped through the dimensions. She loved to have her father take her to the terraced porch overlooking the expanse of the Great Sea, glistening blue and silver far below. With a keen eye and a knowing heart, the dolphin pods could be seen performing their acrobatic dances.

When Joachim was not away working odd jobs or taking supplies to the Brethren scattered about in their small monastic sanctuaries, he loved to be at home cradling his daughter in his arms. She loved to hear his stories and joined him in gleeful singing, while keeping time with her clapping hands. It was not long after she learned to walk that Mary Anna took up dancing while Joachim played the lyre or pipes and I played the frame drum. Mary Anna's favourite thing to do while sitting on her father's lap was to run her fingers through his long grey beard. Her second favourite pastime was to stroke his bushy eyebrows as he tucked her gently into her cradle. Lovingly, they gazed into each other's eyes that glowed like deep candle-lit pools.

In our small courtyard, there was a grapevine arbour in which the birds loved to nest. In the dappled shade of the thick overhanging vines, Mary Anna and I spent three idyllic years before returning to Mount Carmel. In this peaceful setting, I worked with my small loom, fibres, and spindle. While I spun and wove, Mary Anna played upon the court floor's colourfully designed, enamelled tiles, which were surrounded by smooth flagstone. She investigated everything she saw. She would make up little songs that she loved to sing to her parents and the few other adults and children who came from time to time to visit. But most of all, she loved to sing to the sun, dolphins, flowers, sparrows, pebbles, ants, the tethered milk goat, and the three cats that had adopted us.

Mary Anna's mind developed very rapidly, and during her second year, she derived great pleasure from reciting the psalms and sayings that we gave her. Before we left Ephesus, she had begun to learn how to speak and read Aramaic, Hebrew, and Greek. She was quick and very energetic, able to do more than two things at once. Yet, she was calm, unhurried, and always graceful, wise beyond her years. Just as Hismariam had been, Mary Anna was a clear empath, feeling every nuance of energy swirling around her.

There were times when she could be impatient or disappointed in the behaviours of nearby adults. Then, she would stamp her little foot, spin around, tugging at her apron with one hand and putting her other hand to her mouth to quiet an outburst. Her face would blush, tears welling up, spilling onto her cheeks. Squeezing her blue-grey eyes shut and tightly pursing her full lips, she would run to the small garden plot and hide within the tall grasses near the olive trees until the inner storm passed.

Most of those who had come from Carmel for Mary Anna's birth had long since returned to their duties. It was only Ruth, recently widowed, who chose to remain with us. About a year before our departure to Mount Carmel, Ruth married Titus who desired to remain in Ephesus to carry on his work. Joachim continued to assist Joseph of Arimathea when he came several times a year to escort the various Essene brethren, supplies, and manuscripts from Carmel and Qumran to the newly assigned outposts in the rugged Aegean isles and mountainside monasteries. He would then assist those who had completed their assignments to make ready for their return to Galilee and Judea.

We easily met our basic needs with Joachim's readily found handyman jobs and with my bartering of handspun goods, medicinal herbs, and midwifery skills. These resources, together with the stipend of funds and supplies that Joseph of Arimathea brought us several times a year, made our simple life very comfortable.

In the early autumn of 17 BC, shortly before Mary Anna's third birthday, we returned to Mount Carmel, where she was heartily welcomed as a member of our Essene community. On her third birthday, she was consecrated to the Lord Most High, and her care, schooling, and initiations were placed in the custody of the Mount Carmel Mystery School. Indeed, she was no longer ours, as if we could ever have thought she had been.

Now, I will tell you, my friend, it was painful to release Mary Anna to the care of others and to the strict disciplines that gradually replaced her carefree childhood. Yet, we knew the Great Plan, and so we offered up this precious one, even as we had offered up others of our beloved children when we knew that the greater part was to do so. I shall say further that adepts who came to Carmel from Tibet, India, Mesopotamia, Egypt, Greece, and Britain instructed Mary Anna, together with the other young women and men who had been delivered by their parents into the inner sanctuary where secret initiations took place. In this way, all who had chosen to continue their initiations were prepared for their covenanted work to set forth the stage for our coming Teacher of Righteousness.

Fortunately, I was in charge of the young maidens' schooling. In that way, I was able to spend time with Mary Anna every day. However, in my desire to show impartiality to all the maidens within our monastic setting, I rather stoically distanced myself from my daughter. This was difficult for both of us. Once a week, after the Sabbath observance, Mary Anna would spend the night with Joachim and me. How lovely it was to have her sweet presence close to us through the night.

During the warmer months, we three would go out into the warm evening to the grove of cedars under the canopy of stars. Lying on our pallets, our woollen blankets covering us, we stargazed deeply, shared, and prayed into the wee hours. Joachim brought his lyre, and together we sang devotional psalms and made up mirthful songs that bubbled up from our glad hearts.

However, it was not always easy for Mary Anna. Sometimes, the strenuous disciplines, the long hours bent over the scriptures while reading and scribing, the unkind and insensitive remarks of some of the novices, and the sicknesses that required sleepless nights in the infirmary would cause her shoulders to stoop and her face to lengthen in soberness. She felt everything including the growing unrest among the people of Palestine that the walls of Carmel could not keep out.

As the years quickly passed, her understanding of what she was being prepared for often pressed down like a heavy burden. Occasionally, there was tension and pain in her neck and upper back, which Joachim and I would relieve with healing oils and salves. She longed for the respites that took her into the fields to tend the sheep and goats for short periods or into the gardens to cultivate, plant, and harvest. Most of all, she loved to run free through the pastureland grasses, to walk among the cedars and cypresses, and to take a picnic basket out to the precipice overlooking the Great Sea. Mary Anna often felt very alone, with few supportive friends to share her sensitive heart. But those dear souls who drew close to Mary Anna continued to be loyal to her through the remainder of their lives.

When she was approaching her twelfth birthday, her menses began. With two other young women, I took her into the sanctuary grotto that was dedicated to the Great Mother. There, I initiated these precious young souls into the mystery held within the blood, the opening of the womb, and the ripening of the bodies for the energies of the Great Mother.

For one full year, on every new and full moon, I took these maidens, and others who had been recently initiated, into the stone circle and grotto to receive the songs, stories, meditations, and rituals of the Great Mother. After that year, the girls were taken with the older maidens and women to another consecrated site where they learned more about channelling the energies of the Divine

Feminine through their bodies. They were prepared for marriage and the arts of tantric love. They also learned how to keep the sacred energies of their womb and spine held and circulated in certain ways, so that they could heal themselves and others. And of course, we continued to gather during the cycles of the moon to enact the mythic, archetypal journeys of the many faces of the Goddess.

These were the usual disciplines that every young and mature woman well understood. The stricter disciplines, which prepared initiates for the rituals of resurrection and Light Conception, were Joachim's and my offering, which we freely gave to those men and women who responded to the inner call to come to Mount Carmel.

Also, on several occasions between the ages of twelve and fifteen, Mary Anna was taken to the Temple in Jerusalem, where arrangements were made for her to spend as much as three months undergoing further instruction and initiation. In this way, she was provided with an opportunity to become acquainted with the precepts and practices of the larger Jewish community, which were, in many respects, considerably different from those that characterized our small Essene community. As you can well imagine, the discordant energies that our beloved daughter encountered within the ancient walls of Jerusalem were a shock to her highly sensitive nature.

So it was that Mary Anna became strong in mind and body as she met and overcame the many challenges she passed through. Day by day, she dedicated her mind, body, and soul to the cosmic Divine Mother who expressed through her. In this way, our beloved daughter prepared herself to birth many children and become the mother of the Anointed One.

✧

Chapter 15

Anna's Vision on the Mount

The times in which Mary Anna grew in stature were indeed perilous. By the time she was twelve years old, conflict and agitation between the various political and religious factions were constantly disrupting the little peace we had. As a consequence, the Romans had taken all of Palestine well into their hands, and though they tried to maintain peace, it was a very troubled peace. I can still remember how shocked we were by the horrifying news that the soldiers were using crucifixion to keep the many factions in obedience to Rome.

Ever since the Maccabean revolt, in 63 BC, there had been a gradual dispersal of our Essene community away from Carmel to Qumran, the Sinai, Egypt, Asia Minor, the Himalayas, Gaul, and Britain. This caused many of us who remained in Carmel to turn more deeply inward. We also looked for ways to safeguard that which was most precious to us – the lives of those committed to living the Way of the Teacher of Righteousness, and secondly, our oral and written records.

Therefore, we kept to ourselves as a sect and avoided as much as possible going into the densely populated areas. More than ever, those of us who hailed from Mount Carmel clung to our ecumenical ways of brotherly love and forbearance, sometimes in marked contrast to our Qumran brothers and sisters whose ascetic monasticism embraced Hebrew fundamentalism. The growing schisms among our Essene community indeed troubled my soul.

When discontent, violence and oppression strike close to home, it is easy to judge those who fear the empowerment of the masses at the risk of losing their position of authority and wealth. However, I have found that to do so is to add fuel to the fire. My preferred course was to do what I could to pass on the arcane wisdom that empowers internal sovereignty, as it has always been done – quietly, and with an underlying trust in the Creator's plan. This is the essence of the wisdom that I acquired during the course of my long life. And this is the orientation that I sought to share with all of my children, while at the same time honouring their right to learn from their own experience by making their own free-will choices.

So it was in the midst of this increasing chaos, that I chose to walk one day upon the burnt hillside of Mount Carmel hoping to find and heal any remaining survivors of Rome's most recent political demonstration. The grasses of Galilee had been burned in retribution for some wayward folly of the peasant folk, who rose up with the Zealots to decry Rome's and Herod's punitive taxes. And now, homes as well as fields and pasturelands had been burned to the ground. A sore darkness enveloped the hillsides. Dust devils riveted the sky. Vultures hovered over the meagre prey to be found.

Satisfied that we had found everyone who could be assisted, I turned homeward. As the day wore on, my heart became extremely heavy. The sun's almost unbearably blistering heat was intensely amplified by a strong desert wind that whipped black ashes skyward. Covering my face with my shawl, my footsteps slowed by the assailing gusts and debris, I felt a spontaneous lamentation arise from deep within my bowels.

In this way I spoke to God, 'On the hillsides of Galilee, I walk amidst the burning grasses. And the dust flies in the wind. I am tired and alone in my fears of what is coming. An ancient, abysmal feeling wells up and presses upon my heart. I ache in my being.

'Oh my God, what is to become of my people? I know not. Oh my God, I burn in the depths of my being for my people, Israel. Why do I mourn so in my heart? Are we not the Chosen, your Elect? Are we not protected by you, our God? What has become of reason? Little do I know of the passing of time and the sore indiscretions of those who say they know what is best for our small community of followers of Him whose time is nigh. How are we to walk in faith, O my God, when there is so much suffering of mind and soul? O, I of little faith. Come up to the Mountain of the Lord, O my soul. Show me your face, O my God! I quake in the smallness of my being, and the aching of my soul oppresses me. Rise up, O my heart. Be not cast down.'

So I thought and expressed these lamentations to my God as I traversed the burning hillsides of Galilee, awaiting Him whose time was nigh. So many questions pressed upon my mind.

How am I to do this thing required of me? How am I to speak to my beloved Joachim of this distress that oppresses me and burns in my bowels? How am I to meet with my little flock and share with them the substance of my knowing that the time has come for which we have yearned so long? In the midst of great tribulation we have petitioned God to bring us the prophesied Teacher of Righteousness, that we might be lifted from the travails of flesh and the afflictions of our souls in this deepest of nights. A flash of lightning moved across my mind as I reflected upon this.

And so it was in those days that I, Anna, walked amidst the burnt grasses of Galilee. Often, my soul was taken with the lamentations of weariness, and fear beset me. Indeed, it was the crying out of the peoples of the Earth that rested heavily upon my heart. I could feel the entire Earth and knew her great weariness within this darkest of cycles. In my soul, there was a restless torment, as of one lost in the wilderness of a dark night. For, indeed, there was much tribulation among the peoples. No one rested well in our slumbers. It was as if a great calamity would come upon us, and we knew not when, nor of what magnitude. It was a silent aching in my heart and a heavy weight that I carried upon my shoulders as I walked the fields of blackened grasses.

As I continued my walk back to the compound of Carmel, I suddenly felt inspired to climb to the highest knoll upon the mount, where Hismariam had taken her ascension over a century earlier. As if guided by an invisible hand, I made my way to the summit and prostrated my body upon the ground. Within moments, I was taken up to receive revelation of the coming days.

Great was the exaltation of my soul as I stood face to face with the Lord God of my Being, for on His right hand was the Radiant One, whose time was drawing nigh. Into effulgent light I was drawn until all awareness of my individual identity dissolved. Then, the veils were drawn aside, and I saw a new Heaven and a new Earth. And I knew that much travail would come upon the Earth beforehand, even that which would temper by fire the very essence of Earth's creation.

He, who would soon be coming through Mary Anna, then took me aside. Together, we walked in the midst of a most beautiful garden. Here, he placed his arms around me, calling me 'Little Mother'. With a penetrating gaze, he merged his being with mine until we were taken unto the very Throne of the Father. I know not how long I was taken up into the One. When I returned into my separate awareness, he announced that his time had come. The next year would be a great preparation for his entering into Mary Anna's womb.

One who would be his forerunner was already about to enter the womb of Joachim's brother Jacob's eldest daughter, Elizabeth, who had completed her training at Mount Carmel and had returned to Bethlehem to await her time. There were other women who would also be called. Each would receive according to her agreement in Spirit.

Mary Anna would be required to go through several more levels of initiation. After these were accomplished and there was a stabilization of her physical and subtle bodies, the complete impregnation of very vast, high, light frequencies could occur. And, last but not least, her cousin, Joseph, the youngest son of Joachim's brother, Jacob, was to come forward in betrothal to Mary Anna in order to set the stage, activate the Light Conception codes, and provide a strong bastion of protection and emotional solace to mother and child.

Next, I was shown my part. He showed me how my initiations in the great temples of Egypt had prepared me in the Way of the Teacher of Righteousness. This wisdom would be drawn upon during his youth and would assist the Great Work that he was coming to do. This, I secreted away into my heart.

Then, he showed me glimpses of his walk upon the Earth and events to come. The darkest moment was also the lightest; for in crucifixion, he would remove the sting of death. He told me that he was coming to fulfil all prophecy and to anoint all humanity with the redeeming love of the Father–Mother of life. His disciples would demonstrate unto all; that what he did, all could do, and even more. The Divine Plan was laid out holographically. It was decreed in the heavens, and all the players were taking our positions upon Earth's stage. All was in readiness.

Gently, he pressed his fingers into the palms of my hands and blew the Breath of Life upon them. A celestial wind penetrated deep into my flesh and bones, reviving an awareness of my identity in the eternal realms. A healing balm wrapped around my small form until all sadness departed. I knew all was well, even though the mystery school drama soon to be publicly enacted would be misunderstood and not fully received for many centuries to come. This was the time ordained to set a greater evolution into motion within this solar system, galaxy, and universe.

Then he opened my hands and taking each palm to his lips, he whispered, 'Into these hands shall I be born to glorify my Father–Mother. Blessed are you among women. Fear not, my Little Mother, for like your daughter that you presently call Mary Anna, who is my heavenly Mother incarnate, you are likewise born to lift up the Son of Man until all be returned to my Father's kingdom. Hold these words in your heart. Though the night draws a heavy cloak over you, the dawning follows. In that hour, roll back fear's stone that covers the portal called death and emerge into my heavenly Father–Mother's garden, where I await you.'

Thereupon, the Heavens rolled back yet further, and I saw before me a most wondrous sight – the Earth, renewed and transformed! Her waters and lands were resplendent in pristine beauty. Life teemed with robust virility and abundant fertility. All enmity and discord were removed. All life was imbued with a splendor that far exceeded the visions conveyed by the words of the prophets before me. Alas, my heart overflowed with thanksgiving as I rejoiced in the blessings of the Creator, which rested upon me as I quaked with the witnessing power of Shekinah's fiery, indelible presence. Angelic hosts trumpeted, 'Hosanna! Glory, indeed, be to God! Peace, O Immanuel, come among men!'

Joyful tears flowed through my heart, the very heart of the Earth, the very heart beating in all humankind. Indeed, there was but one vast heart that cradled and was the All.

As the transmission of love energies continued I became aware that not only would my grandson represent the Father Godhead, but that his twin-soul would also incarnate joining with Mary Anna to bring down into the earthplane the full return of the Mother Godhead. My soul indeed rejoiced as I slowly gathered myself and picked my way down the mount to Carmel's north gate.

ᔦ

Chapter 16
Mary Anna and Joseph ben Jacob

So it was that, as I came to the outermost gate of Carmel's sanctuary, I beheld two of the brethren hovering over Joachim, who was prone upon the ground. They beckoned me to approach quietly. A great light was upon my beloved. His face shone as the sun. In my inner vision, I beheld Joachim's light body descending with a host of angels, including Archangel Gabriel. The two brothers were speechless, yet magnetized to Joachim in such a way as to be unable to leave his side. Therefore, they looked upon me as one who knew of these things and sought comfort in my knowing.

I knelt at my husband's head, taking his broad skull into my hands. His white, tendrilled hair cascaded through my fingers. Joachim's dark eyes were open, though not seeing the things of this world. In silence, we awaited his return to his body.

When he finally returned, his body began to quake and tremble. Sweat poured from his face, mingled with a torrent of tears. My beloved had also been lifted up. As we looked into one another's eyes, we knew we had both been given the same revelation. One of the brothers poured water onto a cloth and gently washed Joachim's face. We awaited the evening hour, when all were called after supper to come to the sanctuary to receive our news. As Joachim gave voice, I held the space in silence.

Speaking with an inner authority, Joachim reported, 'Our beloved family of saints, peace be unto you. The Great Day of our Lord is upon us. We have been taken up, and we have been shown what is about to occur. We have been given signs and tokens with which to recognize the coming of our Immanuel, even Him long awaited whom we have called the Teacher of Righteousness. He whom the prophets have foretold has come before us and witnessed that the day of His coming is now upon us. His presence is as the sun, and He is even now knocking at the door of that womb which shall bear Him into the world. It has been made plain to us that the promised vessel is one of the maidens who is with us. And in due time, you shall know her identity as one who is indeed blessed among women.

'For now, it is to hold these glad tidings in our hearts. Let neither fear nor envy come upon you as you look to yourselves, wondering who is chosen. There are yet labours to be performed among you, both brothers and sisters, to prepare the way. You will be shown, in your appropriate timing, what each is called to bring as an offering in righteousness to the God Most High. Look into your hearts, and measure well the thoughts that tempt you into the valleys of darkness. Rise up. Behold, the dawning of a New Day is upon us. We must turn away from our petty grievances and anxieties for the morrow. Let faith return and strength gird up our loins. The long awaited day draws nigh. Let each steward be prepared in all things.

'This is our report for this day. In a fortnight, at the hour appointed, we shall come together once again to open our mouths and bring forth writings that foretell His coming. Let us abide now in that peace which passeth understanding. Glory be to the Father–Mother of all life, and praise be unto our fathers and mothers who have come before us. Amen.'

Thus our mouths were opened to bear witness to our community. Then, a great stir arose among us. All felt the excitement of that which was now at hand. Each understood according to each one's capacity and readiness. There was an atmosphere of celebration, and yet there was a hushed silence that fell upon us as we undertook our labours with renewed devotion to God. We made special ceremony to renew our covenants, and we quietly secreted away our communions in Spirit. The young women in training for Light Conception were especially overtaken by a feeling of expectancy. Each of these maidens came to me privately to speak of her desires to be found worthy to play her part. There was a new level of piety that almost became a heaviness shadowing these young souls. Therefore, I found occasion to assist these beautiful women to lighten their hearts.

Mary Anna was especially quiet and removed from the other maidens as the weeks passed. She came to me in silence. Within the bosom of the Great Mother, we rested, cradling each other and abiding until the hour of conception arrived. Always, she was with me on the inner planes, and, as often as seemed appropriate on the outer. Her stature increased day by day. The light of her countenance became brighter, even as her lessons and initiations became more strenuous and demanding. Everything I had learned from the many initiations I had passed through during my long years, I gave to Mary Anna and the other maidens and women who were candidates for Light Conception. We worked tirelessly. Many were the days when there was no sleep at all. At times, there would be some who would murmur; yet, all in all, each who had come to be humbled, tempered, honed, polished, and made a new creature in the Lord, passed their tests of initiation. In that year, there was only one who felt she could not go on and who therefore returned to her parents.

In addition to Mary Anna, there were thirteen maidens and nine women who walked through the mysteries with me that season. Among the young men, there were nineteen boys and five men who also passed their probationary initiations at Mount Carmel. Five of these would also be prepared as initiates to facilitate Light Conception of their seed. It was an intense year. At times, the community bristled with tension, emotional bodies often volatile. Then, we would come together for singing and dancing. From time to time, certain ones would depart singly into the wilderness for fasting and prayer. Our intent was to overcome our lower natures and pass through the gates of the guardian of the mysteries, who keeps the way closed until all is in readiness to pass.

There were secret chambers within Mount Carmel, where the initiates passed their initiations. Some of these chambers held certain energies simulating the passing of the soul through the dimensions and astral worlds. In some chambers, every fear was holographically precipitated. In others, the lusts and desires of the flesh were animated, and the initiate was brought face to face with the beast within their human nature. These were the lower chambers, where the desire bodies and physical body were cleansed and empowered. Once these basic requirements were met, special instruction was then given for opening the higher pathways and spiritual powers. Both male and female candidates learned how to hold very high frequencies in their minds and bodies, how to discern spirits and energies, how to astral travel and bilocate, and how to concentrate their attention for days at a time upon certain patterns, sounds, and dimensional focal points.

It was understood that some of the male candidates who were also being prepared for Light Conception would select brides among the prepared women. So it was that the parents of a number of great souls responded with devotion to their assignments. Joachim and I taught those who were chosen, for we had had much experience through the bearing of our many children. One of these candidates was Joseph, the youngest son of Joachim's brother, Jacob, and his wife, Lois. Joseph was thirty-two years of age at this time and had been a widower for five. He had only been married one year when his wife and baby died during childbirth.

We knew that Joseph was highly favoured of God, for he was already adept at all we had taught him. He had taken advanced initiations in Egypt and India during his young adulthood. We could feel the confirmation of Spirit that what we had been shown in our great Vision would be fulfilled through Joseph and Mary Anna.

When the fortnight had passed, we called the Carmel community together once again. After rehearsing the well-known scriptural prophesies of Enoch, Zadok, Isaiah, Daniel, Micah, and Malachi regarding the Messiah, we revealed more of our vision, as we had promised. Next, we shared our understanding that Joseph and Mary Anna were to be betrothed, and we gave forth our blessing upon this arrangement, should these two agree. As we turned with a questioning look to each one, we caught the glimmer of shining eyes and blushed faces. Then, we understood that these two had already secreted their vow of love, and had perhaps known, well before we did, the plan that was to unfold through them. So it was that Joseph and Mary Anna stepped forward to accept the community's blessing of their right to wed.

Several other couples likewise came forward to announce betrothals, and to relate the dreams that they had had, instructing them to so come together. Among these were my eldest son, Joseph of Arimathea, and his beloved Mary of Magdala, whom he had met three years earlier. It was this small company of men and women who were brought before the canopy of marriage at the same time. Great was our jubilation upon Mount Carmel, for the time long awaited was now at hand.

So it was in those days that I, Anna, began my ministry unto all the souls who had agreed to come forth in that hour. My work was all consuming. My energies were lifted to the Most High, and the focus of my body served as an instrument through which the Lord manifested. My words were few, yet their influence was felt upon each soul. I brought forth the sounds of the winds, the earth, the sun, and the seas. The Breath of Shekinah I blew upon the souls of those who came before me to receive the wisdom of the Great Mother who lived within them. Mighty were the works performed through me.

And mightier still were the combined works of our Carmel community as we prepared for His coming. We laboured tirelessly, as we came together to weave our souls and bend our wills to the Great Work of the Father–Mother God. It was a glorious time in which all within our small community laboured to facilitate the most harmonious passage for the births of the souls who were Light Conceived.

The months passed swiftly. Joseph, who had wed Mary Anna in betrothed commitment, continued to grow in spiritual stature. He had a way about him that endeared him to our community. He fostered humour and good will among all. He also had a talent for unravelling the most complex of riddles held within cloaked doctrines. Within the cumbersome weight of dogma, he brought forth the most hidden truths in simplicity and clarity. The younger boys looked to him as a shining example who could make the way plain and simple. Joseph was truly a Son of Zadok after the Order of Melchizedek, a translated being who often appeared as if out of nowhere. Joseph had been initiated by this ancient one and carried in his keeping Zadok's priestly staff. This staff was hewn from a branch of the hawthorn tree. Within its burls were embedded precious stones, carved symbols, and talismans.

Joseph grew in favour with Mary Anna, who, in her few hours of solitude, wove him a shawl of creamy white linen and fine wool. This shawl she gave to Joseph as a symbol of her devotion. So the days passed, and all within the community were uplifted by the growing love felt when these two would join their voices together to offer psalms and recitations. Every soul delighted in looking upon them as they strolled together hand in hand. To work beside them in the gardens, fields, or seminary, was to be inspired. Every burden seemed to melt away in their presence.

These were to be some of the most carefree days of our lives and we were only occasionally overshadowed by the foreboding challenges that lay ahead.

✑ Chapter 17 ✑

Yeshua's Light Conception

Late one night just before sunrise, during the last week of June in the year 5 BC, Joachim and I were lying upon our pallet, when an immense light came over us. Within the light were four angels: Michael, Gabriel, Raphael, and Uriel. We were drawn up, as within a whirlwind, into a great light-filled chamber. I recognized this chamber as the same one that we had experienced during the times our children had been light conceived. I liked to think of this extraordinarily beautiful place as one of the many rooms within the City of Light that I called the New Jerusalem.

We were pleased to behold Mary Anna and her beloved Joseph entering into the chamber. Others of our family and extended family, living near and far, also entered in. Among these were Mary of Magdala and Joseph of Arimathea, Tabitha and Isaac, Rebekah and Simeon, and Noah who was standing beside a beautiful unidentified woman with long, strawberry blond hair. We were informed that all of these couples, as well as others, would be participating in Light Conception so that the souls who would play their integral parts could make their entrances. Mighty and wondrous things did we see and hear.

The four angels, each in turn, told us that Mary Anna and Joseph ben Jacob had been over-lit with the full presence of the Son of Man. Like Mary Anna, Yeshua would also be born as an avatar capable of anchoring vast fields of cosmic consciousness into the earthplane. And just as Mary Anna had entered fully into my womb without Joachim's physical seed, so it would be with the conception of her son. And as it had been that Joachim's genetics were not required for Mary Anna's earthly expression, so it was that Joseph's physical DNA was not required. Likewise, as it had been with Joachim, Joseph's etheric seed and DNA were permeated with light as he energetically merged with the great cosmic soul that would be his son.

As we heard the sanctuary bell ringing, we once again became aware of our physical bodies touched by the dawn's first light. Tenderly holding each other, tears flowing, our bodies quaking, we lifted our hearts in praise to God on High. At last he was here! No sooner had we expressed our thanksgiving, than we heard a gentle knock at our door, which then slowly opened.

There stood a most radiant Mary Anna and Joseph! Their countenance shone with white light. Inwardly knowing that we knew what had occurred, Mary Anna and Joseph joined us as we silently knelt together and offered up our prayers of immense gratitude. The sweetest fragrance of lilies and roses wafted upon the air. Our hearts overflowed with thanksgiving.

Upon hearing the call to morning prayers, we went before the community to announce what had come upon us. The young women who had been prepared with Mary Anna wept with simultaneous joy and sadness. Each was a worthy candidate, capable of Immaculate Conception of the Son of Man. All had prepared well and had given their hearts to the often arduous task.

Now that Mary Anna had been chosen, the weight of the long months of initiations was felt and lifted up by each maiden, according to her degree of attachment to being the 'Chosen One'. So, in this hour, there was yet another initiation for each beloved soul. Instead of succumbing to disappointment, it was time now to shift their intention to bringing forth other great souls who would be Yeshua's disciples also demonstrating and supporting the Christ initiations.

Instead of going out into the fields to labour, we first attended to the essential chores, and then all gathered into the sanctuary for an entire day of fasting and prayer. Long into the night we prayed. Some continued in this fashion for several days. When all had received a witness and guidance for our next steps, the community of Carmel resumed its usual routine.

Because there is misunderstanding about how Joseph received the news of Mary Anna's pregnancy, I am weaving this account in such a way that you may walk with me between two worlds. Much of this misunderstanding is due to the manner in which your Gospel accounts were recorded and translated. On the one hand there is the story, as it is understood by the human mind, governed by fear and unbalanced polarities. And on the other hand, there is also the story as it was lived by those who are not bound by the limitations of the third dimension.

In your Gospel account, Joseph is described as distraught and ignorant of what had come upon Mary Anna. It is also implied that Mary Anna knew very little about Light Conception. It is said that it took a visitation of Gabriel to convince Joseph that there had been no foul play, so that he would accept Mary Anna as his wife and not bring recrimination down upon her. Thus would the egoic human mind contrive such an explanation, so that those who did not know the mysterious science of Light Conception could make some sense of the story that presented Yeshua's conception as a miracle.

Through the following centuries of darkness, those few adepts who knew the secret mysteries cloaked the meaning, and hid the records that came from the very hands of those who had witnessed the events. Some of these records are still hidden, some are suppressed by Church and state, others were destroyed. Yet that which was hidden is now coming forth when the cycles change to birth an era of light. Many will be surprised when your Bible's multilayered codes are broken.

As I have already shared with you, Joseph well understood what was happening.

Several weeks after the conception, Mary Anna confided that she had received guidance from Archangel Gabriel to make a pilgrimage to the Essene camp at Kadesh Barnea. Then she was to stay in Bethlehem with her cousin, Elizabeth, during the last trimester of Elizabeth's pregnancy, which was also a Light Conception. So, she and Joseph prepared for the journey. Mary of Magdala and Joseph of Arimathea, Tabitha and Isaac, and Rebekah and Simeon accompanied them.

All was brought into readiness for the journey to Kadesh Barnea, a remote Essene encampment in the Wilderness of Paran near the trade route that passes south toward the Sinai. It was here that Sarah and Abraham, the matriarch and patriarch of the ancient Hebrews were prepared to conceive their son, Isaac. It was here that an additional anointing of divine light would be delivered into Mary Anna's womb and into the wombs of the three other women whose lot it was to give birth to three daughters: Mary Magdalene, Sara, and Mariam.

These female children, who would eventually become some of Yeshua's key disciples, would also be initiated into the greater mysteries of resurrection and ascension. Of these, Mary Magdalene, Sara, and

Mariam would play pivotal roles in supporting Yeshua's life and work. So it was that Mary Anna, Mary of Magdala, Tabitha, Rebekah and their husbands responded to the call of Archangel Gabriel, even though it meant travelling under adverse summer conditions in order to receive a greater portion of light. Although I was not physically present, I attuned myself to bilocate from time to time and witnessed many wonderful things that I was asked to hold in my heart.

In this way a new chapter of our lives opened to us. Now that Yeshua had been conceived, we looked ahead to the fulfilment of all that he had come into the earthplane to accomplish. You may well imagine the joy that filled our hearts as you contemplate the children you have welcomed into your life. Whether or not you were the birth parent, to be close to a soul making its entrance into the earthplane is to be close to the heavenly realms. This is also true when one is close to souls taking their departure.

I have shared with you earlier that there are many highly evolved souls taking embodiment at this time to assist Mother Earth through her ascension process. Just as it was true for Yeshua and his cousins, who were light conceived and assisted by conscious parents and a supportive community, so is it possible to participate in Light Conception today. The process of coming into the density of Earth is wonderfully enhanced when parents, relatives, birth attendants, and caregivers consciously choose to lift their vibration into greater light. When there is coherent love present, it is possible to resonate harmoniously with these very sensitive children. With this support, these wondrous souls, who come with the ability to express great love, can accomplish the transformational work of replacing society's dysfunctional structures with those that are more conscious and humane.

Thus, while fulfilling my role as a mother and guide to the light conceived parents and children, I often reflected on the importance of communal family life at Carmel. I treasured Joachim's and my years of raising our beloved children. Reluctantly, I realized that his role as an exemplary father and teacher might soon be coming to an end.

So it was that Joachim and I drew close to one another. As we served our community, we felt the closeness of the glorious light realms as the light conceived babies grew in their mothers' wombs.

～ Chapter 18 ～
Joachim's Departure

Now it is with great sadness that I wish to tell you of the passing of Joachim into the realms of divine light. It was during the time that we were eagerly awaiting the return of Mary Anna from her three months long visit with Elizabeth, in Bethlehem, that Joachim began reluctantly to share his knowing with me that it would not be long before he would be leaving the earthplane.

He told me about dreams that informed him that his time was drawing nigh and that, unlike Hismariam who chose to ascend her physical body, he would be allowing the elements of his worn form to return to the Earth Mother. He was shown that, during his passing into the light, his higher Self would infuse the physical elements of his body with an added portion of consciousness to bless the Earth. Our beloved teachers Lord Maitreya and Maha Babaji were close and began instructing him in the process of consciously lifting up his immortal soul.

After three months passed, Joseph ben Jacob and Simeon took a wagon pulled by donkeys to Bethlehem in order to bring Mary Anna and Rebekah back to Mount Carmel. When they returned, we prepared a formal wedding feast for Mary Anna and Joseph but not for Rebekah and Simeon who had been married before their Light Conception had occurred. After three days of ritual preparation, Joseph and Mary Anna were traditionally wed beneath the canopy of Abraham and Sarah, in the late autumn of 5 BC.

In addition to Mary Anna and Joseph, several other couples were also wed in community celebration. Not all were with child, however. As I have already explained, Mary Anna and Rebekah had been blessed with Light Conceptions, as had also Mary of Magdala and Tabitha. We looked upon these women with reverence. The wedded couples exchanged solemn vows and then we sang, danced, and rejoiced in jubilant celebration.

About a month after the wedding, Joachim came to me while I was labouring in the garden, digging winter root vegetables. He bid me put my tools away and walk with him to Elijah's stone, as we called the sacred altar that Elijah had built shortly before taking his departure within the 'Chariot of the Sun'. Laying everything aside, we walked to the uppermost knoll of the mount.

Not a word did Joachim say to me as we made our way. My heart felt the chill of a nagging foreboding, as the cold December winds penetrated my bones. When, alas, we stood together at the top of the mount, Joachim took me into his arms as we sank upon the dried winter grasses. His face was pale and solemn. Yet, there was a twinkle in his eyes, which eclipsed my fear as I read his body. Still, he remained silent as he tenderly took my hands and kissed each finger and palm, pressing my hands to his parched lips. His dark brown eyes blazed with a fiery energy. It was as though he were the Sphinx itself sitting before me.

Then he lifted me into his lap, cradling me as if I were a child. His chest began to heave with suppressed tears. At last, gasping, tears gushed as a river from his heart. I was stunned, unknowing, not allowing myself to know what this extraordinary emotional outburst might mean. When his tears subsided, my face held close to his in his hands, he began to share his knowing. While gazing intensely into my eyes and speaking in a hushed voice, Joachim explained that he had been out with the sheep and goats, enjoying his communal turn as a shepherd, when he was taken deeply inward. He was shown the Earth and all the light beings who were assembling for the birth of the child we would call Yeshua ben Joseph.

At this point in his story, the countenance of my beloved began to shine as the sun. The wind whipped around us. Joachim's long, curly, white hair and beard danced like fiery serpents around his head. Our heavy, woollen shawls billowed as we clung to one another.

It was now my turn to weep, as I slowly realized that my beloved would no longer be physically by my side. Then, with great resolve I surrendered my will in order to facilitate the Greater Part as I understood it. My chest continued to heave, even as Joachim's had before. Finally, we lay spent, our arms and legs entwined. Our hearts sought each other and wove tendrils of light until a tapestry of eternal love was woven, which our physical parting could not tear asunder. Slowly, we opened our eyes to behold the truth in each other. We are eternally one! In that knowing, there was immense comfort. Shaken and weak, we held to each other as we arose and turned homewards.

The sun broke through thick, grey, clouds as if the hand of God were blessing us. We followed the golden rays of light to our abode where we sought refuge among our Essene family.

We sent word to our children who lived in Galilee and Judea to come and join us in a feast in Mount Carmel. After supper, we called the members of our immediate family to come to our small chamber. Within the dim glow of candles and terra-cotta lamps, Joachim took each child, now grown, into his arms and poured anointing oil upon their heads. Over each one, he pronounced a father's blessing. Our tears flowed. We could not imagine what we would do without Joachim's presence. Over Mary Anna he lingered, placing his hands upon her swollen belly. Light burst forth around us, and each of us was calmed and comforted.

The following day was the Sabbath. After the ritual observances, Joachim called the entire Carmel community to gather in the sanctuary. He explained that he would soon be taking his departure but knew not the exact hour. Each soul went forth to this patriarch of Carmel to receive a blessing. Those of our family who were our sons-in-law, daughters-in-law, nieces, nephews, cousins, and grandchildren, who had not been called to come to our small room, now received a father's blessing from this beloved soul. Joachim had been such a constant companion, teacher, and brother that it was difficult to imagine how our Carmel family could get along without him.

So it was that weeks went by with no further hint of Joachim's departure. However, knowing our days together were far fewer than our personal wills would have chosen, we spent as much time together as possible. We did all the little things for each other that had always opened our hearts to a greater love of God and life. We visited our favourite places around Mount Carmel, especially lingering by the lone cedar tree where many years earlier a robed minstrel played his lyre and pipes, calling me to our rendezvous with destiny. And everyday saw us together in deep meditation where we found deep solitude and inner peace.

When we knew the hour of his departure had come, we came together, emptying our hearts of all that we had shared, and offered it up to the Lord Most High. We knelt in our small chamber, our hands softly caressing each other's hearts, surrendering everything we were to each other and to God. Then, I arose and stepped aside of my beloved. He remained in lotus position upon our pallet. I took my place opposite him, by the door. I burned sweet sandalwood, frankincense, and myrrh incense. As I stood before my beloved, I offered up the psalms of David and the psalms of Hathor, Isis, and Osiris.

Joachim went into deep meditation. I saw his subtle bodies expanding around him in glorious, rainbow-hued, geometric patterns. Energy fields pulsed with his deep, rhythmic breathing, until a deep silence arose, as if the breath were being sucked in. Then, there was stillness as Joachim's last breath passed ever so slowly through his pursed lips. From that point onward, his body was sustained entirely by prana. His beautiful countenance radiated profound serenity as he gradually released his physical focus and surrendered into the Source of his being.

I witnessed the light gathering around him, as he slowly lifted his consciousness in a spiralling fashion from the base of his spine. The serpent energy quickened and rose up. The light increased until Joachim was wrapped in a fog-like mist. His face became transparent. His subtle energy fields spun faster and faster. Then I beheld his spirit lift up through his crown. His glory was magnificent to feel and behold. The silver cord, connecting his soul to his body, spun in a helical fashion, as all his life force moved up and out of every cell of his physical body.

The capstone of the etheric, golden pyramid above Joachim's head glowed with a blinding gold-white light. Every cell in my body was quickened with life force, even as Joachim's body was slowly emptying. It was not that his life essence was entering me. It was that the universal life force was magnified in my body while I held the space for Joachim's full consciousness to depart its focus out of his physical form.

Then Joachim's silver cord snapped.

Slowly the heavenly vision closed, and our chamber dimmed. Joachim's body was still sitting in his favourite meditation position. I remained where I was for hours, continuing to assist Joachim's ascending consciousness. The light began to depart from the form before me until there was but a dim, blue glow surrounding it. When I knew it was time, I gently approached the body, lovingly taking it into my arms and laying it upon the pallet. I removed the clothing, and, using spikenard balm and sea salts impregnated with healing oils, I washed and anointed Joachim's body. Then, from a pottery urn containing oil-soaked linens and sheets of cotton gauze, used for the shrouding of deceased bodies, and for the regeneration purposes I have explained earlier, I wrapped a cocoon of gauze around the body.

I left our room and hurried to Mary Anna and the others to call them to come. Next, I walked around the circumference of the Mount Carmel compound, ringing the small bell that denoted the passing of the soul of one of our community. I performed my ritual washings and joined with those who now were stepping, one by one, into my cell, offering their prayers and blessings to Joachim and to themselves. At last, Eli, who was trained more fully than I in the process of embalming, came with two other brothers to remove Joachim's body to the special room set aside in the infirmary for such purposes.

For three days before burial, we acknowledged the passage of Joachim's soul to a new life. Because our community understood and realized that his departure was taken as an adept who knows how to consciously pass from the physical body, there was something of an air of celebration instead of great weeping and keening. Yet, to be sure, there were tears and sadness because our beloved brother and father was no longer with us on the physical plane.

For myself there was an agonizing grief as I slowly released my immortal beloved who was as my own self. There was a place within my soul that would not be comforted. It was as if my heart had been torn and broken with the memory of our one soul's first rending into male and female. My solace was in the knowing we were one and that the divine love of our Father–Mother God had called Joachim to a greater assignment. I knew Joachim had merged with a larger portion of our over-soul so that he could assist the coming of the Teacher of Righteousness from the other side of the veil. Joachim and I would continue to commune on the inner planes as he fulfilled his ethereal role.

Even though I was comforted in knowing the purpose of Joachim's departure, I still felt the torment within my soul over our mortal separation, which had renewed the sting of the original separation that was God's plan in the beginning of time. So, I resolved to heal my heart by opening my being to the Great Work that was now upon us. The Anointed One, he who would demonstrate the way of a Christ, had come among us. He was here, right here in Carmel! He was within the womb of our beloved Mary Anna and his precious body was growing daily. His great soul was fast approaching its advent into the Earth. How could I lament my loneliness when everything for which I had prepared so many long years was now upon me?

So it was with steadfastness that I directed my attention to the work at hand. Joachim's body lay in a communal cemetery cave near a grove of cedars and cypresses. And though I would come, remembering our love with offerings of flowers and psalms each week before the Sabbath, I turned my greater attention to preparing the young maidens for their Light Conceptions and seasons of giving birth.

৯ Chapter 19 ৯
Yeshua ben Joseph's Birth

I hovered over Mary Anna as much as she would allow me. I loved to place my hands upon the swollen bellies of the beautiful women whose light conceived babies were as my own. I taught them how to commune with the souls who were growing within their wombs. Each soul brought very high frequencies of light directly from the Throne of God. We assisted each incoming soul to hold its latticed patterns of multifaceted energy in perfect alignment. With Metatron and the Archangels, Seraphim, and Cherubim, we wove and encoded the DNA grids with enormous amounts of information. Together, we prepared the frequencies within and around the mothers, husbands, and community, so that these precious souls could come in as harmoniously and painlessly as possible.

Then, in January, we received unsettling news from Judith's husband, Justinian, who had just returned from Rome. He told us that Augustus Caesar had decreed that a census of the Empire's populace be taken during the three weeks following the spring equinox. It required every household to go to the town of ancestral origin, to be registered by the tax collectors and to vow allegiance to Rome. So it was that the community of Carmel came together to discuss our differing opinions about this hardship which was being asked of us by Caesar. Many of us were incensed over having to divide our allegiance between God and Caesar. In the midst of this controversy, our attention was drawn to the loud thumping of Joseph ben Jacob's staff on the flagstone floor.

Silently, we turned to Joseph, who had just opened the scroll containing the words of Micah the Prophet. He then read: 'But thou, Bethlehem Ephrathah, though thou be little among the thousands of Judah, yet out of thee shall come forth that One who is to be ruler in Israel; He whose goings forth have been predicted from of old, from the days of eternity. Henceforth, He shall deliver them, until the time that she who is in labour has given birth; then the remnant of His brethren shall return to the children of Israel. And He shall stand and shepherd His flock in the strength of the Lord, in the majesty of the name of the Lord His God; and the people shall return; for now His dominion shall extend to the ends of the Earth; and this One shall be peace.'

So he read from the prophet Micah, until all began to understand that Creator was orchestrating a divine purpose, using Caesar as an instrument to fulfil prophecy. Joseph suggested that, rather than wasting energy debating, all who were from the House of David and whose families had come out of Bethlehem gather together and pool our resources, so that the necessary journey could be taken as comfortably and safely as possible.

Also to be taken into consideration were the women whose pregnancies were coming full term, including Mary Anna and Rebekah. It was sore to think of the long journey being taken when their bellies were so swollen with child. Therefore, during the next several weeks, Joseph organized our community's resources so that there were plenty of wagons, supplies, and able-bodied men who could make the trip go smoothly. The winter's cold had passed and spring was in the air. The Passover was soon at hand, and the early harvest of winter grains, the lambing season, and shearing of the flocks required our attention before we could begin our journey. There was also the taxed allotment of our harvest to be delivered into the hands of the local tax collectors.

In order that our community be left with a small, core group of men at all times, we divided ourselves, according to our tribes of origin and our destinations, and cycled our leave at different times. With enough of the community moving in companies, there would be little concern for the marauding bands of thieves who robbed the unwary upon the highways. Instead of feeling sorry for ourselves, we chose to 'gird up our loins' and make the best of our unfavourable circumstance.

Then a joyful surprise happened a week before our departure when Rebekah gave birth to a beautiful girl, named Mariam. When we left, Mary Anna and Rebekah were placed into a blanket-laden cart, pulled by two sturdy oxen. The very young and elderly also rode in wagons. I rode a mule. Several other women rode donkeys, camels, or walked. Most of the men and children went on foot. We brought our musical instruments, food, tents, and fodder for the animals. We sang as we walked, told stories around the campfires, and took turns with the necessary duties, which moved us along our way over cobble-stone-paved Roman roads. As we passed by the outskirts of Jerusalem, the road widened and became paved with stones, cut and laid by the Roman garrisons and slaves. Aqueducts and deep wells along the way supplied plenty of water.

We felt protected and well cared for until we arrived within the narrow streets of Bethlehem, which were thronged with tumultuous crowds of people, animals, and conveyances. Roman soldiers were everywhere. Their swords and spears bristled against the sky, and their whips smacked the backs of slaves and naïve passersby who did not know the appropriate protocol. Such clamour I had not witnessed since Alexandria.

Just beyond Bethlehem, near Etam, where I had lived long ago, there was a valley watered by a small spring. This land belonged to a distant relative, who was the father of my son Luke's wife, Abigail. There we took refuge, away from the noise of the swollen village. We set up camp near the well that watered their sheep and cattle. It was good to have our close friends and family around us. We awaited other family members, who would be coming from Galilee, Judea, and Samaria. In order to raise our spirits, we took this opportunity to create a wonderful family reunion.

Joseph ben Jacob's sister, Elizabeth (who was also Mary Anna's paternal cousin) had given birth to her Light Conceived child six months earlier. It had been twenty years since Elizabeth had last conceived. Her womb had been barren the last eight years since the ceasing of her monthly bleeding. So it was that we were eager to welcome this miracle child. In accordance with guidance that her husband, Zacharias, had received from Archangel Gabriel, their child was named John. They also had a grown daughter by the name of Azirah, who was recently married and expecting her first child. Zacharias offered to stay at the Temple in Jerusalem, where he performed his priestly duties, so that Mary Anna and I could stay with Elizabeth in her small abode on the outskirts of Bethlehem. Rebekah remained at the camp with Simeon and her baby while she was still undergoing her time of purification, as the time of bleeding after childbirth was called by the patriarchy. Joseph came and went from the camp every day.

When the first day arrived for those of Galilee to be registered, we went before the census takers and tax collectors in Bethlehem.

It was an ordeal, no matter how philosophically I attempted to look at it. By the time we were finished that evening, Mary Anna's birth contractions had begun. Joseph sat her on Elizabeth's faithful donkey, and we made haste to Elizabeth's small upper room, which was situated above a stable that opened to fenced pens and hillside caves used for animals and storage. Her room was accessed through a breezeway to an inner courtyard that was shared by three connected dwellings belonging to Zacharias' brother, Zenos. Then, Joseph carried Mary Anna up Elizabeth's narrow stone stairs and laid her on the special pallet that had been prepared for her labour. Joseph had already sent a runner to bring Luke to act as attending physician in case there should be any complications.

We were less than three miles away from the hillside caves and fenced stables where Hannah had given birth to Aurianna long ago. I reflected that it had been almost five hundred and ninety-two years since that moment when Hannah and I, her greater self, merged in the humble stable-cave of Naomi's son-in-law. Now, here I was again in Bethlehem awaiting the moment of all moments for which I had taken embodiment so very long ago.

Following Joseph and Mary Anna, Elizabeth carried John upon her hip and a bundle of Egyptian cotton sheets in her other arm. I carried urns of water. Mary Anna's small body quaked as she panted. Her contractions quickened and became more and more intense as we approached the midnight hour. We continually reminded her to breathe as she pushed, relaxing into the birth pangs. Between chewing on a root that lessened the pain, she repeated mantras to her beloved child to calm him and herself. With her eyes turned upwards to the Holy of Holies at the centre of her brain, she prayed and allowed herself to go into a very deep trance state. I checked Yeshua's position and found him coming down the birth canal favourably.

The contractions gradually intensified through the midnight hour. She bore down with great strength for so young a maiden of sixteen years. I encouraged her to sound forth the feelings that engulfed her. Straightaway, Mary Anna's yoni began to open with Yeshua's crowning head. It was good that we had been preparing her body during the past month for the birthing process. Because she had not known the penetration of a man, we had assisted her by applying salves, massaging and expanding the delicate tissues through which Yeshua was now passing.

From somewhere deep in my being arose a litany of sounds. Out of my throat came the familiar song of highest destiny, which the priestesses of Hathor sing to newborn souls. High above us, clearly visible as a stationary 'star' in the heavens, was the Beth Elohim MerKaBa. Hosts of angels, dominions, and elementals gathered and hovered. It was as though all life held its breath as the deepest silence penetrated the very core of Heaven and Earth.

Soon his head, covered with curly, dark, auburn-gold hair, followed by the rest of his small body, lay in my hands! 'Glory be to God in the Highest. Peace, good will to humankind!' the refrains of the angelic hosts resounded. Our chamber glowed with golden celestial light. 'Behold, My Son, in whom I Am come to gather My own. In thee, I am well pleased,' were the words etched into our hearts by God Most High. So did we receive the Son of Man. And, just as he had promised and shown me over a year before, Yeshua had delivered himself into my small hands! Indeed, I was blessed among women, even as was his precious mother.

Yeshua was born in the sign of Aries. His birth occurred about one hour after midnight on the twenty-first day of Nisan, according to the Jewish calendar, which corresponds to early April of 4 BC, according to your Gregorian calendar.

Joseph had remained with us throughout the labour and delivery. Sometimes, he would pace the floor, feeling that he could not interfere with the midwifery in which we older women were absorbed. Adding to Joseph's awkward dilemma was also the shyness he felt because, even though he was Mary Anna's husband, he had not yet had sexual intercourse with her. However, the moment Yeshua began to crown, Joseph was immediately at my side.

Several days earlier, Joseph had gone to the stable below to fetch a small wooden corncrib, which was used to feed the sheep and goats. We had already washed it and lined it with a sheep's fleece and the freshest straw that could be found at this season of the year. Over this, we added folded sheets of soft Egyptian cotton. This humble manger would later receive the infant Yeshua, so that Mary Anna could rest.

John lay in a cradle near Elizabeth's pallet. He had remained wide-awake during the entire birth. Sometimes he would cry, and Elizabeth would give him a breast to suckle while she washed and cooled Mary Anna's face and hands. Then, when Mary Anna required more attention, John would be laid back into his cradle or placed in Joseph's nervous arms. It was in the thick of things that John preferred to be. So it was that he observed the coming forth of his cousin, whose pathway he would open and prepare.

While Elizabeth tended Mary Anna's delivery of the placenta, I gently laid Yeshua upon his mother's belly with the umbilical cord still attached. Then I placed the placenta into preservative oils within a special container to be ceremonially buried later. Joseph hovered over his son and his beloved Mary, as he called her. We abided in silence until the life pulse connecting Mary Anna and her babe had finally subsided, then we cut, tied the umbilical cord, and washed the newborn babe.

Here he was, safely delivered! We praised the Father–Mother God with all our hearts, minds, and souls. We prayed for the strength and wisdom to protect and prepare Yeshua ben Joseph to accomplish all that he had come to do.

We wondered that Luke had not arrived yet, but were thankful that his medical skills had not been required. Although it was still dark outside, a great light flooded our little room as though it were noonday. After we had washed and anointed Mary Anna, we took her to her own bed, which was behind a hanging rug that partitioned the living room. Yeshua was swaddled with the finest woven Egyptian cotton, which Mary Anna had carefully hemmed and embroidered with a colourful geometric design that was common to the lineage of David. We could feel the presence of the Great Ones all around. Communions between the many realms and dimensions were listened to within our hearts, as we silently sat together for the next few hours, watching over the sleeping babe at Mary Anna's breast.

Then, there was a knock at the door. Elizabeth ran to open it and found her landlord and brother-in-law, Zenos standing with Luke, whose fast breathing indicated he had been running. Luke immediately approached his youngest sister and the babe, Yeshua. After washing his hands, he carefully proceeded to examine them and was overjoyed that they both were healthy and robust. As he was trained to do from his youth, Luke later made a written record of this most wondrous of stories. This record although altered, has survived relatively intact down through the centuries and is still known in your day as *The Gospel of Luke*.

Luke profusely apologized for not being present for the birth, but explained that he had been attending another birthing mother, assisting both mother and child to survive a critical condition. I smiled inwardly as I realized that it was my hands, not Luke's, that received Yeshua ben Joseph, just as my grandson had promised!

A short time later, Zenos returned to announce that there was a gathering of celebrants at his door on the street below. Some were shepherds who laboured for Luke's father-in-law. They told him a great host of angels had appeared to them while they were caring for their sheep on the hillside. Others of the group reported they had been awakened from very lucid dreams in which they were told to come to Elizabeth's home. They had known Mary Anna was about to give birth when they last saw her. All had been told to arise and come forth to behold a child, newly born, called Immanuel, Prince of Peace, who was favoured of God, even as was Zacharias' son, John, who would later be called John the Baptist.

As the sun began its ascent, all of these beloved pilgrims were invited to take turns coming up the stairs behind Zenos' main house in twos and threes to sit for a short time of meditation with the sleeping babe. From time to time, unexpectedly, Yeshua would open his wide, almond-shaped, blue-grey eyes to look upon these family members and friends who were among the first to welcome him.

Of my children, there were Nathan, Luke, and Rebekah who came with their partners. Rebekah brought their baby daughter, Mariam. Joachim's and my other sons and daughters were far away. Joseph of Arimathea along with his wife, Mary of Magdala, and his sister, Martha, were counted in the census at Bethany. In a fascinating synchronicity, Mary Magdalene was born the same number of hours after sunset as Yeshua's birth occurred before sunrise on that very same day in Bethany.

Among Luke's father-in-law's labourers, there was a young boy of twelve years by the name of Nathaniel ben Tolmi (bar Tolmi in Aramaic). He had been with the company of shepherds who beheld the angels. In his arms was a newborn orphaned lamb, which he brought as an offering to Yeshua. When he saw Yeshua, he fell on his knees, crying out that in a vision several months earlier he had seen this very child, whom an angel had told him was the promised Messiah. As he wept, his tears fell into the soft wool of his bleating offering. When he looked up, Mary Anna invited him to come forward. Laying a gentle hand upon Nathaniel's head, she looked steadfastly into his eyes and said, 'You, my child, are favoured of

God. He who is now with us has called you to come out of the world and to be as one who is his friend and disciple forever.' Then, she asked Joseph to take the lamb, while she placed the babe, Yeshua, into Nathaniel's tanned arms.

I realize, my beloved friend, that my story is becoming increasingly complex. I also realize that much of what I am sharing with you conflicts with the stories generally accepted by Christians today. Although I am risking confusion and conflict for you, my intent is to bring clarity and open-mindedness. There is so much to be conveyed; and it is being given portion by portion, topic by topic, energy flow by energy flow.

However, do not accept my story blindly; yet give it a chance to work upon your heart and then upon your mind. I remind you that these words are being given in such a way as to open and stretch your consciousness so that you can consider alternatives. It is for you to discern for yourself the truth of what is contained herein, according to its power to uplift, transform, and empower your own knowing.

More than to bring forth another version of the Christ story, it is my deeper purpose to prepare you for the advent of the Christ within your own heart. In this way, you are being prepared for the great changes that are coming upon you. Therefore, open your heart and remember the energies that are witnessed through your feelings.

I shall say further that I am here with you. The very purpose of my coming long ago is the purpose of my being here in this present moment. You need not think that I am distant in time or space, or that what occurred 2,000 years ago has no relevance for your day. You are currently in the process of rewriting your past history. Indeed, some of you have come back from the future for precisely this purpose.

I am Anna of Carmel, returned to bear witness to the birth of the Christ in you. I am here to receive you, just as I received the Anointed One 2,000 years ago! As I bring you a chronology of events and the stories of familiar characters you have studied, know that it is the transmission of transformational frequencies that is more important than the words through which they come. Once you can hear beyond the words, you may remember who you really are and step forward to fulfil your mission by playing your part in this grand drama of planetary ascension that we are co-creating together.

∽

⇜ *Chapter 20* ⇝
The Visitation of the Magi

Although receiving Yeshua into my hands that remarkable day was the fulfilment of the vision I had been given long ago, I did not know exactly how the drama would unfold. Yet I understood, from those visions and initiations I had received that the way would be arduous, even perilous. Although the ultimate purpose of his coming was to exemplify union in God, the sword of separation would be felt to the utmost, until that sword was beaten into a ploughshare. A great responsibility was resting upon our shoulders as we walked through this illusory world which, like a hall of mirrors, was darkened and distorted by ignorance.

To fulfil the Law of Moses, Joseph held the eight-day-old Yeshua while Luke circumcised him and placed the name Yeshua ben Joseph into the records of the synagogue in Bethlehem. Then six weeks later, to fulfil prophecy, which was our agreement as actors within this human play, we took Yeshua to the remnant of Solomon's Temple in Jerusalem to give an offering. Two turtledoves were offered, as was the custom, though the sacrifice of animals was offensive to us. For this reason, we chose not to sacrifice the little lamb that was Nathaniel's offering to Yeshua. And, at the same time, we were willing to acknowledge the entrenched Mosaic tradition so as to fulfil all things.

There was a certain elder by the name of Simeon at the Temple who recognized Yeshua. While looking upon Mary Anna with teary eyes and filled with the grace of Shekinah's presence, the old priest prophesied. 'Yea, my daughter, it will be as if a sword has rent the veil over the Mount of Sion, and you shall not pass through without that sword also piercing your heart.' His saying troubled us because we had seen in a vision that when the sun would be darkened at Yeshua's passing we would feel as though a sword had taken our very lives. 'Mother–Father God, sustain us through that dark night!' my heart cried out.

There was also an elderly high-priestess known as Anna, who stepped forward to hold the infant Yeshua in her arms. She was a seeress who had lived all her life within the cloistered walls of the Temple, and although she recognized who Yeshua was, she kept her counsel, except to press her hand upon Mary Anna's heart. And likewise did Mary Anna place a gentle finger upon this elder's heart and brow, acknowledging the wisdom and love of this one who had acted as a surrogate mother, as well as a teacher, when Mary Anna had come to the Temple as a part of her preparation.

After the ceremony, we gathered at Joseph of Arimathea's elegant home near the Temple. He informed us that a group of wise men had come from the Orient with some of their wives. He was told that they had had an audience with King Herod, and according to knowledgeable members of the Sanhedrin, this company of magi was in search of a child whom they had seen in a vision and whose birth had been predicted in the prophecies of various texts.

The magi were aware of certain prophesied celestial phenomena, including a great planetary conjunction with an unusual zodiacal placement of planets, heralded by the appearance of a comet that had been observed during the previous year. And they were also aware of the appearance of a bright new 'star' in the heavens during the past three months which, unlike other stars, had remained stationary above Judea. They had followed their calculations, based on their inner and outer guidance, which they had interpreted as indicating that this child may have already been born in the vicinity of Bethlehem. Now they were desirous of finding him so that they could acknowledge him as the herald of the next millennium.

After Herod had consulted his chief priests, magicians, and soothsayers, his paranoia increased when he was informed about the prediction of the prophet Micah that a ruler would come out of lowly Bethlehem to govern Israel. Therefore, he sent the company of wise men to Bethlehem to find the child and then return to bring him word. This news rested uneasily upon our ears and hearts, for we knew that Yeshua was the child that the magi and Herod sought.

It was common knowledge that Herod was aging and ailing with dementia. He was given to irrational fits of rage, which he attempted to suppress with opium. We shuddered at the obscene debaucheries and homicidal atrocities that Herod had committed against the members of his family, as well as the peoples he governed. We knew that it was wise to be as unattached as possible from the suffering around us. So we worked with our cellular memory, which held patterns of separation and judgement. And we transmuted our fearful emotions, which seemed to be triggered more than usual in Jerusalem. In peaceful Carmel, initiates were required to go into special chambers in order to feel the discordant, fearful energies that seemed to permeate all of Jerusalem.

I asked my son, Joseph of Arimathea, to send a trusted messenger to find these magi and bring them to his upper reception room for supper. There, they would be questioned concerning their intent and trustworthiness before they were brought into the council room to meet Mary Anna and Yeshua. In any case, the little family would take their leave through a secret underground passage which led outside the city wall at the foot of the Mount of Olives, when we knew it was safe to do so.

We secreted ourselves in a back room, which was positioned over a cistern that was very ancient. Through the centuries, the Brother–Sisterhood had used this room for their meetings. When necessary, they would leave through the underground tunnel below the floor, which had been dug through the rocky crevasse of a natural subterranean streambed. So it was that we took counsel with one another, prayed, and awaited the appropriate action to be taken.

Mary of Magdala, Joseph of Arimathea's wife, had come with her sister-in-law, Martha, from their home in Bethany to be with us. She brought her infant daughter, Mary, with her so that we could feel her presence and give her our blessings. We knew that this girl child was to play an extraordinary role in the years to come. She would be prepared, even as Yeshua, to fulfil all that was required of her.

Arrangements had also been made by Joseph of Arimathea, for a number of his younger siblings to gather with us, including Nathan from Cana and an aging Ruth who came by boat from Ephesus. All of us were filled with wonderment as we took turns holding the seven-weeks-old Yeshua in our arms, while awaiting the arrival of the magi.

Three days later, the twelve male magi and their twelve principal wives came forth to Joseph's large upper reception room to sup and be questioned. I remained secreted away with Mary Anna and Yeshua until word was sent that these magi were indeed those that I had witnessed earlier in a vision. My heart leaped and fluttered with nervous expectancy while we awaited their arrival into the council chamber. At last we heard their muffled approach down the stairs and long corridor. Mary Anna's Joseph opened the heavy, iron-grated door and stood before us smiling.

With solemn decorum, the twenty-four magi slowly passed into the council room to take their positions in a circle around Mary Anna and the babe, Yeshua. Each announced their name and place of origin. Then the three who were hierophants among the Order of the Magi came forward, representing all twenty-four. They read passages from various scrolls and showed us astrological charts, which they interpreted.

Next, they turned to a turbaned Parthian, who had announced his name as Balthazar. He reached into a small trunk made of hardwood and polished brass, and carefully removed a smaller ebony box, together with several silk-wrapped containers of various sizes. First, he placed before Yeshua a censer that burned frankincense and myrrh, which he lit. Next, he placed at Mary Anna's feet several vials of precious oils and ointments. Balthazar brought forth a robe of purple silk, embroidered with gold and iridescent rainbow-coloured fibres. This robe was indeed fit for a king. It was small, made for a child.

Finally, Balthazar opened the small, ebony box and removed a broad, beaded collar of lapis and gold, which had belonged to the Egyptian pharaoh Akhenaten. Beneath it, was a menat, the ceremonial necklace of Hathor, which represented the union of male and female principles. This, too, was reported to have belonged to the household of Akhenaten's mother. These treasured items were tokens to assist Yeshua to realize that he was born of the royal bloodlines of King David and Pharaoh Akhenaten.

In this way, Yeshua was acknowledged by these great beings who understood that before them was the Anointed One, whose star they had followed.

৩

⇜ Chapter 21 ⇝

Egyptian Sojourn

With concern for Yeshua and other innocent babes, we took counsel with one another. After carefully considering all aspects of the situation, we agreed upon a radical change of plans. The angel Gabriel had appeared to Mary Anna's Joseph in a lucid dream and had advised him not to return to Mount Carmel. Instead, Joseph was counselled to take Mary Anna and their child directly to Egypt, and to remain there indefinitely until he received guidance that it was safe to return. We reviewed the records and shared our memories. We realized that it was to fulfil prophecy that, like Moses, a Messiah would come out of Egypt unto the peoples of Israel to call them out of the wilderness.

Joseph of Arimathea called a trusted friend and messenger to go that very night to the households of those who were of the Brother– Sisterhood. The word was given to make certain preparations of supplies, horses and wagons, as was Joseph's custom when he went abroad with his boats. Others were told to go to Bethlehem to warn Elizabeth to take John to Martha's home in Bethany until the danger had passed. Those Essene brethren and families who still remained in Bethlehem after the census were encouraged to make their way back to their homes. The word spread among the households of Jerusalem and Bethlehem that it would be well to safeguard their children.

Preparations were quickly made for the departure of Joseph, Mary Anna, and Yeshua to Egypt. Under the cover of darkness, Joseph of Arimathea and his servants escorted them to the port of Joppa. There, a boat was quickly loaded with the necessary supplies and crew for the journey to Alexandria. In order to avoid arousing suspicions, Joseph returned to Jerusalem, and I returned to Carmel.

The magi then returned to Herod and reported that, since they had not found the child in Bethlehem, they would continue to follow the new star to the southwest. It had been indicated in their dreams that such a one as they were looking for might be found among the desert peoples. Consequently, the magi took their leave of Judea and made their way southwest to the Sinai and Egypt.

Soon thereafter, the infant Yeshua went with his parents to the bustling city of Alexandria. They were introduced to those members of the Brother–Sisterhood of Light who facilitate safe passage and refuge for anyone requiring it. Still taking precautions, the little family secretly made their way to Heliopolis. When Yeshua was less than a year old they took up residence with Isaac and Tabitha, in Tabitha's parents' home in a nearby village. For the next seven years, my beloved grandson was surrounded by a host of adoring aunts and uncles who were with him during his most formative years.

In the summer of 2 BC, Mary Anna gave birth to fraternal twins, James and Jude. Another male child, Joseph the Younger, sometimes called Joses, was born the following year. In addition to his three brother playmates, there were his light conceived cousins, Sara, the daughter of Isaac and Tabitha, and Mariam, the daughter of Rebekah and Simeon. Yeshua also came to know numerous distant cousins who lived in Alexandria, Heliopolis, and Thebes, most of whom were descendants of my daughter Aurianna. Because we kept careful genealogical records, it was possible for Yeshua to meet many of his relatives over the eight years that he lived in Egypt.

Among Yeshua's cousins, the one he loved most was Rebekah's daughter, Mariam, who had moved to Egypt with her parents when she was one year old. Mariam conveniently lived nearby at his Aunt Mariamne's spacious home. But Sara had moved to southern Gaul with her parents when she was three, so there was not an opportunity to really become acquainted with his dark-skinned cousin.

Outwardly, Mariam was beautiful and graceful, yet reserved. To know the inner Mariam was to find a profoundly wise and sensitive soul, so attuned to the nonphysical dimensions that it seemed as though she were barely present in this one. It was this tendency to be otherworldly that became more and more evident as Mariam endured many hardships and losses through the years. These inward qualities enabled her to serve as a faithful confidante to Yeshua and many others throughout her life.

It was in Mariam that Yeshua confided his deepest thoughts, because she could always bring herself to be fully present for him, no matter what he shared. She would straighten her spine, breathe deeply, open her heart, and be there. No other child could do what Mariam did so naturally. Yeshua loved Mariam as a sister. He even had fantasies that someday he might marry her. They were devoted friends who understood each other better than anyone else.

As Yeshua grew in wisdom, he especially loved to hear stories about his ancestral family, including the great Pharaoh Akhenaten. Both of his parents were wonderful storytellers, assisting his active imagination to place him into the scenes they described. His aunt Mariamne was a skilled dramatist, dancer, and singer, whose every gesture and word made her stories come alive. The vast repertoire of stories that his parents, aunts, and uncles shared with him covered great epochs in human history, touched on the sacred legends of the Egyptian gods and goddesses, and opened vistas into the natural world. So it was at a tender age, through the loving assistance of his family, Yeshua began to be enriched and empowered in his love of humanity, his ancestral lineage, spiritual mysteries, and the diverse wonders of nature.

Like his uncle, Joseph of Arimathea, Yeshua easily mastered languages. He could speak fluent Egyptian and Greek, as well as his family's native Aramaic and Hebrew tongues. He poured over ancient papyri and inquisitively touched carved hieroglyphs. With his father's assistance, he learned how to decipher the cryptic messages of the Brother–Sisterhood within the texts. Yeshua was by nature very curious, and he loved to go with his father into the libraries, pyramids, and temples along the Nile.

From time to time, Mary Anna accompanied Joseph and Yeshua on their journeys, thus taking her initiations in the temples of Isis, Hathor, and Horus. She also took initiation in the Great Pyramid. Memories of having been an adept in previous incarnations in Egypt came easily. All that Joseph and Mary Anna experienced in Egypt prepared them for the support they would continue to give their sons and daughters as their ministries unfolded.

Yeshua stayed with his relatives when his parents were away taking initiations. Occasionally Yeshua accompanied his father on journeys that took him to temples to the south, where legends had said the Queen of Sheba had taken the Ark of the Covenant for safe keeping during the time of Solomon. He also enjoyed going into the nearby temples of the Giza Plateau, which he knew he would revisit some day.

As reported to me by his mother and other relatives, Yeshua accomplished much in the eight years he lived in Egypt. The process had begun of removing the few, but necessary, buffering veils that his consciousness received at birth. The vast cosmic energies that came together as one composite within Yeshua were very intensely experienced by his physical, emotional and mental bodies. Removing the necessary veils that protected his denser bodies continued for much of his life.

His parents carefully explained his unusual experiences as those that are common to initiates who are taken into the mysteries of Osiris-Isis-Horus, which include the Rite of the Sepulchre. Angels and ascended masters taught Yeshua and his parents that a new manner of personal and planetary ascension was to be cultivated from his infancy, and that Yeshua would later demonstrate this for humanity. These revelations were both challenging and comforting. Challenging, because from time to time the task ahead seemed overwhelming. However, the increased solace and radiant hope that accompanied these insights caused any anxiety to subside.

Yeshua could see beyond surface appearances, and realized that he had a gift for healing the injured and lame. He saw energy fields, heard peoples' thoughts, and felt everything anyone might be feeling. He would have a precognition dream, a thought, or a vision and the event would come to pass. Sometimes Yeshua shared his inner life with his family, but most of the time he kept his experiences to himself.

In other ways, he was as ordinary and simple as any child; however, he was exceptionally curious, always asking questions, experimenting, constructing, and looking into things. Yeshua could also be very stubborn once he made up his mind about something he knew was his next step, even though the adults thought it would not work, or not be safe, or that he was not old enough. So it was that he assisted his parents and relatives to let go of their overprotection towards him, when he felt that his freedom to discover himself was being limited.

Yeshua loved to play and laugh. His high soprano voice was angelic of tone and frequency. His father taught him to play the harp, which he accompanied with the psalms of David. Other musicians, such as his aunt Mariamne, who were skilled with the native instruments of Egypt, taught him how to play solo pieces, as well as how to harmonize with others. Some of his teachers were Pythagorean adepts, who taught Yeshua sacred geometry, mathematics, astronomy, astrology, harmonics, and geomancy.

Like his mother, Yeshua was quick and able to undertake several tasks at once. However, unlike Mary Anna who appeared to be unhurried and calm, my young grandson would flutter about like a butterfly from one project to another. In your day, you would call him a hyperactive child, a dynamo of energy. He slept little, and when he did, he could fall asleep in an instant, anywhere, anytime. He enjoyed spending time on the rooftop sitting under the stars. He might take clay, string or pigments, and fashion various sculptural designs. Often, when he was not running from here to there, he could be found sitting very, very still, communing with the unseen ones.

As a clear empath, Yeshua was also very sensitive. Occasionally, he would double over in pain when an energy he was feeling passed through his body. Sometimes, he experienced an inexplicable outburst of emotion that was very difficult for him to control. It was as though a great storm came out of nowhere, buffeting Yeshua's mind and body until it finally subsided, leaving him spent and confused. He did not like those times and, frankly, his emotional upsets were trying for anyone around him, especially his mother. It was difficult for those who were near him from day to day to understand the extremes Yeshua demonstrated. How to assist this child to temper his emotional body was a challenge for his parents as well as for Yeshua. His heart's desire was to be like his parents, who always seemed to be unruffled. He desired that no one be harmed or adversely affected by his unpredictable emotional tempests as they came and went.

By Yeshua's seventh year, his body was long and lean. He was almost as tall as his mother and he loved to look straight ahead into her eyes, place his hands on her shoulders or her chin, and with deep feeling or lighthearted mirth, call her 'my beautiful little mother'. He was always respectful of his mother, even though his emotional storms would express in a way that was disturbing to Mary Anna. She taught him to breathe while allowing the energies to pass through his body, not speaking, just feeling them moving in and around him. She explained to him that what he was feeling was the pain of the world that was caused when love was not acknowledged by humanity. This pain, she also understood, although she experienced it differently from her son. For Mary Anna, it moved upon her as abysmal grief; with Yeshua, it was as if all the elements found expression.

His family often wondered how this child was to master himself. The road ahead seemed rocky, indeed. Finally, his father, setting the example of the master high alchemist, assigned him the task of embracing and transmuting every expression of energy without judgement.

When the tempests of fiery rage, heavy depression, terrifying thoughts, and oceans of sadness found a home in Yeshua's mind, emotions and body, he often sought the comfort and solitude of a nearby cave. This deep cave was near the homes Joseph and Simeon leased from their sister-in-law Tabitha's wealthy father, whose properties were numerous. After they had first arrived, the family had often sought refuge in the darkness of this cave for days at a time when vigilance was required.

As the months had gone by without incident and after learning that King Herod had died, in February of AD5, Joseph received word from the angel Gabriel that it was now time to return home. Several weeks before Yeshua's eighth birthday, Joseph and Mary Anna invited their relatives to come together for a feast day of celebration prior to their departure back to Carmel, which would include a pilgrimage to Mount Sinai.

On the evening of the feast, before they left Egypt for a new life, Yeshua asked Mariam to walk with him a short distance from the merrymaking. Beneath a grove of great date palms, beside an ancient well, Yeshua and Mariam embraced and promised that they would always be faithful to one another. Mariam gave Yeshua a necklace that she had made of coloured glass and alabaster beads, shells, and small pieces of lapis. Yeshua gave Mariam a sheath of papyrus upon which he had written psalms that had come from deep within his heart. These gave expression to his love for the One God, his love for all life's bountiful wonder, and his love for her.

So they vowed allegiance to one another and to the divine plan, however it would play out or wherever it would take them. Yeshua kissed Mariam's tear stained cheeks, squeezed her hands, and led her reluctantly back to the music and dancing. Having exchanged their heartfelt gifts, they playfully dipped fruit and flat bread into bowls of date paste and honey. Laughing, they tenderly placed their dripping fingers and sweet offerings into one another's mouths.

Two days later, Joseph, a pregnant Mary Anna, Yeshua, James, Jude and Joseph the Younger left Heliopolis together with Simeon, Rebekah, Mariam and several other adult cousins. Faithful assistants joined them in a caravan of camels, donkeys, and ox carts. They began their pilgrimage trek to Mount Sinai by following the same path Moses had taken with the Israelites across the desert to Etham. They journeyed south to the narrow strip of land that was bordered by the Red Sea on the west and by a rugged range of mountains on the east. This wilderness range culminated in the towering escarpments of Mount Sinai where Moses received the Ten Commandments and many higher spiritual teachings.

‿◠

ᔆ Chapter 22 ᔆ

Rite of Passage on Mount Sinai

High on the rocky face of Mount Sinai were the remains of an ancient hermitage of the Wise Ones that predated the coming of Moses and the Israelites. A group of Essenes were the caretakers and guardians of this sacred site and powerful energy vortex. It was here that the Ancients had taken initiation into the mysteries during previous rises of civilization, long before the Exodus of the Israelites from Egypt, and it was here that their physical bodies had been interred at the time of their transitions. There were also secret caves and crypts that were used for regenerative purposes and high alchemy. This most ancient reserve of wisdom was kept secret and hidden. When Yeshua arrived, it was still being used by the Essenes as a repository of records and catacombs. The monastery of St. Catherine of Alexandria, constructed many centuries later, still exists in your day.

When Yeshua arrived at Mount Sinai with his family just a few days before his eighth birthday, they were invited to climb up the steep ascent to those pinnacled places where Moses had brought initiates long ago, around 1300 BC. The sweeping panorama was breathtaking. And the realization that this was the site of Moses and his sister Miriam's great visions was awe inspiring. It was to be here that Yeshua would experience his first Rite of Passage.

Shortly after his eighth birthday, Yeshua was taken into one of the caves that had been carved to form a large 'temple' cavern. Here he was inducted as a probationary initiate into the Essene Order of Melchizedek, which was patterned after the higher priesthood administered by Moses and Miriam. After Joseph had taken vows of secrecy and oaths of allegiance, he vouched for his son's qualifications even though Yeshua was only eight and this initiation was ordinarily for boys who were twelve or older.

Yeshua was then led blindfolded to the highest crags of Mount Sinai. There, he was left alone without food or water for four days and nights. This was the first of Yeshua's initiations, which took him through the rigours of governing his flesh and passions. While he had experienced much preparation as a young boy in Egypt, now it was time to pass from childhood into the responsibilities of adulthood and to begin his life's destiny as an Essene Covenanter. You would call this rite of passage a vision quest.

Yeshua was instructed to remain within the circumference of a small circle and to find shelter among the stones. He circumambulated a walking meditation, weaving patterns of sacred geometry from the centre point to the outer circle, and then he would come back into the centre again to sit in stillness until called to move outwards again.

Within the circle, Yeshua experienced the thought-forms of the 'burning bush' left by Moses. He watched primal fear take numerous forms before his eyes. Demonic creatures seemed to cajole him to jump into the fire or leap off the precipice; others laughed at, spit at, and mocked him. In many ways his discernment was tested. The sun was as a furnace by day, and the moon was cold as ice at night. Shivering at night, Yeshua called upon Ra, the power of the sun within his belly, to warm and comfort him. Faint-headed during the scorching heat of the day, he imagined himself within a cool, moonlit, green oasis of his childhood.

Thus, he passed the four days, communing with every creature and elemental energy that introduced itself. Great eagles, hawks, falcons, and vultures called to him as they spiralled overhead. Ants and flies crawled upon and occasionally stung his body. Serpents and scorpions approached his body and slithered on. In this way were his patience and awareness tested, as he realized that the least of God's creatures were also the One God with as much a purpose and right to live as he had.

Yeshua understood that the serpents represented the life-force energy of the embryo god/goddess that lay coiled at the base of his spine. He remembered the teachings of Thoth, Serapis Bey, and other Great Ones. He contemplated the uraeus symbol of the cobra goddess, Buto, who spreads her mantle at the time of enlightenment. She was often depicted at the initiate's third eye, her crowned head covered with the feathered wings of Nekhbet, the vulture goddess.

Yeshua called forth the anointing light, as he remembered stories of the Benu bird or Phoenix, when the initiate's old identity is left behind, as if burned to ashes. The Phoenix takes flight when the fiery serpent energy appears to take wing and spirals up the spine. Yeshua thirsted for enlightenment's anointing nectars and imagined them being poured into the cup that rests upon the altar within the inner sanctum of his skull. He hungered for the fulfilment of the initiate's flight into the realms of union with the One God. Identifying with Horus's ascending consciousness, he imagined himself depicted as the winged sun disk, pushed forward by a scarab beetle, Kheperi-Ra, through the Gate of the Sun. So it was that my beloved grandson remembered and rehearsed the stories of Osiris, Isis, Set, Nepthys, Horus, and Hathor during his hours upon Mount Sinai. In this way he found internal peace and satisfied his soul's hunger and thirst.

It was Yeshua's courage and love of God expressing in him and in all forms that enabled him to pass this test. Angels stood around him, even though there were times when their presence could not be felt. By the last day, Yeshua had opened his heart and crown sufficiently to behold his body below him, his soul taking flight into the cosmos, wherever he willed it to go. My grandson began to understand how it was that his father and mother could appear to him even though he knew they were in the monastery far below. There were also times when he could hear his parents speaking to him, even though they were not physically present.

Now that he knew how to astral travel and to bilocate his consciousness, he determined to test his ability by taking his Ka body, or etheric double, to the tent of his father and mother. He was delighted to find them supping upon a mid-afternoon respite of goat cheese and dried fruit. When they saw him, they beckoned him to eat; so he did, amazed that his very hungry physical body could feel the nourishment coming through the ethers. This revelation brought Yeshua great strength and comfort, which later helped him meet the more arduous initiations of mastery that were still ahead of him along the path of his life.

When the four days of his initiation were finished, Joseph and Simeon came for him. Yeshua's physical condition was weak, but he felt a victory of spirit that made the long, perilous trek down Mount Sinai at night easier than when he had passed this way blind-folded four days earlier. The glow of the rising sun rose to greet him in triumphant celebration. When, at last, he caught sight of his mother, he ran headlong into her outstretched arms, causing both of them to fall to the ground. Laughing and crying at once, Mary Anna took her son into her lap. For a few moments, Yeshua allowed himself the comforting pleasure of being a child, while Mary Anna washed his sunburned skin and offered him sips of refreshing, life-giving water.

Then, helping his mother up and cradling Mary Anna's tear-stained, smiling face in his hands, Yeshua said, 'My beautiful little Mother, my time has now come to enter into my heavenly Father's work. His kingdom reigns within me. It is time for me to be about His business.' And so he stood up, lifting his mother with him, and turned to the others who had gathered, enigmatically saying, 'Peace be unto you. I have come of age. I now prepare a banquet, even as my Father in heaven prepares a great feast for you. And I say to you: Let us come and enter in, for we have found favour with God and humankind.' Then, lowering his head, Yeshua turned away and walked to the shelter where the ritual washings were done.

Mariam, who was watching from a short distance, took a deep breath, clasped her hands to her heart, and almost swooned with love for Yeshua, who had instantly become her hero. Mary Anna and Rebekah called the Brethren to come to prayers around a low table filled with crocks of goat's milk and honey, platters of cheeses, flat breads, dates, and mugs of water. Yeshua took his place with the men, a broad though weary smile upon his deeply tanned and sunburned face. His blue-grey eyes sparkled like the sun upon rippling water. He offered the prayers of thanksgiving to the sun, angels, and the Mother of Life. Then, he broke the bread and gave to each one before giving his own shrunken stomach relief. So was the nature of Yeshua ben Joseph revealed as a testament of compassion from the days of his youth.

Several weeks later, the families of Joseph and Simeon followed the ancient route of Abraham and Sarah to Hebron and then they continued onwards to Bethlehem and Mount Carmel.

౸

Chapter 23

The Homecoming

Word had been sent ahead and I awaited the return to Mount Carmel of Mary Anna, Joseph, Yeshua, James, Jude, Joseph the Younger, Rebekah, Simeon, and Mariam. Often, I perched with the young children in the late afternoon on the hillside overlooking the road which snaked its way across the Plain of Sharon below. This was the same road Joachim had travelled when he returned from India. Now, I was looking as I had before, my heart aching to reach out and touch my beloved children, who had long been away from me.

We had heard in advance that Mary Anna was pregnant with her fifth child and that Rebekah was ailing with a disease that afflicted her blood, bones, and skin. Some thought she had leprosy; however, we chose to diagnose her condition otherwise, and we agreed in advance that we would not have her put away from our community.

How would Yeshua look, now that he was in his ninth year? My new grandchildren, James, Jude, and Joseph the Younger – what would they be like? And Mariam, so sweet a presence! How had the years in Egypt changed her? So many questions pressed upon my mind and heart that hot, blistering day in June of AD5 as I took my turn with the very small children out upon the hillside. We had heard they were on their way. Could this be the day?

Absorbed in the picking of herbs and identifying their names and uses for the children, I was astonished to hear the large bell of Carmel begin to toll. Someone else had spotted the approaching caravan, from a higher vantage-point upon the mount where the sheep and goats grazed, and had run down to tell the good news. There were shouts amid the blowing of horns. And then the young boys and girls, who could ride like the wind, quickly mounted the draft horses, mules, and donkeys. Off they went in a cloud of dust to meet these strangers whose story had been rehearsed over and over. Whom would they meet? Would their expectations be fulfilled?

The processional journey had been slow and steady. The hot afternoon sun danced upon motes of dust. Shimmering haze blurred their upward ascent. The younger children who were with me tugged at my apron and skirts, pulling me after the mounted welcoming party. All the bells began to toll. Horns blew; cymbals and tambourine frame drums beat ecstatic rhythms. High and low voices sang out, as the entire community of Carmel ran from the gates to the first round of the long, winding road. There, most of us stood waving our arms, garlanded with branches of olive, palm, and cedar. I could not hold back my tears any longer. I wept and laughed and sang, until all I could do was gather my hands to my breast and pray with an immense gratitude for the safe return of my beloved family.

Through the thick, yellow dust, the caravan approached the last turn, rutted by a recent cloudburst that had unexpectedly poured sweet rain upon our fields and gardens. Then I ran, children in hand. Mary Anna waved from her seat upon a large mule, her small body revealing the silhouette of one with child. At her side strode Joseph. Behind her, straddling the mule, was her youngest child, Joseph the Younger, now almost three years old. Running ahead were two red headed boys, whom I instantly knew were James and Jude. Where was Yeshua? My eyes glanced from one beloved to the next. Then, through the haze, I saw the ox cart carrying Rebekah. Inside the cart was a young girl, cradling a still body in her lap. A bladder containing water hung by her side and a tarpaulin stretched overhead, giving protection from the burning sun. Walking beside the ox was a tall, deeply tanned boy, whose bright eyes and smiling teeth flashed as he caught my searching gaze. Riveted, as if by a lightning bolt, I quaked with recognition: my God, it is Yeshua, a man in a boy's body!

Yeshua called out to Jude to come and take the ox's tether and goad. Then, as fleet as a deer, Yeshua left the roadway and flew upwards, leaping from stone to stone. He was in my arms in less than a minute. Then stepping back, we stood facing each other, eye to eye. Although only eight, his strong arms curled around me as though he were a bear, lifting me off the ground. Laughing a contagious laugh, Yeshua spun me around and around, all the while looking into my eyes. He had the most extraordinary eyes I had ever seen. 'You are just like my mother, only you are still yourself. So I shall call you NaNa, my little mother. Come. Come and see my beautiful mother!' whispered Yeshua in my ear as he gently set me on the ground.

Taking my hand, he led me excitedly to Mary Anna. Joseph stopped the mule and helped his beloved wife to dismount. Once her sore, strained legs could hold her upright, Mary Anna was in my arms. How wondrous our reunion!

Arm in arm, with Mary Anna in the middle, Yeshua and I walked among the pilgrims, hugging and kissing each one as we went. When I came upon Rebekah, who was with Mariam in the ox cart, my heart burst with agony for her affliction. Open sores covered her face, causing one eye to be swollen shut. I reached into the lumbering cart to place my hand upon her gaunt form, and placing my ear close heard her faint words, 'Mother, I have come home to you. I know you can make me well. For this I have prayed.' These were the barely audible words Rebekah spoke from a place of faith in her heart. It was indeed hard to look upon Rebekah's beauty wasting away, her face ashen and her eyes glazed by pain. Then, I looked up into my granddaughter Mariam's doe-like, golden eyes. Such wise and noble beauty I had not seen among all the maidens born of the light, except the one you call Mary Magdalene, the daughter of Mary of Magdala and Joseph of Arimathea.

Slowly, we made our way to the south gate of the Carmel compound. Nathaniel, the shepherd boy who had held the infant Yeshua in his arms, then came forward and offered to assist. He was now sixteen years old and had recently completed his probationary initiations in the Mount Carmel Mystery School. Nathaniel gently lifted Rebekah from the ox cart and carried her into the infirmary, accompanied by a weary Simeon and a solemn Mariam. I introduced him to everyone and then explained to Yeshua who Nathaniel was and that the little lamb that he had given Yeshua at his birth was still very much alive. We agreed that we would later find the little lamb that had become a grandmother sheep many times over.

One by one, the tired pilgrims dismounted from carts and steeds. Children milled about, asking questions, getting acquainted with cousins, and making friends with those about whom they had only heard stories. Yeshua was pressed to answer dozens of questions all at the same time. The children hung on him, begging him to lift them up and whirl them around, as they had seen him do with me. When the weariness of the journey caught up with him, Yeshua gently excused himself and went with his father and Simeon to the men's dormitory and bath.

This homecoming was bittersweet. On the one hand, here were my beloved children returned to me. On the other, Rebekah's sore condition deeply troubled my heart. Reluctantly, though in good faith, I will now share with you the sad departing of Rebekah. Though her faith was strong, her condition continued to worsen over the six months after her arrival in Carmel. I stayed with her in the infirmary night and day, as did others of the family. We did all that we could to heal her fading body. Her spirit waxed strong and her inner beauty grew as we took turns caring for Rebekah's basic needs. Although her voice was silenced to our outer ears, we could hear and feel her love of God and the angels who attended her. When it came time for her soul to lift upward into the light, we all gathered around. I could feel Joachim's presence and gave thanks that all our children had been spared until now. This beautiful being freely moved on into the greater realms of light in order to fulfil her part from on the other side of the veil.

Mariam, Rebekah's only child, was bereft beyond comforting for almost a fortnight, until one evening when Yeshua came to her where she knelt beside her mother's grave. Gently, he picked her up and held her close to his heart. Where she had grown numb of spirit, he blew his breath until Mariam began to shake. At last, the venom of bitter anger toward God and toward me for not saving her mother began to depart. Because her father, Simeon, had gone with Joseph to Qumran a week after her mother's death, Mariam felt utterly alone, desolate, and betrayed.

Yeshua continued to blow his breath into her heart until her sobbing began to subside. Holding his cousin fast to his bosom, he waited until another wave of grief and anger crested, before resuming breathing into her heart. Torn by sobs and screams, she beat her fists on his back. 'Why? Why, O my God? Why did God take my beloved mother?' she lamented. All Yeshua knew to do was to hold her, until the months of futile hope and deep anguish that had frozen into vacant-eyed numbness were dissolved. Then, Yeshua led her to his mother. Mary Anna took Mariam to her bosom and adopted her as her own child. So it was that Mariam became Yeshua's sister. Remembering the promise that she had made to him long ago in Egypt, she then proceeded to devote herself to fulfilling her vow that she would be his eternal friend and confidante.

∽

∽ Chapter 24 ∽
Yeshua's Childhood

My beloved friend, there is much more that I desire to share with you regarding those five formative years between AD5 and 10. Yeshua returned to the homeland of the Hebrew peoples to receive the counsel of Essene elders and the imprinting of this ancient soil where the prophets had once walked. In him would be fulfilled all that the prophets had spoken.

During the latter part of the year of their return to Mount Carmel, Joseph ben Jacob began establishing himself as a builder and fine craftsman in the new village of Nazareth, named after the Nazirite Essenes, an easy day's journey from Mount Carmel. Nazareth was located five miles south of Sepphoris and ten miles south of Cana, where Joseph's parents lived. Mary Anna's brother, Nathan, had acquired land in Nazareth and proposed that Joseph use it to build a home that would support his growing family. So it was that Joseph and Mary Anna moved into a modest, but more spacious home, in the early spring of AD6. From Nazareth, Joseph took his trade to the nearby bustling Roman town of Sepphoris, where Yeshua often accompanied him as his apprentice. Occasionally, Joseph also facilitated the design and building of Essene communal structures throughout Galilee and in the desert near the Salt Sea.

Whenever Joseph could, he also brought Yeshua to Mount Carmel and to Qumran, where he would stay for months at a time taking probationary initiations. Of these, I will say more later. You have in your tradition that Joseph was a carpenter. But, I will add that he was much more than a simple, itinerate handyman. Indeed, he designed and built buildings for public and private use. He was also known as a master craftsman of fine woods, musical instruments, and the tabernacles of synagogues. And to the initiated, Joseph was known as one who knew the 'Crafting of the Soul'. He was an adept who held within his countenance the substance, frequencies, and mathematical codes of the Ark of the Covenant. Joseph was looked upon as one to whom initiates came to receive certain rites of passage into the Way of the Teacher of Righteousness.

During the extended months that Yeshua lived in Carmel, he spent a great deal of his time with me. In Carmel, and also at Qumran, he took many of the initiations. He lived with the older boys and celibate men in a communal dormitory. His dress, possessions, and daily routine were simple, straightforward, and communally uniform. To look at Yeshua as he went about his labours with the other boys, one would not perceive him being treated any differently than the others with whom he shared his life.

Yeshua spent long hours in the library reading, translating, and transcribing the ancient texts which had come out of Alexandria, Greece, Persia, India, and the Himalayas. He was quick to learn the different languages, and he enjoyed communicating with anyone who would enter into various philosophical perspectives and dialogues with him. Long before the sun rose, he could be found walking amidst the fields of grasses, alone or with his mother when she visited, sitting in meditation beneath the ancient cedars, or absorbed in the text of some ancient scroll or papyrus. Like his father Joseph, he slept little. He took his turn at the various communal chores without complaint. Whether it was the cleaning of floors, latrines, and the kitchen, or the tending of children, flocks, or the lame, Yeshua went from one task to the other with great sensitivity, gentleness, and a light heart.

He had begun to gain a mastery of the emotional storms that still swept through him. In many ways, Yeshua was the perfect child. But before you put him on a pedestal, I will also tell that on occasion he played jokes on the children, adults, and me. There was one time when Yeshua was attentively rubbing my feet on one of our long walks to gather herbs. Unbeknownst to me he tied my sandal laces together when he placed my sandals back on my feet. When I got up to continue our walk, I lost my balance, falling into Yeshua's waiting arms. Then, we both merrily laughed as he whirled me around. Whirling me around seemed to be one of his favourite past times, when he thought I wouldn't mind or when he thought I was being too serious.

Yeshua also had challenging days when he surprised everyone with complaints and stubbornness. And when an unpredictable emotional storm came on such a day, our community found it best to leave Yeshua alone. Occasionally, during particularly challenging inner storms, Yeshua would seek me out, and we would go for walks or go into our favourite cave, where I kept the space for him to work it out. Then we talked and shared deeply from our hearts until peace and love were found again.

During the times our community gathered for feasting and celebration before and after certain high days, Yeshua loved to teach the other children various games that he had invented or expanded upon. Some of the games tested physical prowess, some honed mental acuity, and some were just for laughter and play. In one such game, my grandson ran like the wind ahead of the other children, only to dodge to the right or left, falling behind a child who was lame. Then, in an instant, the unsuspecting child would be picked up and perched on Yeshua's thin shoulders. Off they romped, laughing giddily, the child flapping his or her arms like a bird.

While Yeshua was in Egypt he had acquired something of the rich heritage of Egyptian, Hebrew, and Persian temple music and folk dances, which he learned from his Aunt Mariamne and his Uncle Ezekiel. By his twelfth year, he had become an accomplished singer, composer, and musician. He loved singing the psalms of Akhenaten, David, and Zarathustra. He rejoiced in the dialogue of Krishna and Arjuna. He was given ample opportunity to share his unusually advanced understanding, as well as his sweet, perfectly pitched, soprano voice when we met for morning and evening prayers, the Sabbath, weddings, and other festive celebrations.

Yeshua took his second rite of passage into manhood when he was twelve at the hand of his father, within the new synagogue at Nazareth that Joseph had assisted in erecting. He amazed the elders with his knowledge and wisdom of the Torah and other ancient texts of Enoch, Zadok, and Moses. However, it would be another twelve years before he appeared before the priests of Levi in Jerusalem for his rite into true manhood, as this tradition was practised by the Jews in that day.

Also during Yeshua's twelfth year he entered more deeply into the serious matters of the mystery school. Among other teachings, I assisted him to understand how to hold and circulate the Breath of Life within his body, until his heartbeat slowed to an almost imperceptible flutter. Into the caves upon the Mount we would go together, to test his understanding of pranic flow and how to move through the veils of the astral worlds.

Some of these caves were hollowed out in a fashion to create specific acoustical sounds. Deep trance states could be accomplished when these sounds were consciously made and heard. I would use my voice, accompanied with my frame drum, Hathor sistrum, and bronze bells. Yeshua brought jugs of water, pallets, oil lamps, and the herbs that would sustain our vigils. Sometimes, we stayed deep within the caves for as long as a week. I came to know Yeshua very well as we shared deeply during these retreats.

Together, we would take etheric journeys into the inner retreats of the Masters. One of our favourite bilocation journeys was to visit a number of places in Britain. I promised him he would some day physically travel to that ancient Celtic land and take initiation at the hand of his uncle, Joseph of Arimathea. His uncle and his parents had already agreed that Yeshua would be taken to Britain for three years at the age of thirteen.

As Yeshua approached his thirteenth birthday he undertook his first level initiation into the Rite of the Sepulchre. All our work prior to this initiation into the mysteries had prepared him to go into the 'death' state and to return his soul to his body through the process of resurrection. So it was that I took Yeshua into the secret chamber located behind a false door in which I had placed my body from time to time, when it had been appropriate for me to depart the earthplane for an extended time.

As the long hours passed, I looked into the future and saw all the arduous tests Yeshua would be put through, and there was a part of me that wished Yeshua could simply live as a man, albeit, a man who could love and serve much. So it was that initiating my grandson was also an initiation for me. In this way, at the tender age of twelve, Yeshua began his preparation for publicly demonstrating the crucifixion and resurrection initiations. Throughout the remainder of his earthly expression, Yeshua knew death to be an illusion, and with each resurrection experience that followed through the years, he brought more light into the elements of his physical body.

Also at this time the signs of pubescence began to become apparent. His lanky form continued to lengthen. His hands and feet had outgrown the rest of his body. Yeshua's body was unusually strong for one so slender and tall. He allowed his silken, dark, auburn hair to grow long in the manner of the celibate Essene initiate. He was over a hand's length taller than his mother and me. I shall always treasure in my heart the memory of Yeshua's infectious laughter, as well as his stony stubbornness when it was time to put his determination, courage, and wisdom to the test. I was privy to his childlike spontaneity, curiosity, and playfulness.

Occasionally, his mastery of the full range of emotion, which he had developed over the years of his childhood, seemed to evaporate. There were times when the least annoying disturbance would incite a flood of tears. Sometimes he would bend over and guttural screams poured out unexpectedly. Then, Yeshua would sit down, shaking, while he attempted to embrace and transmute the energy as he had been taught to do by his mother and father when he was a child. There were even times when the elementals out-pictured his inner storms. Dark clouds appeared out of nowhere as a torrent of rage or grief moved through his body. Lightning struck the crags and cedars, as deafening thunderclaps rumbled down the mount into the valleys below. Rain poured down, filling the almost empty cisterns with welcomed drinking water.

I could feel Yeshua's potent life-force energy surging in his developing groin. Whereas he had once been carefree in his open expression of delight with the embraced warmth of the maternal bodies of his mother, grandmothers, aunts, and the curious femaleness of his cousins, Yeshua now seemed to withdraw into a reserved shyness. Often he would go into the bathhouse for ritual washing in order to gain clarity for his mind and body. He often took extra turns with the sheep in the fields away from the others so that he could have sufficient space to sort out his feelings. This was complicated by the various contradictions within the scriptures he had read, the ambiguity of what others said and practised, and the reality of the sexual life-force energy running rampant in his own body. During such times and as he gained increasing mastery, Yeshua turned to his mother less and less. This was a difficult time for Mary Anna, though it was a necessary preparation for freeing her son to fulfil all that he had come to do.

Once a poisonous snake bit Yeshua while he was removing it from the Carmel compound. Stunned with disbelief, he screamed while squeezing the serpent until it died in his hands and became like a staff. Then, he stood rigid, not allowing anyone to come near him. While standing absolutely still, with his eyes closed, for almost an hour, Yeshua summoned the venom to be transmuted by the life-force energies that streamed through his body.

Over the years we all came to know my grandson's unusual powers. Although the other boys tried to include him in their camaraderie, Yeshua found himself more and more alone. Just as nature and prayerful communion provided his mother with comfort and solace, so it was with her eldest son.

Yeshua was gifted with prodigious insights into the mysteries. Sometimes he would meet an energy field of consciousness about which he would ask me for further explanation, or for guidance as to where he might go within the scriptures and codices for greater illumination. Always I would encourage him to turn inward for answers within his own heart. We often had discussions of the various points of view of the different religious sects, doctrines, and practices.

So it was that I taught and prepared my beloved grandson for his coming initiations, which would eventually assist him to rise from the sepulchre when the time of fulfilment of prophesy was at hand. His life would demonstrate to humanity that death holds no power for those who know that death is an illusion.

❧

❧ Chapter 25 ❧

Mary Magdalene and Mariam's Childhood

I shall share with you now, according to the desire of your heart and mine, the nature of the developmental years wherein Young Mary, later known as Mary Magdalene, the twin-soul of Yeshua, was raised and prepared for her great work. While her father, Joseph of Arimathea, continued to live and work in Jerusalem, Young Mary grew up with her mother, Mary of Magdala, and her Aunt Martha at their spacious country home in Bethany. She rejoiced in the beauty of its open and sunny inner courtyard, and the light which filtered into the surrounding rooms. Martha had never married, so it was a great blessing when her older brother, Joseph, and his first wife, Eunice Salome, created their second home in Bethany and asked Martha to caretake it. Joseph had then spared no expense in expanding Martha's abode, when his new wife, Mary of Magdala, came to live with her, about fourteen years after Eunice Salome died. Martha carefully prepared it as a sanctuary of light and cultured beauty. Throughout her lovely home were collections of art from Greece, Egypt and other places near and far.

It was in this environment that our Young Mary, as we called her, developed her sensitivity to growing things and to the people who sought out her aunt and mother for advice or remedies. Young Mary loved her mother with a possessive love that was almost ferocious, much like a lioness protecting her young. When she was small, she would watch her mother and aunt like a hawk, and then pretend she had the same healing skills they had, as she treated her dolls, the small household animals, fowl, and lame birds. It soon became evident, when the injured animals revived, that this child had a gift for healing.

Young Mary loved to walk out into the desert with her mother at sunrise and sunset. There, she befriended many wild animals and made them her pets. Some of these pets were lizards, snakes, rodents, birds, wild dogs, and cats. The aging and ailing Martha did not particularly like her niece's menagerie, and insisted that the animals be kept in the stable away from the main household. However, Young Mary could sometimes be found secretly nursing one of her pets in the closet of her room; or a box containing a family of newly born kittens might be found by Martha during her cleaning. The last straw came when Martha opened one of her storage baskets and found a poisonous snake coiled inside. From then on, Young Mary could not bring home snakes!

Mary of Magdala travelled to her home village of Magdala every solstice and equinox to officiate as high priestess at the temple grotto of the Goddess – the Divine Feminine aspect of the Godhead. On these occasions, her daughter always went with her. So it was that, at a very early age, Young Mary learned of the Great Mother – her rituals, ceremonies, songs, rhythms, and cycles.

As a small girl, she could be seen sitting in stillness, staring with her golden eyes, holding a focus for hours on end. Sometimes a milky vapour appeared before her or wrapped around her. In this mist, those with eyes to see could behold angels or beings from other dimensions and worlds. At times, food, coins, jewellery, statuettes, or sweet perfumed oils would precipitate in front of my granddaughter or in her hands. She would blink, smile, intensely laugh, and then share the treasure with all. She kept little for herself, loving to give the fruits of these magical moments to those who were her family and household helpers. As she grew older and other initiate maidens compared themselves unfavourably with her, Young Mary refrained from publicly sharing her magical gifts. She avoided as much as possible the shunning and cutting remarks of her peers' jealousies. Often, her pillow was wet with tears because she felt lonely and misunderstood. In looking to her mother and her invisible friends for comfort, she found purpose and direction for her life.

Adding to Young Mary's challenges were the averted glances and hostile remarks of the orthodox Pharisees and the aristocratic Sadducees, when she and her mother would go into the marketplace or visit other cousins in the villages between Bethany and Magdala. When they were home in Bethany, they seldom went out into the streets and rarely ventured into the throngs of Jerusalem. The reason for secreting themselves away and traveling incognito was that the Jewish patriarchal priests and their wives had become increasingly antagonistic toward the worship of the Divine Mother or Holy Shekinah.

By placing themselves as intermediaries between the seeker and God, the priesthood sought control over people's ability to have direct knowing of God within. The Shekinah's ways of direct revelation they distrusted and often abhorred. They despised Isis, Inanna, and other representations of the Great Mother, because they could not make use of the Goddess for their own purposes. The women who were strong in the old matriarchal traditions were perceived as threatening, because they could not be easily controlled, and also because they held powers the priesthood coveted for itself. Therefore, many of the men in positions of religious authority looked down upon women generally as temptresses responsible for the fall of humankind and the corruption of flesh. Most husbands kept their wives and daughters as ignorant possessions and virtual slaves to their physical pleasures and their need for heirs. Those women who were known for their worship of the Goddess were often branded whores and harlots.

This state of affairs was further complicated by the fact that Joseph of Arimathea held the position of adjunctive counsellor to the Sanhedrin – the legislative and judicial governing body over the peoples who practised the so-called Law of Moses. So it was that this delicate situation required a certain amount of secrecy concerning Joseph's relationship with his wife, who was a high initiate and priestess of the Goddess. Thus, Mary of Magdala and her daughter retired to a rather obscure life within their own home.

In this climate of distrust, Young Mary grew wary of men, especially those in positions of authority. Her sensitive nature questioned such a dogmatic and hypocritical system that had such an impact on the relationship between her father and mother. Although she was repelled by these conditions, she was attracted to those men who, like her father, were kind and wise, and who could appreciate her beyond her outer beauty and femaleness.

It seemed to her that her father was never home enough. She thrived when he was near, and would become withdrawn and sullen, not eating for a day or two, whenever Joseph of Arimathea left for Jerusalem or went on long journeys to places she longed to visit. When her beloved father was home, he would take Young Mary on his knee and tell her stories of his adventures and share gifts from his travels. These gifts were beautiful to be sure, yet not as precious as were Joseph's loving arms and kind, thickly bearded face. Young Mary loved the smell of her father's manliness, and she made her desire for his attention well understood by the entire household.

Young Mary only encountered her mother's grown children, Thomas, Matthew, and Susannah when her mother visited them in Capernaum and Magdala. By the time Young Mary was seven years of age, however, there were two younger siblings with whom she had to learn to share her parents' attention. There were now Lazarus, who was five years younger, and Young Martha, who was just a babe, six-and-a-half years younger. As Lazarus grew older there continued to be a close rapport. With Martha, however, there seemed to be an old karmic pattern of distrust and competition that was only resolved years later.

When she was in her ninth year, Young Mary heard the exciting news that her cousin Yeshua had returned from Egypt, and that her parents were planning a special journey to visit her grandmother at Mount Carmel and to meet relatives she had only heard about. What would Yeshua, James, Jude, Joseph, Ruth, and Mariam be like?

It was with great enthusiasm that Young Mary packed her things and set off with her parents and younger siblings for Mount Carmel to meet her Aunt Mary Anna, her Uncle Joseph, and her cousins. As it turned out, the experience of meeting Yeshua and Mariam was far beyond anything that Young Mary could possibly have imagined. When Yeshua and Young Mary looked into each other's eyes, they instantly recognized one another, as a piercing light moved through their hearts. Both of them felt as if they had been struck by lightning.

When Mariam and Young Mary beheld one another, there was a similar experience of soul recognition. In their case, however, the quickening of divine light was accompanied by a dark shadow. Because they both loved Yeshua, there began to be an awkward rivalry between them, as they both attempted to claim Yeshua's full attention. This thorn of contention between Mariam and Young Mary grew over the years as they came into their maidenhood. It was this thorn that became the great test of divine love, which moved both of them through their probationary initiations.

So it was that Yeshua grappled with the intense feelings that arose within his heart, and was torn at a young age between these two great loves in his life. He knew that his destiny was entwined with both. But how?

During the next four years, Young Mary came to Carmel with her mother on several different occasions. And although Yeshua was thrilled to see his cousin, he also felt relieved when it was time for her to return home to Bethany. He often encountered her in his dreams, and even though he missed Young Mary, he was glad to have only Mariam present at Mount Carmel while he focused his energies on the many tasks that required his attention.

As for Young Mary, that first meeting with Yeshua at the age of eight constituted the pivotal point of her life, and from that point onward she began to know ever more fully who she was and for what purpose she had incarnated upon this Earth.

So it was that when Young Mary became thirteen, she was brought to Mount Carmel by her parents during the time of Yeshua's final preparations to leave for Britain with Joseph of Arimathea. Her mother had already begun to initiate her into the mysteries of the Order of the Magdalene at the Great Mother's grotto at Magdala. However, she had never been required to commit to any consistent discipline. So it was with high hopes and expectations that I began my work with the one you call Mary Magdalene.

It was not easy for Young Mary to leave the comforts of her Bethany home and the luxury of having very little requirement for attending to the affairs of homemaking. Such domestic concerns were well attended to by her Aunt Martha and her maids. So it was something of a rude shock when the pampered young lady attempted to adjust to the communal requirements of sharing everything, living in rather austere conditions, and surrendering her freedom to do as she pleased to the strict codes of monastic conduct, ritual, and routine. Furthermore, having learned to distrust the dogmatic, authoritarian, patriarchal orientation of the Pharisees and the Sadducees, she found herself beginning to rebel against the discipline of our tradition-bound Essene community.

For most of that first year she balked and was petulant, attempting to win favours and special treatment through her charismatic manipulations, which had worked so well back in Bethany. So it was that Young Mary could be seen pouting, teasing the other young girls and boys, running away, and sometimes standing in resolute defiance against the rules that had governed and maintained the Mount Carmel community for centuries.

There had never before been such a one to question Mount Carmel's entrenched authority, which disturbed the peace among the young and old alike. To have this rebellious adolescent in our midst was like living with a wolverine that felt cornered or a hornet baring its stinger. Her mother could not persuade Young Mary to bend to the standard expected of those who sought initiation at Mount Carmel. We all wondered if she would make it through her first year.

After her mother and younger siblings returned to Bethany, Young Mary went through a very difficult period for a number of months. She went on hunger strikes and refused to eat. She would hiss and spit like a wild animal when invited to remember neglected assignments. We did not know what to do to help her feel at home at Mount Carmel. Mary Anna came to see if she could help, but even her attempts to comfort her niece were refused. So great was Young Mary's influence upon us that it was as though a dark cloud hung over our community, no matter how we tried to place our attention on the common goals which ordinarily brought us great peace. So the months passed into the winter season. Cold winds, sleet, hail, and frost bit deeply into our reserve of patience. More and more of the community turned away from her, ignoring her, refusing to give in to Young Mary's rebellious manipulations, sullen depressions, and defiant withdrawal into herself.

Whenever I went to my beloved granddaughter, my heart anguishing for her well-being, she would avert her eyes. Looking down, tears welling up, she would run past me, as if she were freeing herself from a captor. Once, when I found her crying in a dark storeroom, I took her into my arms, only to have her begin screaming, tearing my robe and apron, her eyes maddened with grief and heartache.

'It's your fault that I am here. I don't want to be here. I hate you! I'll never forgive you for taking me away from my mother and father,' she screamed. As I let her go, I felt confused and tortured by the demons of self-doubt, remorse, and guilt. I, too, began to question the traditional methods of teaching the ancient mysteries, and wondered if Young Mary was right in demanding reforms. I did not know what to do. So I gave our young rebel up to the Lord Most High and asked Archangel Gabriel to help me find a way to heal her heart. I also began to look at Mount Carmel through Young Mary's eyes.

Among Carmel's elders, it was decided that Young Mary would be escorted back to her home in Bethany. On the evening of that choice, she became very ill with a disease that affected her heart and lungs. High fever, chills, and deep coughing racked her thin body. Mariam, who also had her pallet in the young maidens' dormitory, came to me with the news of her cousin's worsening condition. I gathered several other women who were skilled at healing to come with me. We took Young Mary to the infirmary.

Although Mariam had endured Young Mary's stinging barbs and had continually compared herself unfavourably with her cousin, she now began to feel a love for her cousin that she had not felt before. Mariam also began to realize that she, and only she, understood Young Mary, from whom everyone else had become alienated. She understood her longing for her parents, her moodiness, and her rebellion against Mount Carmel's strict discipline and piety. In short, she understood why her cousin had become aloof, withdrawn and numb.

Mariam understood her cousin to be more like herself than anyone else that she knew. The essential difference between them was that Young Mary did not hesitate when there was an opportunity to be an active reformer of the outer world, while Mariam preferred to invisibly harmonize discord on the inner planes. So Mariam came along that night to be with her cousin, whose silence spoke louder than words that she was determined to leave Carmel one way or another. When we told Young Mary of the elders' decision to let her return to Bethany, her face brightened. However, the many weeks of starving herself had taken their toll. The fever intensified. Her spittle carried blood.

Mariam responded with a courageous resolve to support her cousin with every ounce of strength she had. She brought her pallet and laid herself down beside Young Mary. Placing her blanket over both of them, Mariam wrapped her arms around her cousin's frail body that in turn sweated profusely and convulsed with chills. Through it all, they both somehow found deep healing. From time to time, I relieved Mariam so that she could attend to her bodily needs and ritual washing. As Mariam nursed her, Young Mary found a loyal friend with whom she could open her aching heart.

And so it was that these two began to truly know each other. They found solace by bringing healing balm to one another's broken hearts. However, there continued to be a barb of jealousy over their mutual love of Yeshua and their suppressed fantasy that he would someday choose one over the other in marriage. Although this thorn continued to test them through the remainder of their early years, they opened their hearts to each other as only soulmates can, once they see through the veil of distrust.

A messenger had been sent to Bethany to summon Mary of Magdala to come and be with her ailing daughter, assess the situation, and perhaps take her back to Bethany. During the days while we waited for her mother, Young Mary began to change before our very eyes. Although she was weak, she began to welcome the rich herbal broth and the gentle caresses I gave her. At last, a glittering light gathered in Young Mary's golden eyes, as Mariam recited secret love poems she had written. She enjoyed brushing her cousin's long mahogany hair, which like her own raven black hair, was very densely curled. With new ears, Mariam listened as no one had before to this one's childhood stories of loneliness and of her great love for her mother and father. Of all her stories, the romantic fantasies and troubled dreams that Young Mary had of Yeshua were the words Mariam listened to with every beat of her heart. She discovered that her cousin's trials and dreams were just like her own. So these two bonded and healed as they emptied their hearts out to each other. Mary of Magdala arrived to find in her daughter a matured young novice who had passed a most arduous test.

Including Young Mary in the decision-making, the elders of Mount Carmel now agreed that she could stay as a probationary initiate until she was sixteen. Then she, Mariam, and other young probationary initiates would go to Egypt to receive further initiations, if they proved successful with those they would take at Carmel. So it was that the next two years passed harmoniously, as Young Mary and Mariam grew in stature and waxed strong within the Great Mystery. Both of these young women developed a growing sensitivity to the ways of Spirit. They searched deep within themselves and found a profound, abiding love for the One God/Goddess.

They knew their purpose was to restore life to that which was dead within the minds, bodies, souls, and outer institutions of humankind. Claiming the prize of self-mastery was the pearl of great price they both sought. Thus, embracing, balancing, and unifying the polarities within themselves became the goal of these two young women, who found in each other a perfect mirror. They also knew that their lives were integrally entwined with their cousin, Yeshua. He became their constant guiding star and the mystery they most desired to unveil.

So it is that I have shared with you some understanding about the personalities of these two young maidens. In future years, Young Mary would become Yeshua's beloved consort. Mariam, his adopted sister whom he called Mary Grace, continued to be his loyal friend and confidante.

෨

⤟ Chapter 26 ⤟

Yeshua in Britain

Now let me share a portion of all that could be said about my grandson's experiences in the British Isles, which Yeshua and his uncles later reported to me. I will give you a brief summary of the places he visited and the initiations he passed through between the ages of thirteen and sixteen. Of his many initiatory experiences, my favourite was the final initiation Yeshua took inside the Tor at Avalon shortly before returning to Mount Carmel and Nazareth.

The journey to Britain included stops along the coastline of the Mediterranean where Joseph of Arimathea deposited initiates, manuscripts, supplies, and news at their various destinations along the way. They braved the typical late winter and spring high seas, which Yeshua found very exciting once he got his sea legs. Needless to say, he was glad to finally stand firmly on Britain's verdant land, meet his uncles Andrew, Josephus, and Noah, and begin his adventures, from which his etheric journeys had only provided glimpses.

He had spent his thirteenth birthday with relatives in Gaul, one of whom was Sara. She looked amazingly like his cousins Mariam and Young Mary, except that she was taller and had the darker complexion of her Egyptian mother. That rendezvous was wonderful, and here he was now in the Covenant Land of his Hebrew forebears and the land where his maternal grandmother had been adopted as a Celtic princess. The months ahead were full of promise.

Yeshua enjoyed getting acquainted with the uncles he had never seen before, as well as getting to experience a new side of his Uncle Joseph – that of a Druid high priest. It was known that Joseph of Arimathea would leave for Palestine within two months and would return every year, for the following three years, until his nephew's initiations in Britain were completed. Yeshua's other uncles gladly took their young charge under their protective wing.

Andrew, during the thirty-one years since he had come to Britain in 22 BC, had become the chief architect of the small monastic communities of Celtic Druids on the Isles of Avalon, which had expanded substantially under his supervision. Before going further let me explain that Avalon was the name used for two isles: the smaller isles of Avalon in what is now called Glastonbury and the much larger isle of Mona now called Anglesey off the western shore of Wales. Josephus was now in the early stages of establishing major Druid-Essene universities at these two locations, with a library that eventually contained thousands of books, manuscripts, and scrolls, many of which were transported to Britain by Joseph of Arimathea from all corners of the Roman Empire. Both Andrew and Josephus chose to be celibate monks, while Noah's spiritual path embraced the intimate understanding of the feminine heart as a married man.

Noah had been twelve years of age when he first arrived in Britain. Ten years later he met and married a red haired, Celtic princess whom he called Ariadne. Her brother, Llyr Llediaith, had begun his reign as king of the northern branch of the Silurian kingdom in Kymria or Wales, several years before Yeshua's arrival in ADIO. Noah was recognized as a bard within the Druid Orders. If Yeshua had a favourite uncle, it was Noah, who was more like his father than anyone he knew. And, I will tell you this, my dear friend, there is a good reason for this similarity. Both his father and his Uncle Noah carried the same soul stream that expressed as the ascended master Saint Germain many years later. Like Saint Germain, Noah became a very well known adept who knew the secrets of physical immortality, and kept the same body for well over six hundred years. Your records refer to him as the Merlin Taliesen, who prepared Arthur Pendragon for his role as King Arthur of Camelot.

So you see, Yeshua was well connected. It did not take long for his uncles to introduce him to the royal families of the various tribes, to fabled chieftains, magicians, bards, and Druid priests and priestesses. His first initiation occurred during the celebration of Beltaine fertility rites at Avalon, when he was inducted as a probationary initiate into the Order of Druids. I know you may be very curious about what Yeshua may have experienced as the Beltaine fires burned on the Tor. However, if I were to tell you about this and all the other empowering stories my grandson shared with me about Britain, they alone would fill a book.

In addition to spending time in the summer country of Avalon's fabled isles and the west country you call Cornwall, Devon, and Somerset, Yeshua's uncles also took him to the great stone monuments of Stonehenge and Avebury, where he learned about the powerful forces understood by geomancers. He followed the electric and magnetic ley lines, feeling the surge of energy that occurred at the 'dragon points' where they crossed. Usually at these crossings there were stone circles or other monolithic monuments of stone that acted like acupuncture needles to harness and channel the combined telluric, lunar, solar, and stellar energy for specific purposes known by the Druids.

He also connected deeply with the consciousness of Gaia, the Great Mother Earth, by entering into many of her natural and manmade underground chambers and caves. And, just as I promised him, he met the elemental and fairy realms as he meditated in fairy rings, by springs and lakes, on mountain crags and by bonfires. The inter-dimensional portals at these places were very easy to pass through. Here, Yeshua also learned more about the measurement of time and the influences of celestial bodies.

Throughout Britain, except to the southeast, where Roman rule was all too evident, Yeshua made ceremony with Druid high priests and priestesses within sacred groves, and meditated beside the source of babbling springs, lakes, and running waters. Deep within the tunnels and upon the highlands of this ancient land, he learned how to listen to the oracles of unseen worlds. He also learned incantations and discernment of spirits, and how sexual energy could be used for good or ill.

During his second year in the British Isles, Yeshua devoted a substantial amount of time to exploring the neighbouring island of Eire or Ireland. Here, as in Britain, he found the angelic realms very close and accessible, as he communed with beings of Inner Earth, fairies, and the elementals of earth, water, air, and fire. Yeshua's last year in Britain was primarily spent on the island of Mona, the great Druid sanctuary, off the coast of west Kymria, as well as the isles of Avalon that you presently call Glastonbury. It was at the Avalonian site of Chalice Hill and the Tor, just a month before his departure, that he took his last initiation in Britain.

There in Avalon, in the area that became the crypt of what would later be called the Mary Chapel of the great Glastonbury Abbey, Joseph of Arimathea had built a small mud and wattle structure that served as a sanctuary for observing Essene practices. Nearby was a spring and well house that provided water for ceremonial and community use. The well house also protected one of the entrances into the underground initiatory tunnels that led to cavernous chambers beneath Chalice Hill and the Tor.

At this ancient well, my sixteen-year-old grandson met with his Uncle Joseph, who was clothed in the white robes of a Druid high priest. He led his nephew through a labyrinth devoid of light, except that born of the sun within the soul. In a chamber of great crystals both massive and tall, the young initiate was left alone to meditate beside a small inner lake which reflected his every thought and feeling. Into the cold water he plunged, diving deep into the abyss, until a faint light began to shine in the distance.

No longer breathing as does a human, Yeshua surrendered into the remembrance of his soul having taken the form of a dolphin. Upward through a narrow passage he swam, until his body broke through the dark water. Emerging from the deep, shivering with cold, he found himself in a cavern, sealed from the world above. Over the doorway, written in the ancient language that his uncles taught him, were the words of Thoth-Hermes, 'As above, so below'. Seeing a beckoning light beyond, my grandson crossed over the towering door's threshold. Great beings, over seven feet tall in stature, arose from great stone benches to greet him.

Accompanied by these beings of light, Yeshua climbed a steep, narrow, spiral stairway and crossed over a stone bridge into a grand cavern hewn out of stone and built of finely crafted masonry. There, in the midst of the well-lit room, was a large, round, crystal table surrounded by twelve stone chairs. No evident source of the light could be found, as he looked all around. No shadows were cast in this place. Everything and everyone glowed from within. Yeshua trembled with this self-illuminating energy and knew it would be important to recall this experience and its particular vibration in a future hour.

Then, one of the great beings took him by the hand. This one was ancient, several thousands of Earth-years old. Yet, his translucent face shone with a sparkle of wit and sublime wisdom. Torak announced that he was one of the high priests who had survived the sinking of Atlantis. He had gone with the ships of light into the underground city of Thoth beneath the Great Pyramid. When the Earth's waters finally receded, revealing the ancient lands now called Britain, Torak went with his bride, Torhannah, to bring a Divine Feminine balance for the Earth's people who still grieved. By doing so, it was hoped that humanity's survival against any future holocaust would be assured. So it was that Torak and Torhannah chose to linger through time upon the face of the Earth.

Torak intoned remotely familiar words into Yeshua's ears, assisting this young initiate to remember the languages of light and the blue stargates of Orion and Sirius. He said he was of a lineage of seers and magicians who held certain wisdom inviolate from the tampering of the sons of the darkness. Those who loved and feared him knew him as a Merlin.

Now, let it be said that my beloved grandson tarried with Torak for a night and a day, though the passing of time was not measured, as you know it. It could well have been years, the sharing with this great soul, who no longer reckoned the passage of time by the movement of the external sun.

Torak bid Yeshua to sit very still and to meditate. Stooping low, he touched Yeshua's chest, and then turning around, he silently walked away. Torak knew the more empowering choice was to leave the boy to find the answers he sought within his own heart. As Yeshua sat there, very ancient memories began to quicken and to take form within his mind. Then a mysteriously warm draft of air wrapped itself around him as if it were a soft cocoon. Drowsily, his head began to nod, lulled by the delicate chime of bells.

As the highly refined tones took him ever more deeply inward, he became aware of Torhannah's presence who announced that she represented the Divine Mother, just as her beloved Torak had said. Yeshua's heart opened more and more as he slowly became aware that what he had thought was the sound of bells was actually the eternal Mother's voice. Surrendering into the infinite liquid sounds of her love, he felt as if he were floating upon a vast ocean. Without any effort at all, the gentle tide carried him into her vast heart. Weeping with remembrance, in a silence deeper and louder than any sound could utter, the Mother of Life spoke to every cell of Yeshua's young body attuning the matrix of his form to remember its cosmic origins and birth.

She shared how important it was that he feel and express the healing and nurturing energies of the Divine Feminine that dwelled within him throughout his life. She explained that he had entered upon the earthplane during a time of great darkness and suffering that was caused by humanity's attempt to separate the Divine Masculine's objective mind from its Divine Feminine intuitive heart.

Opening his vision, she showed him the perils and desecration that would occur upon the Earth Mother through future years. This, she said, was the result of the increasing masculine imbalance. She reminded him that he and a group of cosmic companions had come to assist humanity to stop this downward imploding cycle of separation and devolution. Through humanity's free-will choice, life could consciously join with the living Earth Mother, who was already beginning to align her consciousness to her ascending return into the realms of light and union.

How long he sat there receiving insight upon insight, while in dreamlike repose, he knew not, until the pressure of his Uncle Joseph's hand on his arm woke him up. Enthusiastically, Yeshua began to report his experiences and to pelt his uncle with all the many questions he so desired to have answered. But, before he could finish a sentence, Joseph mutely gestured the signal that communicated silence was to be honoured. Then, by a much shorter and easier route, as so often occurs when an initiation is completed, my grandson left the Tor's inner chamber by ascending another spiralling stone stairway that led to a hidden exit situated at the top of the great earthen mound. Near an ancient circle of standing stones, Yeshua emerged into the cool night air and the reflections of silver light cast by a full moon upon the dewy grasses and waters of Avalon. Today, this exit is buried below what remains of St. Michael's Tower.

Yeshua had hoped that he could share his experiences with his uncles upon his return to the communal building, where he was pleased to find a feast laid out for him. However, the elders reminded him that it was better to hold his experiences inside his heart for a time, allowing them to magnetize increased insight. Rather than dissipating the power of his initiation by talking about it, the wisdom gathered from his experiences could then deepen through his coming days. Thus, his confidence grew in his ability to find answers and empowered guidance within the ample treasury of his own mighty I AM. And, in this way, he continued to understand how his small self could be tempered and aligned with a greater purpose than bringing glory to itself.

But more important still, my grandson began to fully understand the nature and work of the Divine Mother whose empowering and loving presence heals the suffering of the world. He learned how to be still and allow her presence to comfort him in those moments of feeling lonely or confused. Likewise, let us linger and absorb the energies of Divine Love's nurturing embrace. Attune your ears and you may hear the delicate chiming of Torhannah's silver bells calling you home to the Divine Mother's heart. Breathe and also receive the essence of an elder brother whose exemplary light shows the way.

෴

♬ *Chapter 27* ♬

Yeshua Returns from Britain

I fondly remember the day that Yeshua returned from Britain. Before sunrise one August morning I was compelled to rise and walk to my favourite precipice that overlooks the Great Sea. I had created a small altar here many years earlier. As I knelt beside the familiar stones and prayed, I began to be absorbed within an ocean of bliss and ecstasy. When I began to sense my body again, the early rays of the sun were beginning to penetrate the deep dark of the night. Within my inner ears I heard, 'I am come!'

As my outer vision focused into clarity, I scanned the horizon. Yes! It was a small fleet of sailing boats, their lamps bobbing like dancing stars. As they approached in the dawning light, I beheld the colours and design of Joseph's heraldic banner appliqued upon the main sail of the leading vessel. I removed my shawl and began to wave it upon the gathering breeze. The shore was rocky and dangerous; consequently, the boats could only pass by at a distance as they sailed to the small port of Dor a few miles to the south. Nevertheless, they were close enough for me to see the individual forms of the crew. It would be at least another day before Yeshua arrived.

Then I saw him! Yeshua waved, and the next thing I knew, he was diving into the sea. I watched, somewhat alarmed at first, but then taking a deep breath, I could clearly see that he was a very strong swimmer. His lean body surfed the waves as he guided himself to a narrow spit of sand along the towering cliffs. He gathered himself up, a small bundle tied to his waist, and began to climb upwards. Long ago, the ancient ones who once lived here had carved handholds and narrow ledges so that they might be able to escape captivity by marauding nomadic tribes. So it was that Yeshua had explored this precipitous path as a young boy, and he remembered it well. Indeed, this treacherous route was one of the many tests of courage and intuition he had passed on a foggy, moonless night shortly before going to Britain.

My, how he had grown these past three years! Now, he towered above me, grinning from ear to ear. His long, wet hair smelled of the sea. Salt and sand glistened on his tanned, sweating body. My heart ached with a swelling ecstasy, as I surveyed the extraordinary beauty of my grandson. He breathed deeply, once the effects of the long climb had gradually subsided, restoring his lungs to normal breathing. We stood there, looking at one another, so very joyful to be together again! It was easy to see that his uncles, Joseph of Arimathea, Andrew, Josephus and Noah had done well in preparing this young man for his coming tests. Suddenly, we both broke into peals of laughter, until we began to shake all over. We were not able, nor did we desire, to stop this unexpected return to childlike innocence and joy.

Yeshua swept me up in his arms, as he had long ago, upon his return from the Sinai. Around and around we whirled until we both were dizzy, laughing all the while. Finally, we came to ourselves, realizing that the day had already begun in Carmel. A distant bell could be heard for the gathering to morning prayers. Nearby, were the sounds of bleating and the merry jingle of sheep and goat bells. Then, we heard a welcoming hello as Nathaniel Bartholomew strode into view. Nathaniel was the shepherd boy who had kneeled before Yeshua when he was a newborn babe in Bethlehem, and had been one of his most ardent friends and confidantes during the five years Yeshua was at Carmel, Nazareth, and Qumran. Nathaniel had hoped to accompany his friend to Britain, but the elders had decided that it would be more empowering for Yeshua to go alone. Except for those occasions when he was with his uncle, Joseph of Arimathea, Yeshua was to undergo his initiations into the Order of Druids with relatives he had not known before.

Yeshua ran into Nathaniel's arms. They were almost the same height, slender and deeply tanned. Nathaniel was twenty-eight and still unmarried. He was overjoyed to see his beloved friend again. Weeping, he held Yeshua fast to his breast, kissing his cheeks, which had grown a light beard. As I beheld these young men rejoicing in their reunion, my heart beat so fast that I could not speak. Finally, realizing that Yeshua was really here, Nathaniel Bartholomew held him at arm's length, looking deeply into his smiling, blue-grey eyes. Then, after embracing one more time, they began to run for the west gate. I was left with the sheep and goats, but it didn't matter. I could be still, and take into my heart the glad news of his coming.

After Absalom came to relieve me of the herd, I was met at the gate by Mariam, who was beside herself with joy over Yeshua's return. 'We must prepare a feast for my beloved brother!' exclaimed Mariam as she grabbed my arm, hurrying me toward the great kitchen. Everyone was milling around Yeshua, plying him with questions and embraces. Community ritual was set aside. Young Mary held herself back, peering from a doorway, taking in her cousin, feeling tidal waves of joy and passion rising and falling in every cell of her body. What was she to do with all this energy now that her matured body betrayed a woman's love for a man? She commanded the angels to return her to calm and dignity.

Suddenly, Yeshua caught her gaze. Dumbfounded, he looked down, his face blushing with the heat of a passion that came from a place so deep in his being he could not determine its depth. Catching this poignant moment of intense, though embarrassing pleasure, everyone began to smile and laugh. Yeshua took a deep breath, gathered up the children one at a time to ride on his shoulders, and began to run around the inner court. Then he leaped over a low stone fence and darted among the fruit and olive trees. The children squealed and flapped their arms like birds. As I joyfully looked upon this scene of innocent play, my memory returned to Yeshua as an eight-year old boy arriving from Egypt and the Sinai.

Noticing Yeshua's fatigue, Nathaniel came to Yeshua's rescue and told the children to return to their assignments. Then these two beloved young men walked to the baths after which they went to the great dining room to take refreshment for their hungry bodies. No matter that it was not the communal hour for breaking the morning fast. Steaming bowls of oatmeal, millet, and kamut were put before them. Fresh goat's milk and cheese, loaves of dark bread and wild honey were also provided. It was plain to see that the reforms Young Mary had catalysed were underway.

After an evening of intense sharing with the entire community of Mount Carmel, Yeshua departed for a weeklong visit with his family in Nazareth, which was just twenty miles away. Mary Anna and Joseph were expecting Yeshua's arrival, and they were delighted with the way his three years in Britain had transformed their son from a precocious youngster into a maturing young man. A grand family reunion was enjoyed by all. Yeshua was overjoyed to share his experiences with his parents, brothers, and sisters – James, Jude,

Joseph the Younger, Ruth, Thomas and Simon. In this way, Yeshua was able to integrate his initiations by sharing only those experiences that he knew would benefit those who listened.

Mariam and Young Mary were in the process of preparing to leave Mount Carmel in late October, with a number of adults and other young people, to begin more advanced initiations in Egypt. They knew that they would not be seeing Yeshua again before his departure to India. Consequently, the intensity of their desire to renew their acquaintance with their favourite cousin was readily apparent when Yeshua returned to Carmel from the week with his family in Nazareth.

They spent every moment they could with him. Mariam and Young Mary had bonded so closely that the shadow of jealousy was barely discernible, except for an occasional biting word or fearful glance. They made a pact with one another to find their way through the intense feelings they both felt toward Yeshua and their mutual destiny with him.

When it came time for them to leave for Egypt, Joseph of Arimathea escorted Young Mary, Mariam, and the others to Alexandria on one of his freighting boats. Docking for a month, before continuing his trade route, Joseph showed them the wonders of this rather sophisticated city and introduced them to a number of their distant relatives who later took them on to Heliopolis. Isaac and Tabitha had brought their light conceived daughter, Sara, to Egypt several weeks earlier, and were waiting to greet them when they arrived at their Aunt Mariamne's home. Mariam and Young Mary had heard stories about their dark-skinned cousin that aroused their curiosity, and they were very eager to meet her.

So it was that the rest of us had the immense pleasure of Yeshua's presence at Carmel and Nazareth, prior to his departure for India. He would leave the following April, shortly after his seventeenth birthday. How good it had felt to Yeshua to be with his beloved parents and younger siblings again. The three years' absence had seen much change in the children who had been Yeshua's playmates. Now that he had matured through his initiations and had much more refined sensitivity of subtle energy, Yeshua looked to both his parents with deeper insight and acknowledgement of their journey that had prepared them so well through the years. Although they appeared to be quite ordinary and went about their work unnoticed, it did not take long for Yeshua to discover that both his father and mother had more spiritual powers than he had realized before he left for Britain.

Often he would take his mother or father aside. In privacy, he asked for their counsel concerning how to go about cultivating his spiritual gifts. On such occasions, he also asked deeply probing questions about what the angels had said concerning him and the work he had come to Earth to do. Of Yeshua's brothers, James and Joseph the Younger seemed the most interested in his spirituality. They loved to join their older brother and parents in lofty discussions and long meditations. Jude, however, was more taken with the wonders of the natural world which he demonstrated by cultivating his mother's garden and raising animals.

As the months passed, Yeshua's esteem for his humble father increased. He so desired to follow his father's example. Although he had not known his grandfather Joachim, the stories that I told him about Joachim's great spiritual strength and devotion inspired my grandson. When he realized that much of the wisdom that these two men had gained had come from their years spent in India, his eagerness to depart and gather the same wisdom for himself multiplied everyday. Even though the journey would be long and dangerous, he vigorously applied himself to the necessary preparation for leaving as planned. James, of course, also felt that he must go. And when young Joseph also implored his parents to let him go with his brothers, he was firmly told that they would pray on the matter.

Joseph of Arimathea understood that it would be wise to have a close relative act as the boys' guardian, since their father would be staying in Nazareth. After taking his daughter and the other young initiates to Egypt, Joseph proceeded to southern Gaul and Britain, as was his custom. While in the Languedoc, he met with his half-brothers Isaac and Jacob. When he informed them of the news that Yeshua would be taking pilgrimage to India, Jacob immediately knew that his dream of advancing his initiations in India could now be realized. He gladly accepted the invitation to go with his nephews.

Consequently, Joseph of Arimathea returned to Palestine, Jacob immediately went to Nazareth and Mount Carmel to meet with family members he had not seen in many years. It did not take him long to make the necessary preparations that were required to accompany his nephews to the Indus valley and high Himalayas.

Looking at Jacob, who appeared no more than forty years of age amazed me because his appearance was so much like his father's at the time we first met. Having received his advanced initiations in Egypt, Jacob had also mastered the secrets of longevity. Thus, his robust appearance made it very difficult for most people to believe that he was sixty-two years of age.

One of Joseph ben Jacob's cousins, who had made a number of journeys to India as a trader, was hired to act as a primary guide and outfitter for the expedition. It was agreed that the boys' father, as their spiritual advisor and overseer, would also be one of those who travelled. However, because of worsening physical infirmities that had recently begun to affect his eyesight and joints, the long journey to India was ill advised. It was decided that Joseph would remain close to home, or so it would seem to the uninitiated.

Because Joseph had mastered the manipulation of subtle energy in inter-dimensional time and space, he would bilocate as often as possible in order to be with his sons. On other occasions, when necessary, he promised to teleport his physical body. Yeshua had seen his father do both, so he knew his father would keep his promises. The remainder of us who knew how to bilocate and/or teleport, would join them from time to time. An overjoyed Joseph the Younger was ecstatic when his mother, who was against his foreign travelling at such a young age, consented he could go.

Several days before their departure, many of the family gathered at Mary Anna's home for a farewell gathering. After a simple meal, we celebrated with music and dancing, and then brought forward the gifts we had prepared for the pilgrims' journey. I made pouches for my son, Jacob, and my three grandsons, into which I placed all kinds of healing herbs and oils, healing stones, and protective amulets. Mary Anna had woven strong belts of brightly dyed spun linen, which she gave to her brother and three sons. Upon these belts hung intricately carved wooden bowls and painted gourds for drinking and eating, which both she and Joseph had crafted. Joseph gave his brother-in-law and sons heavy over-cloaks, which could be spread out for sleeping or fastened overhead for protection from the sun or rain. Before they went to Egypt, Mariam and Young Mary had each woven Yeshua a robe of finest wool, which they had given to Mary Anna to keep for this occasion. Nathaniel gave each of his friends a pair of sturdy sandals.

Then, at sunrise, on a bright spring day, I embraced these courageous souls so dear to my heart, not knowing when I would be seeing them again. With Jacob blowing a ram's horn and taking the lead, they mounted their camels, each with a pack camel following. They would rendezvous with a caravan of traders at a campsite near the Sea of Galilee and then make their way to the great mountains of the east.

Although excited and completely supportive of their pilgrimage, this time I found myself somewhat melancholy, knowing I would miss being with these grandchildren during the coming years they would be away. This occasion seemed to be another opportunity for detaching from my human desires and aligning to a greater plan. There was comfort in knowing that I could join them on the etheric plane, and perhaps, even teleport my body when it was appropriate.

ᴖ *Chapter 28* ᴖ
Yeshua Reports His Journey to India

It would be seven years before Yeshua returned from his travels in India and the high Himalayas. In those days while Yeshua was in India, I remained in my station at Mount Carmel, continuing to teach the young women and men. I assisted in their full comprehension of those energies that are aligned to their Creator. I taught them how to prepare their minds, bodies, and souls for the initiations that would prove their commitment to the highest truth of oneness within them. Many came, and few left the training once it had begun because they had been interviewed thoroughly and were required to meet high standards. No one entered the Mount Carmel Mystery School, regardless of age, unless they were found capable of meeting the tests.

Over many years and indeed many generations, I continued as the head of the initiatory school of the young people at Mount Carmel. Also, from time to time, there were couples and individuals who came to me to receive the initiations and disciplines of Light Conception, so that they might bear forth highly evolved children. Some sought my wisdom pertaining to the practices involved in attaining cellular regeneration and physical immortality.

There is little to report of those years we awaited Yeshua's return. Therefore, I shall resume our story at the point when my grandson returned to his parents' home in Nazareth at the age of twenty-four, in the late summer of AD21. There had been many changes in all of us during the intervening years. Mary Anna was now almost forty-one years of age, even though she appeared to be no more than thirty, and Ruth was almost sixteen. Esther Salome and Simon were thirteen. Some of my children and their descendants had passed on to the other side of the mortal veil, and there were other souls who traversed the veil to take up bodies on this side.

Needless to say, when the news arrived that Yeshua had come back with his brother James and his Uncle Jacob, there was a family gathering at Mary Anna's home to celebrate. With mixed feelings, we were told that Joseph the Younger had chosen to remain in India as a married householder. He had been welcomed as a son-in-law by a wealthy rishi, and had established himself as a promising Ayurvedic physician. Then, my grandson revealed that his father, Joseph, who had teleported for the last time to India, during the month before Yeshua and James were to begin their return to Palestine, had ascended into the light and would not be returning.

Yeshua explained that he would share his story with the extended family later, after James, Jacob, and he had given a full account to Mary Anna. So it was that a week passed before we came together again. Mary Anna was in silent retreat the entire time. She had confided to me several months earlier that she had been called on the inner planes to come into Maha Babaji's presence. She did not share with me all that she had heard or seen, but she did reveal that Joseph was taken up into the light and that he would not be returning to her in the physical. She was resolved to hold him in her heart and to carry on as best she could without him. It had not been easy.

Although material comforts were abundant, loneliness often disturbed Mary Anna's peace. Yet she brought herself out of the potential valleys of depression with renewed vigour and constant availability to ease the pain of others whose losses were greater than her own. Thus, Mary Anna was challenged to achieve a greater balance between her highly developed feminine nature and to express her latent masculine abilities. Her providential skills increased, as did her extraordinary wisdom and compassion. Her counsel and presence were sought by many, and seldom did she have time to consider her widowed condition, except when the night hours grew long and her bed knew no comforting warmth.

Yeshua and James were now returned to her. Fully matured, these young men made their presence felt in Mary Anna's small but comfortable home. It was clear that they had come into a stature of which she was proud and grateful. Yet, there was an ache in her heart that arose whenever she beheld her son, James, whose countenance was so much like his father's. Tears spilled from her eyes when she looked upon him during those first days after his return.

After Mary Anna had had time to embrace all that Yeshua, James, and Jacob told her about their experiences in India, and particularly that which concerned her husband, she prepared a feast, and invited family and friends to gather around. So it was that Yeshua began to share with us the highlights of his seven-year pilgrimage to India.

Yeshua called us forth in the evening hour, just after sunset. We prayed and gave benediction upon our day's affairs and our bounteous supper meal. Bodily hunger satisfied, we then took our places in the outer court of Mary Anna's home. In this sweet and sublime garden, we found repose and solace. The sweet fragrance of citrus blooms, jasmine, and roses wafted upon the warm, tranquil, late summer breeze. All were hushed and deeply inward. Even the very small children, who gathered around Yeshua's knee, and the toddler who sat on his lap, were unusually still. A deep peace prevailed, unsullied by any thought of sorrow or anxiety for the morrow. We waited in silence until Yeshua sighed and began to give utterance.

These are the words I recall him speaking to us:

'My beloved family and friends, into whose presence I am returned after a long journey. I am now of a man's stature, and the Law of One does rest within me, though not all is yet fulfilled in me. Of this, I am now certain: I await the full awakening when God comes and dwells permanently within my consciousness. This, I also know: it is not I who doeth the works, but my Father–Mother who moves and breathes me.

'You now look upon me as one who is returned to you. You remember me as son, nephew, brother and cousin. But I say to you, this is both a truth and an untruth. I am Yeshua ben Joseph, and I am he who transcends my family name to receive the name unspeakable. So have I returned to you, as I am held in the balance of yesterday's fading memory and tomorrow's realized dream. I am with you fully in this present moment.

'Now, I shall say to you further that I bring you greetings from my earthly father, Joseph. I represent to you, as well, the fond greetings of my brother, Joseph the Younger, whom many call Joses, who has made the choice to remain in India.

'During the course of our wanderings over the past seven years, my brothers and I developed a deep love and appreciation for our Uncle Jacob, whose enlightened and compassionate presence enriched our travels immeasurably. From time to time during the course of our pilgrimage, our beloved father, Joseph, walked with us. Both the wealthy and the poor welcomed us. And, with these we were invited to impart our wisdom.

'We read from sacred texts, and traced the lineage of that wisdom to Atlantis and Lemuria, even to golden eras before. So ancient was this wisdom that I quaked in the magnitude of those great minds that had gathered these truths and set them to writing. Very quickly, I learned to read, write, and speak in the Sanskrit language. Several of the vernacular dialects I also learned in order to converse with the native peoples.

'We tarried for four years in the countryside, villages, and cities of the Sindhu (Indus), Ganga (Ganges), and Brahmaputra rivers. We encountered many great Hindu and Buddhist teachers along the way, who have mastered their souls on the physical plane. And many wonders did I behold. Into the high places I wandered without purse or scrip. As the lilies of the field, I was arrayed with raiment and sustenance sufficient for the day. Into caves and great temples I was taken, where I received many witnesses of our heavenly Father–Mother's supernal light.

'My beloved father was a wonder. I had not fully appreciated him during my childhood. Before my eyes, he became a wonder-man. He had made it known to us before our departure to India that he would often be bilocating and would occasionally be teleporting from Nazareth at key points in our journey. And so it was that he magnificently served us as a guide and introduced us to various masters and adepts. We rejoiced at his unpredictable appearances on these occasions and became increasingly appreciative of our father's extraordinary example.

'Let it not be supposed that he ever took pride in his abilities or displayed his gifts to aggrandize his small self. In outward appearance, he maintained a calm, reserved, and unpretentious mien. Often, his full-greying beard revealed an infectious smile. At times, he would break forth with a whistled tune, a comic tale, or a joke that would lighten the air that had become heavy with some scholarly discourse or wounded ego's pious lament.

'My father seemed invincible. Nothing tired him. Nothing ruffled his feathers. And if there were occasions when he was fatigued or irritable, I was not privy to them. Yet, I also knew that he embraced his humanity, and was compassionate towards the human condition.

Certainly, he desired that I not put him on a pedestal to worship him, even though at times my unabashed adoration of him became so great I could not help myself. It was at such times that he would assist me to reclaim the energies I projected onto him. Gently, he suggested that I expand my veneration of him into a deep reverence for the Father–Mother's glory, which dwells within my own heart and that of all life.

'What a mirror was this father of mine! He knew exactly the moment when I was giving my power away. Never did he take it for his own purposes, but he would call me to heed and follow the leaking energy until it came back to me. This was not always easy. Sometimes my thoughts and feelings flew on a circuitous route, taken and qualified by anyone, seen or unseen, who coveted power to bolster their perception of an inadequate or insecure lower self. So did my father teach me to also know my connection with the whole of life. He taught me reverence for the life force, and showed me how my energy substance could sustain and empower life or, conversely, be drained away by my inattention, ignorance, or naivety, to feed the phantom addictions of those untransmuted aspects of myself that still identified with fear, conflict, and lack.

'We ventured into the cities of Kanyakubja (Kanauj), Benares (Varanasi), and Pataliputra (Patna). We bathed in the River Ganga (Ganges) and chanted the names of God; the Creator (Brahma), the Sustainer (Vishnu), and He/She who returns all that is to its formless origin (Shiva). We also celebrated the Great Mother's many names and attributes in temples and outdoor shrines. My father taught me the nature of the fakirs, saddhus, and tantricas, which further expanded my understanding of the mind–body relationship. Through his example of wise compassion, I came to appreciate every path leading to God, no matter how ascetic, transcendent, or immersed in the physical senses.

'In Benares, my father introduced me to a tantric master of the Sound Current and high alchemy practices, who was also a very fine musician. This wise man, a grandson of one of my father's gurus, had become a trusted friend during those years when my father had been in India many years earlier. This teacher took me on as a student, and taught me how to hear and follow the infinite inner sound, how to play intricate rhythms upon the tablas, and how to strum the many-stringed sitar. I learned how the ragas, played at different times of day, altered my states of consciousness and affected my breath, internal organs, absorption of energies, and moods.

'I was apprenticed for a year with this master, and worked as a craftsman in his household. He was married to three women, all of whom were very beautiful and gracious. That year was a time of cultivating my appreciation for aesthetic refinement, applying the subtle nature of life-force energy, and expressing the nurturing feminine quality of my own soul. While living with this cultured and highly spiritual family, I made the discovery that I need not own anything. Simply by appreciative attention, my requirements and preferences were supplied.

'In this household, were nine daughters and thirteen sons. With one of the older daughters, I felt a great mutual attraction, and with her I learned the ways of high tantric love. This is a very highly refined science and art for raising and expanding consciousness. I share this with you so that you may understand that I hold sex to be a powerful endowment of our Creator Source. Through discipline and conscious devotion, sex can be a direct path to the true Self as an expression of divine love. Sex, however, if expressed through the untransmuted energies of the lower chakras, governed by the animal centres of the unawakened brain and toxic bodily organs, can bring sore affliction that dominates and devours the souls of woman and man.

'Jealousy, lust, avarice, rage, guilt, shame, abuse, and degradation can sweep the innocence of the sexual flow into tortured paths of self-judgement and endless rounds of karmic restitution. In order to become a high initiate who masters all energy through its rightful use, one must confront this great creative force within one's self, together with all the genetic and soul memories connected with it.

'During that wondrous year in Benares, I came to know myself, like my parents and grandparents did before me, as a master of these most beautiful and powerful, refining, initiatory energies. We also learned and practised body postures, pranayama (conscious breathing), and the cleansing of mind and body. We used mantras (words of power) and mudras (hand gestures that activate the body's energy circuits) and experienced how to reach different levels of samadhi (awareness of the Absolute) through many forms of meditation.

'I learned that even my body is consciousness, which paradoxically holds the entire universe within it. By my using it as an intricate map,

I could locate, communicate with, direct, restore, enliven, remove and rebuild every inward and outward reflection of my consciousness. I also came to know that I was sovereign unto myself, so long as I was aligned and attuned to my omnipotent Creator Source, my mighty I AM. I realized that I was free and not dependent upon another. Yet, how lovely and empowering are relationships nurtured by the heart, when we know that we are all flowers within the garden of the Beloved, who gives life equally to all its creation.

'I was grateful that our father took us into such a school, where life's important matters were practised liberally, with wise conscience and compassionate discipline. I will invite James to share his experience later. Although we differ in our philosophies toward the physical plane, and I feel my brother's judgement of me from time to time, I am glad for my experience and our father's support of us both.

'So our father, Joseph, assisted us to follow the path he had trodden long ago, when he was preparing himself to be our father. However, it was not only for the sake of being our father that he had gone to India in his youth. Clearly, it was to attain mastery so that he could be of the greatest service to humanity.

'When my time was complete with my master teacher (guru) and my tantric lover, our father then led us to a village in the lower Himalayas. My brothers James, Joseph the Younger, and Uncle Jacob accompanied us for a year and then they returned to Benares. Joseph had spent most of his days with our Uncle Jacob in the home of one of our host's physicians, who recognized my brother's inherent healing gifts. So it was that James, Joseph and Uncle Jacob later returned to the great temple complex. James continued his studies in the library, Joseph began his formal Ayurvedic medical training. Knowing that we were in good hands, Uncle Jacob prepared to journey to many other sacred places in India.

'Reviewing our experiences, I now realize that our father knew more than he was willing to share with us at that time. At any rate, well before taking his departure from the earthplane, he carefully prepared us for our first meeting with the one called Babaji. That encounter, the first among many, would forever transform our lives, as you will come to see. After we have had some refreshments which my beautiful mother has prepared, I shall continue my story.'

∽ *Chapter 29* ∽
Yeshua Meets Babaji

Later that evening Yeshua gathered us together again and said, 'Now, my beloved ones, I will share more fully about our experiences with the great master, Babaji. You have heard of him through my grandmother, Anna, and my grandfather, Joachim. My father's words concerning Babaji were few. I did not know why my father spoke so little of this one. Yet, when we met face to face, at the abode of one of his disciples, I began to understand. This great master, who is known as 'The Immortal Yogi', appeared to be a young man in his thirties who had clear, brown eyes and long, black hair. So powerful were the energies that emanated from his presence, that I could barely maintain my conscious state. When I saw my father go to him and kiss his feet, I began to see my father in a new and revealing light.

'Babaji placed his hands upon my father's head and slowly lifted it, so that they could look into each other's eyes. Tears spilled from my father's eyes, as a golden light spread throughout the room. Soon, I began to tremble, as did my brothers, James and Joseph the Younger. We sat very still. Slowly, the heavens opened to our inner vision, revealing rank upon rank of angels, masters, and saints. Next, we saw a corridor of light open to our view, and we were invited to follow Babaji. By this time, I was aware that Babaji's form had changed into the most luminous body I had ever beheld. Directly before us was the sun, a radiant orb of intense white light. The central energy began to spin, gathering us into its vortex. Then we were taken into the very centre of our solar system's sun. There we were greeted by beautiful solar beings who said they were known as Helios and Vesta.

'After we had been taken into and had merged with the sun, we were returned back to our bodies. Babaji smiled and assured us that this was the first of many such journeys, utilizing our sun as an interdimensional portal. Turning directly towards me and raising his hand, Babaji beckoned me to come forward. My father took my place beside my brothers and my Uncle Jacob, as I went forward to lie prostrate before Babaji, my hands upon his bare feet. Communicating telepathically, he then gave me the maha-mantra: 'I Am the Light.' Gently, he laughed and touched a finger to the crown of my head. As if it were a lightning bolt, a piercing light shot through Babaji's finger, striking me mute. So I remained for many weeks.

'James, Joseph and I, together with our father and our Uncle Jacob, remained with Babaji for a full year, having experiences I am informed from within that I am to hold in my heart. After the year had passed, Babaji told us that it was time for James and Joseph the Younger to return to the temple in Benares. There, Joseph would continue his Ayurvedic studies and James' path would unfold among the monks at the great library within the temple complex, where he would abide until it was time for us to return home. Uncle Jacob was asked to accompany them, resume his studies with James, and prepare for travelling to other sacred sites.

'After my brothers and Uncle Jacob left, Babaji became mysteriously quiet. My father and I had few interactions with him physically, but on the inner planes, we were constantly together. We spent most of our days in meditation, eating little food, bathing in the ice-cold water, and tending a small garden. We slept very little. Then, one night, when the moon was full in May, my father and I were called on the inner planes to attend a gathering within a sacred valley high in the upper Himalayas. There, we experienced our bilocated bodies coalescing to stand around an altar. A chalice and a bowl were on the altar. Behind the altar stood Gautama Buddha and one who announced that he was called Maitreya Buddha, a representative of a lineage of energies called the Cosmic Christ.

'As I looked, my very core melted. I wept. The door of my heart flew open, as if all eternity revealed itself. Through the door of my heart, a gentle, clarifying wind blew, transforming my being. Then, I was told telepathically that I must bring my physical body to this valley where I was to enter a monastic community, far removed from the world. My father turned to me and took my hands, pressing them to his lips. Tears flowed. Our hearts merged as we went outside, walked off a distance, and lay beside one another upon the snow. When we awoke, we noted that the snow had melted from the great heat that abided in us. All around us, in a circle twelve feet in circumference, were white, alpine flowers growing in an emerald field of fine-cropped grass. They gave forth the sweetest perfumed scent, which filled our nostrils and nurtured our lungs.

'Then our consciousness returned to our physical bodies. We opened our eyes and gazed at one another lying on our pallets in the small room. How long we simply gazed and drank each other in, I know not. Perhaps we might have continued in this manner indefinitely, except that a soft knock attracted our attention. Babaji entered, carrying thick, woollen robes, fur boots and leggings, and empty leather packs. He said it was time to go into the retreat of the masters whom we had met last night.

'Little did I know then that my beloved father, Joseph, would not be returning with me. I was so taken up with the exquisite, tantalizing feelings of being with a true avatar that I hardly noticed my father's loving looks, which spoke more to me in hindsight than in those few remaining months we had together. So it was that Babaji escorted us through extraordinarily high mountain passes. Finally, we came to the sheer wall of a granite cliff that had foot and handholds carved in it. It was required of us to rope ourselves together, take off our packs, and then pass our packs along on a rope to the first one who arrived at the other end of this precipitous passage. However, this was not the last test of our determination to arrive at our destination.

'After several more days of long trekking, we came to a deep gorge where we could hear the distant echoes of a roaring river below, which appeared as a thin, white ribbon. There was no bridge. Nothing could be seen that would convey our mortal bodies across this narrow chasm. I sat down, puzzled and somewhat downcast. Had Babaji erred? I searched his glowing face, which was expressionless, except for a twinkle in his eyes. I looked at my father. He, too, gazed back at me with no hint of being disturbed or unsettled by our state of affairs. All of a sudden, a great weariness came over me, which I recognized as primal fear. We had come through snowstorms that seemed to part before us, allowing a warming sun to bathe us as we passed through. Even an avalanche had been turned aside at the very last moment, just as I was about to lose my composure. Now how were we to carry on? I knew there was no turning back.

'I closed my eyes and went deeply inward, commanding my mind to be still and my heart and belly to relax. A great wind arose, tearing at us as if to send us flying. Flying? Yes, that was it! Then,

I looked inwardly and saw Babaji gathering the elements and the forces of gravity. With my inner vision, I could see him creating an etheric bridge across the chasm. And then I opened my eyes. There was no sign of him anywhere!

'Remembering that the different dimensions and all forms within them are simply energy vibrating at different frequencies, I shifted my focus of perception by changing the frequency of my consciousness. Looking through my third eye, I saw him walking in midair as calmly and confidently as if he were strolling through a grassy meadow. My heart raced with excitement. I already knew about such things as levitation and teleportation, and had achieved a certain measure of success at levitating my body. I still had much to learn about teleportation. Now with my increased inner vision, I was really seeing how such things are done.

'Then, I realized that my father was preparing himself to step off the edge of the abruptly ending trail by shifting his dimensional focus to a more subtle realm of being. He looked back toward me and smiled. 'Yes, my son, you, too, can do as you see me doing!' were the comforting words he transmitted to me telepathically.

'Was I sufficiently prepared? I would soon find out! The wind stopped, as I watched Babaji and my father walking confidently across the expanse of seemingly empty space. Babaji had almost reached the other side when I felt a whoosh of spirit building an enormous sense of lightness throughout my body. It felt as though I were more air than clay. I began to sense my feet rising. Yes! I was levitating! And, as I looked down at my body, I could see through it as if I were a ghost. With my attention fully on the etheric forms of Babaji and my father, I placed one foot ahead of the other out into space. At least that is what it would have looked like to you. But to me, it was as though I were walking on solid ground, although it was more like what you might think walking on a cloud would feel like. I proceeded slowly, keeping my breathing very even. I felt suspended and supported. What a marvel!

'When I arrived on the other side, neither Babaji nor my father looked at me. With their physical bodies reconstituted, they simply continued onward. I paused, breathed in the manner I had been taught to recalibrate the frequencies of my subtle and physical bodies until my perception of the physical plane was as it had been before. I admit that I was a little disappointed at first that I was not acknowledged for accomplishing this great feat. Then, I realized that this was a gift of Spirit, not my ego's doing. So, I accepted and acknowledged the One who works the ways of miracles. I prayed for sincere humility, brushed off any thought of false pride, and followed behind my father.

'Onwards we walked for several more days. At last we arrived at a high vista point that overlooked a green valley. As we descended, the trail became paved with large, smooth flagstones and round, river cobblestones. Grasses and blooming shrubs softened the endless horizon of towering, granite escarpments and distant, snowcapped peaks. With every step, my strength renewed with increasing vigour. Sweet birdsong greeted my ears, and the buzz of bees and flies. With the descent, the dwarf scrub brush gradually turned to stands of shade-giving evergreens and broad-leafed trees. Cascading streams and waterfalls fed verdant fields, which pastured all manner of animals. Whether I was in an altered state of consciousness, dreaming, or really present in my physical body, I will leave for you to determine. As for myself, all that I experienced felt as real as my sharing with you now.

'I was very happy to find myself in the lovely valley I had experienced before with my inner vision. In this valley was a small village filled with some of the happiest people I have ever met. Perched on the narrow terrace of a sheer cliff was the monastery that I was told would be my new home for an indefinite number of months. Babaji motioned to the attending monks above to lower the large basket that was used to haul us up with the assistance of a winch and pulley.

'Upon climbing out of the basket, I was pleasantly surprised to find Babaji and my father passing through an inconspicuous door. Out of the indigenous stone was carved the entrance of a beautiful temple, which was located in a former cave of large proportions. I stood in awe and wonder! It was simply designed, yet resplendently decorated with statuary of the deities representing the many attributes of our Father–Mother God. One of the monks then showed me to the monks' cells and invited me to leave my pack in my new home. I noticed that the monks who served here wore different robes denoting some were Hindus and some were Buddhists.

'Babaji then escorted us back to the village, where we entered a small house that served as Babaji's residence whenever he visited this sacred valley. My father was invited to refresh himself with a warm bath, a gentle massage, and a nap, while I sat in the quietude of Babaji's small, cloistered garden. This comfortable, yet very modest home would be my father's temporary abode.

'Now, as I look upon your nodding heads and yawning mouths, I shall bid you a restful sleep. I invite you to return on tomorrow's eve for the conclusion of my story,' said Yeshua as he placed two sleeping children into the arms of their parents and walked quietly to his room.

ॐ

⮞ *Chapter 30* ⮜

Joseph ben Jacob's Ascension

'**M**y dear ones, peace be with you. We are gathered together in this fashion so that we may be fed as the shepherd feeds his flock. So may we receive gladly of this feast of glad tidings that lies before us.

'I shall now share with you my most treasured memories of what I experienced during this past year, in that beautiful and peaceful valley in the high Himalayas. My father and I lived comfortably in our respective places. We were in constant communion with the masters and their consorts, male and female, seen and unseen. We walked with Babaji daily. We held vigils every night, as we embraced all humanity in our hearts and extended our prayers of light to Mother Earth. It was our deepest desire to facilitate a peaceful evolution for this beloved planet, whose birth pangs are great.

'The memory of the last days I spent with my earthly father is like precious treasure held in my heart. I would have you know that my father and I witnessed many people in their light bodies from every quadrant of the planet come to this great ascended master retreat, joining with us while their physical bodies lay sleeping. We were all given instruction and prepared for our various tasks. During the night you also go as spirits to various ascended master retreats to be tutored and given assignments, which you fulfil while your physical bodies and minds slumber. I am come to support your awakening through my example so that you may consciously play your important roles in the light of day.

'As summer approached in the high Himalayas and the time for our departure drew near, Babaji took me to a very remote cave where I was to remain alone for an indefinite time. There was snow all about and freezing temperatures all day. I took no food and only minimal raiment. After removing my boots, I was led into the dark recesses of the cavern. I could feel the energies of many initiates who had come before me. There would be no fire and no source of light or warmth. Babaji bade me remove my cloak and arrange it as a cushion upon which to sit. Then, he anointed me and rubbed my naked body with ashes. After blessing me, by placing his hands upon my head and shoulders, he departed from the cave and rolled a stone over the entrance.

'I was in total darkness. The cavern was fairly large, and a gentle draft of air circulated from some obscure crevasse. Right away, I set myself the task of surrendering my will to the Source of my being. Although I knew that I could teleport my body out of the cave, I was resolved to come to know the Father–Mother God of my spirit, transmute any lingering attachment to my physical body, and learn further of my mission. So, I slowed all my vital signs, as my Grandmother Anna taught me in my youth, and instead of lying in a sepulchre, I remained seated in a full lotus posture. I felt comfortable and blissful. Although I did not know how long my body would be enclosed within the cave, I did know that my consciousness was free to enter the vast realms beyond time. I also knew that my body's angels would carefully attend it.

'While thus meditating, I was assisted to awaken to the remembrance of the divine being I am, as are you and the whole of life. My entire body began to intone the maha-mantra: 'I am the Resurrection and the Life.' I continued to meditate on those words until I knew with absolute certainty that I AM the Resurrection and the Life!

'While I was practising this mantra, my father appeared to my inner vision. Gradually, he began to look more and more like a very tall pillar of light within a great sphere of golden white light. I could see that his physical body remained seated just as my Grandfather Joachim's body had when he passed into the light. As he slowly lifted his etheric arms as would a crystalline butterfly, a golden-white light radiated from his heart. I could feel this great light enter my heart as if it were a tidal wave of love. This experience will be a blessing of comfort to me through all my days.

'Then the brilliant shaft of light coming from his heart became a dazzling expanding ball of light, which began rotating incrementally faster and faster. It gradually encompassed my father until no further distinguishing features could be seen. Then slowly, ever so slowly, my father's essence lifted up until he entered into an even greater sphere that I recognized to be our sun. I felt great, ecstatic joy! No thought of sorrow crossed my mind. It was not until after Babaji came for me, and I had returned more fully to body consciousness as I was walking away from the cave, that I realized I had witnessed my father's ascension from the physical plane.

'A silent and tender Babiji escorted me to the place near the temple where my father's body lay. It did not smell of death, but emitted a sweet fragrance, as of lilies, for a week. Then, his body was placed upon a great funeral pyre of flowers and wood, as is the Hindu custom. In the consuming flames, the elements of our Earth Mother returned from whence they had come. And so it was that I gave my love and honour to our father and our mother's husband, at his passing.

Let us pause now and offer our prayers and psalms to the memory of Joseph ben Jacob.

⤐

'And so do I now give you a witness that death is nothing and that our father lives on, his immortal consciousness quite accessible through our prayers. Believe as you choose. Of this, I am now certain: every initiate embarked on the journey into self-mastery, must remove the last vestige of fear concerning physical death. I am come to invite you to follow the example my father set and that I shall set for you, thus fulfilling all things.

'I realize that some among you are sceptical. You question and doubt my sayings because I appear to be human and one of your relatives, the son of a carpenter. However, it is only because you have forgotten your own empowered divinity that you question my sayings. But I say to you in a time yet to come, when I have accomplished all the masters showed me, I will come to you and will give you an inner witness. Whether in this body or another body in a time far distant, your soul shall come to know my Father–Mother God who has sent me to be an example of eternal life.

'I shall now leave you to contemplate and rejoice in the good news that I have given you. James, Uncle Jacob, and I have returned safely into your midst. Our brother, Joseph the Younger, abides in India where he renders valuable service to the multitudes as an esteemed physician. Let us, everyone, say a prayer of thanksgiving for all that is ours, for we are amply provided with every good thing.

I am here on the earthplane to do my Father's will, and to prepare the way so that you may return to the One who is calling you to rest from your soul's long journey.

'So I have shared my treasured memories with you, even as I fulfilled all and more than was my intention when I set out on my pilgrimage to India as a young man. With the assistance of my beloved father, Uncle Jacob, my brothers, and my wonderful teachers, I have matured in wisdom and self-mastery. I now understand the wondrous workings of my physical and subtle bodies. I have witnessed the power of focused and expanded states of consciousness that can accomplish what would be called miracles to most people. I have always enjoyed the nurturing beauty and touch of the feminine nature in women. Now I have come to honour my own internal feminine that continually balances my masculine expression. My heart has been opened to the suffering of the world, and with compassion I honour every soul's path of evolution. I have overcome my mind's fear of death. My remaining desire is to open myself completely to my Father–Mother's presence.

'That desire prompts me to leave you again next spring, after making an appearance and an offering within the Temple of Jerusalem during Passover. I am called to pass through the desert of the Sinai, renew acquaintance with the Brother–Sisterhood there and then proceed to Egypt for further initiations.

'Until that time, I am with you. We have plenty of time to become reacquainted. Let us now make merry and celebrate our many blessings. Come, my little ones, let us go to the table and partake of the sweet refreshments my beautiful mother has laid out for us. Come, my brothers and sisters, let us take up our instruments and sing a glad song. Praise be to the Father–Mother who gives birth, sustenance, and homecoming to all life!'

‿

Chapter 31

Yeshua's Egyptian Initiations

The weeks in which Yeshua abided with us after his return from the Himalayas were profound and enlightening to all who were in communion with him. We all benefited by his presence, as he continued to grow in spiritual stature and strength. We encouraged and delighted in Yeshua's frequent visits to Carmel, one of his preferred destinations, as he travelled and acquainted himself with the diverse populace and countryside you call the Holy Land.

On the spring equinox of AD22, part of our family gathered to celebrate at Mary Anna's home in Nazareth. Yeshua announced he would be traveling to the Sinai and Egypt for an extended stay, and that he might include a visit to Greece before returning home. As we discussed Yeshua's approaching pilgrimage, it was decided that many of us would go to Jerusalem for Passover. So we gathered as a caravan and made our way to the gated city, which was outwardly magnificent but inwardly corrupt.

Although Yeshua had visited Jerusalem with his father on numerous occasions, it was the first time I had accompanied my grandson inside the City of David. On the day before Passover began, Joseph of Arimathea and I walked with Yeshua through the ancient, narrow streets thronged with all manner of pilgrims, merchants, and Roman soldiers. Needless to say, Jerusalem was radically different from the way it had been six hundred years earlier, when I first came to live there.

During Passover week, Yeshua, who was now almost twenty-five years of age, spent most of his time in the Court of the Scribes discussing, reading, and expounding upon the Law and the Prophets. The elders marvelled at his knowledge and wisdom. Some sought to test and discredit him, setting snares whereby they might catch him. Throughout it all, my grandson maintained a calm, assured manner. When least expected, he would insert a parable or a riddle or a joke to lighten the air. As the days passed, crowds began to gather around him to hear his words. The high priest of the

Temple looked on with a grave expression and sometimes knitted brow. Who was this young man of Galilee? How was it that one from Nazareth could expound the scriptures with such authority? The high priest became increasingly anxious as he began gathering information concerning Yeshua.

It was customary for any man designated as a rabbi to be married in order to officiate in the synagogue or Temple. Although Yeshua was not married yet, sincere questioners, sceptical interrogators, and awestruck listeners began to address him as 'Rabbi'. For the most part everyone marvelled at the breadth and scope of my grandson's teachings, which opened the well-worn scriptures to expanded heights and practical application.

Thus the people began to wonder about this one who had come into their midst. Could he be the Teacher of Righteousness prophesied? Some continued in their self-righteous scepticism, while others turned to Yeshua with a flickering hope for liberation, awaiting a charismatic leader's light to kindle their hearts into a bonfire.

Yeshua was aware that the time had come to begin gathering his team of active supporters and to do whatever was required to prepare for what was coming. Except for the prophetical writings and the small glimpses that Yeshua and the close family had received through the years, little was known about what lay ahead. Yet, there was a knowing that being well prepared for any eventuality would see us through our challenges. Those of us who had been initiated in Egypt lent our understanding to Yeshua, which supported his inner guidance that being in the temples of the Nile was his next step.

We remained in Jerusalem for three weeks. Joseph of Arimathea hosted many of us in his three Jerusalem residences. During this time, Yeshua met with a number of his cousins and friends to discuss his traveling plans and to invite them to accompany him on his pilgrimage to Mount Sinai and Egypt. Of these, John ben Zacharias, Lazarus, Judas Iscariot, and several others from the Qumran community planned to go as far as Mount Sinai where they would stay until guided to return to Qumran. Mariam and Nathaniel had much earlier declared their intention to accompany him. Their son, Benjamin, who was in his fifth year and who was born with a crippling palsy, would remain with me in Mount Carmel.

Mary Magdalene had also expressed earlier that she was guided to accompany him. However, they would not accompany him to the temples because she and Mariam had already taken the initiations that would assist them to support Yeshua. They, together with Mariam's husband, Nathaniel, would stay in Heliopolis with their aunt, Mariamne. James ben Joseph and John ben Zebedee both expressed their desire to undertake advanced initiations in certain of the Egyptian temples. And almost at the last moment, James ben Zebedee and his friend, Andrew ben Jonah, also chose to join the pilgrimage.

Let me remind you again that such journeys as Yeshua's pilgrimages to Britain, India, and Egypt could not have happened were it not for his uncle Joseph of Arimathea's business acumen and generosity. Because we, as Essenes, were accustomed to communal living in which harmonious collaboration and the sharing of our abundance was practised daily, it was possible for Yeshua's support team to come together easily and to prepare harmoniously for their expedition to Egypt.

It was arranged that the companions would depart with Yeshua on the next full moon. Word was sent ahead to my daughter, Mariamne, that Yeshua and a number of relatives would be traveling to her home in Heliopolis by way of Mount Sinai. Joseph of Arimathea hired several clever and trusted guides to oversee the journey, and outfitters provided enough camels, horses, oxen, and donkeys plus conveyances for everyone's comfort.

Along the route to Mount Sinai, Yeshua's company rested at a number of small isolated camps and communities. At the various stopping places along the southerly, inland trade route, there were followers of the Way of the Teacher of Righteousness who were overjoyed to give their hospitality. When they reached the foot of Mount Sinai, some of the elders recognized Yeshua and remembered him as an eight-year-old youth taking initiations there. Everyone was welcomed into the peaceful Sinai sanctuary that has served humanity for eons. A remnant of the Brother–Sisterhood of Light continues to this day to endure the isolation and hardships of this place in order to serve humanity within its powerful planetary vortex.

There were several of Yeshua's companions who took initiations at Mount Sinai, and all were invited to read the scrolls and tablets of the monastery's rather extensive library. Numerous scrolls from the Carmel and Qumran libraries had been sent as gifts, while the others were used in exchange at the Sinai, Heliopolis, and Alexandria libraries.

Except for John ben Zacharias and the brothers from Qumran who stayed on at Mount Sinai, the pilgrims then trekked northward along the Red Sea. They travelled primarily before and after sunrise, resting in the afternoon and early evening in order to avoid the scorching heat until they reached the welcome comforts of Heliopolis, which served as a primary home base and rendezvous point. Relatives gladly opened their homes and provided support without recompense for those who would be taking initiations. They welcomed Nathaniel Bartholomew's carpentry and masonry skills and Mary Magdalene and Mariam's help with the household.

My granddaughters also saw opportunities to serve the infirm and gave much of their time to carrying on their healing work throughout the surrounding community. Egypt was well known for its pure essential oils and medicinal practices, so these tireless women were happy to replenish their healing supplies and to gather more knowledge. Mary and Mariam also met with some of the priests and priestesses who had initiated them earlier. On certain feast days of Isis and Hathor, they participated in the ancient rituals dedicated to the Great Mother. When possible, Nathaniel also joined them.

Yeshua and the other four male initiates, his brother James, James and John ben Zebedee, and Andrew, met with key priests who could pass on the necessary empowerments and who could mentor them along the way. Because Nathaniel's choice was to support Yeshua in a different way, he only occasionally participated in these meetings. Although Mary Magdalene and Mariam would not be accompanying Yeshua, he often included them because he valued their wisdom and mastery.

It was determined that all the initiations would be taken in the traditional manner that begins in Nubia, far to the south. Now let me explain the process, by saying that the ancient Egyptians saw the Nile as a metaphor for the human body, particularly the spinal cord and its more subtle neural pathways. They knew that the path enlightenment takes begins at the base of the spine, and like a river, flows upwards to the brain. So it was that they constructed temples that simulated the journey of enlightenment. In this case, because the Nile flows from south to north, the initiate would begin their journey in the south and proceed through the subsequent temples, culminating at the Great Pyramid, represented the 'Holy of Holies' in the brain.

At each temple the initiate experienced the various initiations which tempered, refined, and opened the life-force channels. In order to progress to the next temple, the initiates proved that they were ready to meet, unify, and alchemically transmute the opposing forces of love and fear, light and dark, spirit and matter, life and death. Although all the temples enacted the Osirian mysteries, each temple enacted a particular aspect of the archetypal journey of Osiris, Isis, Horus, Set, and Hathor. These mysteries involved Light Conception, crucifixion, and resurrection.

Yeshua and his faithful friends travelled up the Nile sometimes by barge and other times on foot or by donkey in order to avoid turbulent cataract white water until they arrived at the Temple of Isis on the island of Philae. This was a long and arduous journey – one that very few of the native Egyptians ever accomplished in a lifetime. Again, I will say that the magnitude of this pilgrimage could not have been accomplished within such a relatively short period of time, if it had not been for the companions' spiritual readiness, communal cooperation, and the financial funding they received from Joseph of Arimathea.

Yeshua, James ben Joseph, and John ben Zebedee underwent their initiations at more or less the same time at the same temples. Because they had already taken advanced initiations in India, the additional experiences in Egypt further refined their consciousness and strengthened their constitution and character. Now that they were in the Motherland, out of which all they had learned in India had come, they humbly and gratefully received any added portion that could be gleaned.

Their consciousness was opened to the subtle energies of the mythic, archetypal realms, and they were tested according to the practices of the priesthoods in those days. Although much of the original power of the ancient mysteries had been lost, the purity of the Osirian, Pythagorean, and Cybeline Orders was maintained by a secret remnant of high initiates and adepts who still functioned as officiators when required. Great beings of the Brother–Sisterhood of Light facilitated the rites of initiatory passage on the inner planes.

I will now share some highlights that occurred in several of the temples that Yeshua later described to me.

One of the first temples encountered was Kom Ombo, the initiation chamber of the crocodile god, Sobek. Having successfully passed the qualifying tests to enter the path of the initiate at the Temples of Isis and Osiris, the novices were then required to test their intuition and face their greatest fears with regard to physical survival. They swam underwater through a labyrinthine passage that passed through a pool of hungry crocodiles. Through the process of mastering the lower centres of their animal nature, which clings to security, lust, and competitive power, the heart and intuitive centres were cleared and opened. In this way, the initiate was prepared to receive the higher alchemical energies that activated greater spiritual powers.

The goal of all this work in the temples was to attain enlightenment, as the archetypal High God Horus demonstrated, when he attained his highest spiritual body called the Sahu. The halo depicted around a saint's head or the hooded cobra at an Egyptian deity's forehead symbolizes the attainment of the Sahu, and the precursory light anointing called the Uraeus. Activating the Sahu and Uraeus also signifies that the initiate has been anointed within the brain centres by a very high vibration that permanently changes neurophysiology and consciousness, thereby allowing the experience of conscious immortality. Those souls who have attained this mastery are called a Christ, Buddha or ascended master, whose destiny it is to function openly or secretly as a planetary server.

Yeshua knew that the same path Horus followed was also his own. In fact, the similarities between Isis and Osiris and his own mother and father, as well as, Horus and himself were strikingly clear. Because of his experiences in India, he knew that he was well on his way to achieving his highest immortal light body.

Now you can see that the initiations that prepared Yeshua or any initiate, past and present, have very little to do, if anything, with religion. They have everything to do with changing one's fear-based perceptions and behaviours. An initiate who has once perceived a limited, self-centred identity awakens to having compassion towards all life as an expression of the Divine Self. The path of enlightenment requires an ethical and expanded relationship with self, others, polarities, time, and space.

So it was that, having successfully completed the arduous initiations at Kom Ombo, Yeshua and his companions proceeded down the Nile to other temples including Edfu, Luxor, Karnak, Abydos, and Dendarah. At Dendarah, they lingered for six months in the temple dedicated to Hathor, the goddess of healing love. Here, the primary focus was the opening of the heart centre through the balancing of feminine intuition and masculine intellect. This union of polarities was achieved by cultivating and disciplining sexual energy balanced through love and mindfulness.

At the Hathor temple of Dendarah in Yeshua's day, the young initiates were invited to bring their sexual energy forward in order to master this powerful procreative life force. This was done only after passing increasingly difficult preliminary tests. When the initiates' hearts were sufficiently clear and open – meaning, much of the subconscious 'shadow' material had been brought up into conscious awareness and healed – they could then engage in ecstatic rituals with the Hathors through inter-dimensional contact.

Sometimes initiates remained in the Temple of Hathor at Dendarah for months or years, until the tests were successfully passed and various astrological conditions were ideal for certain individual and group initiations. As a consequence, Yeshua and his companions abided at Dendarah for six months, learning more about the keeping of time, the goddess Hathor's cycles and rituals, and how to channel life force and sexual energy (Sekhem) within the body. Yogic disciplines of breathing, postures, toning and chanting, meditation, tantric arts (internal energy practices), purification and cleansing of body, mind, and soul were given. For those who sought full enlightenment in order to be of service to others, initiates were also given higher levels of regenerative practices, sexual energy practices, and the conscious conception, birth, and rearing of children.

You may have never heard of these unconditionally loving ascended beings, but they are very active today assisting humanity and Mother Earth through the ascension process. Their expertise with sound healing and the alchemy of transmutation through love is available to anyone who chooses to call on them for assistance.

On the occasion of Yeshua's last initiation at Dendarah, I bilocated my consciousness in order to be one of the Hathor high priestesses who witnessed this most beautiful empowerment. When you are ready, like my grandsons and granddaughters, you may also realize internal empowerments such as those the Hathors facilitate according to your asking and belief.

∽ Chapter 32 ∽
The Great Pyramid Initiation

So it was that Yeshua, his brother James, and his cousin John, progressed through all of the advanced enlightenment initiations of Horus representing the human journey that unifies and ascends the spirit/matter connection as an embodied soul. From Dendarah, they went to Abydos, the ancient temple site that commemorates the resurrection of Osiris. Here, they participated fully in the Rite of the Sepulchre.

As I have shared with you before, the Rite of the Sepulchre was not new to Yeshua, whose first sepulchre initiation took place in Mount Carmel when he was twelve years old. It was my privilege and responsibility to introduce my grandson to the ancient ritual of 'dying' and resurrection. He completed the final rite with Maha Babaji in India nearly twelve years later. Going through the process again in Abydos gave him new insights as well as an opportunity to assist his brother and cousin.

Just as I represented Isis in Yeshua's first experience, so it was that Isis herself brought forth the full presence of the Divine Mother within the tomb at Abydos where these three faithful friends lay for three days. As the wings of her love enveloped them, all fear stilled and the life force within her vast energy field resurrected every atom into a new awareness of eternal life. Yeshua owned every thought and reclaimed the energy he had previously projected outwards into the astral realms that hold discordant emotions and disempowered thought-forms.

In the secret chambers of Abydos, Yeshua met with enlightened beings who have directed the seeding of ascension codes into human DNA, including his ancient ancestor, Akhenaten. He also took the initiation of the elements of earth, air, fire, water and ether. He went deeply into the atomic structure of his body and found the entire cosmos within himself. He studied the infinite weaving of light into the ascension matrix that is called the Flower of Life.

Through the understanding of electromagnetic fields, sacred geometry, and the three-fold nature of light, sound, and colour, he took his body completely into a field of light that was impermeable to involutional spin factors. In this way, Yeshua took complete control of the forces of life and the illusion of death. He continually contemplated and spoke a mantra that he received in India: 'I AM the Resurrection and the Life!'

After Abydos and a rather leisurely journey by barge down the Nile to participate in the temples of Memphis, Yeshua, James, and John rested for several months in Heliopolis, awaiting the return of the others who were still completing their initiations. Mariamne's spacious home offered quiet and peaceful surroundings that allowed integration of all that they had passed through. Yeshua enjoyed this time of repose, solitude, and familial sharing. If the trials of Britain and the Himalayas had been intense, the Egyptian initiations, taken all together over a relatively short period, were even more arduous and trying for the soul.

Yeshua was grateful for all the preparation he had received, his companions' support, and for the wise teachers who had supported his journey into self-mastery. Now he welcomed a time of refreshment and reconnection with his cousins Mariam and Mary Magdalene. With Mariam he found a deep consoling peace and with her husband, Nathaniel, he could relax into laughter and celebration. With Mary Magdalene, Yeshua felt an awakened desire for courtship. They both sensed a divine timing in their being together in Egypt. Now, a spirit of freedom helped them to cultivate an intimate, though celibate, relationship.

During this time of renewal, while waiting for the rest of his companions to arrive back in Heliopolis, Yeshua was taken inwardly to council meetings with the Brother–Sisterhood of Light. He was introduced to the master plan for the public demonstration of resurrection and ascension to humanity. The plan was designed to assist a very unconscious and stubborn people to know how they might overcome every fear. Since the greatest fear was of death, he was told that a complex, multidimensional process would be undertaken, which would indelibly imprint the resurrection and ascension principles into all life through all time and space. Thus it was that a foundation was laid in Egypt for Yeshua's later mission.

Yeshua's final initiation in Egypt, as is the case for all initiates who are sufficiently prepared, was in the Great Pyramid. This, the largest of the pyramids, which represented the chamber in the human brain where enlightenment occurs, had been designed long ago to serve both as an individual ascension chamber and as a planetary ascension chamber. Although it stands somewhat dormant in your day, its true function will be fully restored when a sufficient number of human beings are ready to make the transition from separation consciousness into unity consciousness. When that pivotal point is reached, a chain reaction will occur, synergistically awakening other vortices that focus energy within various etheric grids located on, above, and within Mother Earth.

I will now give you a brief account of Yeshua's initiation in the Great Pyramid located at the necropolis of Giza on the west side of the Nile. Nathaniel travelled overland to the Great Pyramid with provisions and a wagon, while Yeshua and six companions began their underground journey by accessing an ancient underground chamber below Heliopolis,. Standing by the heavy iron door to the chamber was a very old guardian priest who had been awaiting them. He took them through a series of chambers whose doors operated by sound frequencies and compatible resonance. They passed through unharmed.

Then they journeyed through a long, narrow, descending tunnel under the River Nile where they occasionally came upon catacombs heaped with bones and the decaying corpses of those people who could not afford burial in the necropolis. There were various junctions; some gated, others were dark, gaping holes. Everyone carried lamps, small flasks of drinking water, and sufficient faith that they would somehow get through this ordeal.

Guardian priests met them at three different junctures. The initiates were tested to determine their readiness to proceed, and then the stationed priest led them through the next segment of the long journey. When they finally arrived at the very large chamber located directly beneath the Sphinx, many hundreds of feet below the surface, they were astonished that they no longer required their lamps. Here, they were greeted by a conclave of twelve ascended masters, including Serapis Bey and Thoth, who showed themselves in physical bodies. Yeshua recognized this room from the childhood stories that his father and mother had told him when he lived earlier in Egypt. He was told that the Sphinx had had a 'consort twin'. The still visible Sphinx represented the masculine solar principle. The second Sphinx, which represented the feminine lunar principle, had been desecrated – her stones used to build some of the smaller Giza pyramids.

The masters issued various instructions and passwords, which took the initiates to the underground city further below them. After they had received refreshment, each was assigned a specific role that would support Yeshua's initiation in the Great Pyramid. James went alone into another chamber below the Sphinx, where he was taught how to maintain certain sound frequencies that would be 'broadcast' into the Great Pyramid. Priests led Andrew and James ben Zebedee through adjacent connecting tunnels leading to chambers within the small and middle pyramids. There, at these strategic points where coordinates and harmonics could be struck, they would also broadcast specific sound frequencies into the Great Pyramid.

Yeshua, Mary Magdalene, Mariam, and John ben Zebedee were escorted through mysteriously lit passages to the vertical shaft that is now called the 'Well'. They were then required to proceed on their own through a convoluted, ascending tunnel to what you know as the 'Pit' of the Great Pyramid.

The ascent to the 'Pit' was fraught with challenges. Because they had successfully completed the various initiations that had taken them through primal fears, they easily passed upwards against the gravitational and magnetic forces, which pressed down upon them. There were times when they felt almost weightless, their bodies vaporous. Then they found themselves in complete darkness – a darkness so dense that a flame could not be sustained. Each one felt completely alone. In order to continue, it was required to remember and put to use all the wisdom they had gained throughout all of their previous initiations. There were times when they felt so faint, dizzy, and disoriented that to go on was an immense test of fortitude and communal support of one another.

Onwards, through passages that your sonic devices and psychics have detected, the companions passed. Their extrasensory abilities were heightened as they progressed. They began to experience a luminescence radiating from within themselves and a golden photon energy, called 'vrill' by the Atlanteans, emanating from the stone walls, almost like an ethereal phosphorescence. They also began to hear sounds, which echoed in such a way that, if they listened carefully, they were guided in their upward ascent. It was a test of refined discernment of the various tones and the geometric angles that were impressed into their minds, which created a kind of mental map.

When the 'Pit' was reached they rested, meditated, and grew in resolve to complete their mission. Mariam took her assigned position just below the base of the pyramid directly under the King's Chamber far above. Mariam had mastered the skills of concentration and had passed most of the levels of the Rite of the Sepulchre. Because she had Yeshua and Mary Magdalene's blessing and knew Nathaniel was praying for her just outside the pyramid, she reassured herself that she was not alone. However, feeling the heavy blackness enveloping her beating heart, and remembering the stories of those whose hearts ceased to beat in this place where she now lay, caused doubts to rise like monstrous shadows on the screen of her mind. Mariam embraced her fear, and became 'Isis' in the Great Pyramid's abyss for three days. This was Mariam's supreme test that prepared her for the assignment she would fulfil later, when the present hidden initiation was outwardly dramatized for humanity to feel and see on Mount Calvary.

Yeshua, Mary Magdalene, and John ben Zebedee pressed on. They ascended the low, steep, inclined passages. At last, they reached the chamber that you call the 'Queen's Chamber'. Again, they rested and meditated for several hours, until they received an inner signal that it was time to proceed. In accordance with his instructions, John remained in the 'Queen's Chamber', where he began to intone specific sound frequencies. Yeshua and Mary continued the symbolic Path of the Initiate as they ascended the 'Grand Gallery' passage, and then stooping low, finally entered into the 'King's Chamber'.

The 'King's Chamber' was designed to function as a great resonance chamber. Once they were inside, they began to sense the glorious combination of sound frequencies that were being intoned by all those in their variously assigned places, including a number of priests and priestesses who were stationed in hidden chambers within and beneath the Great Pyramid. In this way, all aspects of their mental, emotional, and physical bodies were attuned and calibrated to the inter-dimensional music of the spheres, thereby aligning their consciousness with specific solar, stellar, and galactic energies.

Although much of the energy that had been transmitted to initiates in former times was no longer available, the energies generated by planet Earth, when augmented by those of the ascended masters, were still sufficient to transform the Great Pyramid into an extremely powerful virtual reality chamber.

Mariam and Mary Magdalene had each undergone initiation in the King's Chamber eight years earlier. Consequently, they were now qualified to serve as the attending priestesses of Isis at Yeshua's initiation. After leading her beloved cousin to the red granite sarcophagus, within which he would remain for seventy-two hours, Mary Magdalene took her position at the doorway of the 'King's Chamber' and sealed the entrance energetically with mudras and intonations. Acting as a Magdalene high priestess of Isis, trained in the powers of concentration and simultaneous realities, she energetically connected all the participating disciples into a grid of oneness. Everyone who was involved in supporting the individual and planetary scope of the Great Pyramid ascension initiation began to transmit frequencies that focused vibrations of light, sound, and colour into the sepulchre where Yeshua lay.

The 'King's Chamber' began to vibrate with a subtle timbre as a multidimensional geometric matrix was created around the sarcophagus. Within this atomic accelerator, Yeshua's physical body began to glow with translucent light, as it was gently infused with the divine blueprint of the Cosmic Christ. And for those who witnessed, according to our capacity to receive this blueprint, we too were awakened to our full potential.

Now, I shall say further that the sarcophagus within the 'King's Chamber' was positioned in such a way that the subtle energies that were generated by the powerful vortex of the Great Pyramid passed directly through the pineal gland of the initiate within the sarcophagus. Thus, far from serving as a monumental tomb for one of the ancient Egyptian pharaohs, the Great Pyramid was and is, not only an initiation chamber, but also an extraordinarily powerful ascension chamber. It was designed to help initiates awaken to the full remembrance of their true identity. This, my beloved friend, is the secret of the pyramid.

In this instance, however, the initiation ceremony was not simply a matter of facilitating Yeshua's individual process of spiritual awakening. In a carefully orchestrated way, Yeshua's crucifixion, resurrection, and ascension initiations were facilitated in the Great Pyramid so that the entire Earth and all of humanity could be seeded collectively for planetary ascension in your day. I would ask you, my friend, to contemplate how you might take advantage of this seeding of ascension consciousness in your daily life. Surely, when you realize that you have access to great assistance each day, your challenges can be met with faith and hope instead of fearful dread.

Every soul that was destined to play a significant part in supporting Yeshua in the public enactment of crucifixion and resurrection was present at this particular point of preparation. In addition to Yeshua and his close companions, there were those of us who knew how to teleport or bilocate who came to the Great Pyramid to participate. Others, who played lesser roles, came in their light bodies during sleep, and later remembered fragments of what they had seen in their dreams. For all consciously participating, this rehearsal assisted us to be emotionally detached so that we could play our parts in the divine plan. In this way every step of Yeshua's mission was orchestrated and imprinted into the planetary consciousness.

Although the essential portion of his initiation within the King's Chamber took place within the first twenty-four hours, Yeshua remained in the sarcophagus for another forty-eight hours in accordance with the sign that had been given to Jonah the Prophet. As the story goes, Jonah had a profound shamanic experience of death and rebirth in which he spent three days and three nights 'in the belly of a great fish that had swallowed him.' Let us also remember that as Yeshua did, so did the others. During this time, Yeshua and the other supportive disciples experienced much of the public resurrection demonstration that was yet to come as an interactive virtual reality. We were opened to the pivotal choices that aligned our lives to our highest personal realization and planetary service. When the Great Pyramid initiation was completed, all participating inside made an easy exit through a concealed door.

As we bring this summary of Yeshua's Egyptian initiations to a close, I wish to further reemphasize the importance of cohesive group action, which this story illustrates. Yeshua could not have accomplished what he did without the willing companions who came together to prepare themselves to be the most qualified support team possible. Likewise, we could not have achieved what we did without the vast consciousness, focused dedication, and impeccable example Yeshua provided for us.

While I have said, and will continue to stress, that 'all that Yeshua did you may do also, and even more may you do,' allow me to explain that your initiatory experiences may express differently than Yeshua's. Yes, Yeshua was and is an extraordinary being whose task encompassed a planetary and cosmic scope of ascension activity. Your personal life, which just as importantly will contribute to the success of planetary ascension, may not impact as many as did Yeshua's. While your responsibilities to humanity may not be as great as those of my grandson, like Yeshua, you also have the same personal responsibility to increase in self-mastery, co-create harmony where there is conflict, and add your enlightened, loving presence to the collective ascending body of consciousness.

As a Son of Man and an Elder Brother, Yeshua set an example of what is possible for every human when there is an alignment with love and unity. Because of the cosmic scope of Yeshua's and Mary Magdalene's mission to assist all humanity to awaken, they in turn received cosmic levels of assistance. Whatever your mission is, you will also have all the support you require to succeed. In this awareness, you, like your Elder Brother, can receive encouragement and hope along the way until you realize yourself as a Christ.

There is no requirement for you to go to the Great Pyramid in this lifetime. Yet, I would ask you, have you had experiences in which you felt as though you were in a sepulchre, your limited identity and life dying, as a new identity and life emerged? Have you recognized a pattern of increased willingness to align your ego nature with a greater power, an enlarged sense of caring for others' wellbeing, and an ability to be more compassionately present in all your relationships? In these simple, though significant ways, you are also successful in your Christ initiations.

৵ Chapter 33 ৵

The Way Is Prepared

Now, I wish to bring you up to date about the good news regarding Mary Anna's marriage to Ahmed, an Egyptian Essene brother from Heliopolis. Shortly after arriving at his Aunt Mariamne's home in Egypt, Yeshua became acquainted with Ahmed, who sat next to him at one of Mariamne's well-attended feasts. Instantly, Yeshua could feel his mother's presence and knew this sensitive and devotional man was a suitable husband for her. Without delay, an invitation was extended, Ahmed travelled to Nazareth, and within seven months the very happy couple were married

After completing their Egyptian initiations, Yeshua and his companions enjoyably spent almost six months in Greece, the Aegean islands, and Ephesus, returning to their destinations in Galilee in the autumn of AD24. While they were in Mount Carmel, I was delighted to find Yeshua and Mary leisurely walking hand in hand in the garden and openly showing their affection for one another whenever they were together. Everyone nodded their approval, though to be quite honest, there was still an aspect of my human nature that secretly desired Yeshua and Mary to settle down into a relatively stress-free life of home and children. However, I also knew that the Greater Part had been chosen, which caused my heart in equal measure to both soar and tremble. Responding to the community's questioning looks and self-conscious smiles, Yeshua announced his formal betrothal to his beloved Mary, which would occur on the November full moon.

So it was that two years after marrying Ahmed, Mary Anna invited close family members to attend a simple, yet elegant betrothal ceremony for Yeshua and Mary Magdalene in her home in Nazareth. Glad to have the loving assistance of her older children, a radiant Mary Anna held her year old son, John Mark, on a swollen lap, pregnant with her ninth child. After the festivities, Yeshua and Mary Magdalene announced that they would soon be departing to the Orient. All of the companions who had gone to Egypt with Yeshua agreed that they would also travel with them.

Yeshua explained that it was important to contact various masters in India, Tibet, Nepal, and China. In the late spring of AD25, they joined a caravan of traders that was going to India. The trade route followed the same course Yeshua had travelled before from Damascus, Palmyra, Selucia, Kabul and then the Khyber Pass to the River Ganges. During the winter months, they gratefully rested in Varanasi and enjoyed Joseph the Younger and his family's warm hospitality. After their welcomed rest, they pressed on to their various destinations in the Orient.

This pilgrimage greatly expanded everyone's awareness and appreciation of the Buddhist teachings of Siddhartha Gautama that had spread throughout the lands they visited. They also found the brilliant consciousness of the Chinese Taoist master, Lao-Tzu, highly illuminating. One of the treasures Yeshua brought back to be placed in the Mount Carmel library was a well-worn manuscript of Lao-Tzu's *Tao Te Ching*. This cross-pollinated synthesis of potent spiritual teachings and practices of inner alchemy from Egypt, Greece, Britain, Palestine, Mesopotamia, India and China had a profound influence on the now mature Yeshua ben Joseph and his devoted disciples.

John ben Zacharias returned to Qumran from Mount Sinai after Yeshua had made it known to John in a dream that he would soon be returning to Palestine. John was told in the dream that it was time to begin his public ministry, which would prepare the stiff-necked Hebrew people for a demonstration of the Christ. As Malachi had prophesied, a forerunner would sow the seeds of resurrection through the law of purification and repentance. In this way, the old fear-based identity and behaviours would be encouraged to 'die' (to be cleansed and transmuted) in order to be raised up into a new creation in God ('at-one-ment' with the One I AM).

So it was that John ben Zacharias, Joachim's nephew through his eldest sister's daughter Elizabeth, was quickened in his knowing that it was time to relinquish his hermitage status. It was his lot to take a message of redemption, as he understood it, to the children of Israel (Isis-Ra-Elohim). During the autumn of AD26 John went forth with a small company of dedicated followers, including Lazarus, the brother of Mary Magdalene, and Judas Iscariot. All of these brothers had accompanied him to Mount Sinai in the spring of AD22 where they had remained in seclusion for over three years.

Now, rumours of John's fiery, charismatic presence and outspoken exuberance, which had won both favour and criticism from his Qumran brotherhood, went before him like a mighty wind stirring sleepy consciousness awake. Having first gone out to the scattered Essene communities around the Great Salt Sea, he then ventured farther afield eastward of the River Jordan to Edom, Perea, Decapolis, and Caesarea Phillipi. Word was left with every Essene household and community in Galilee, Samaria, and Judea, including Jerusalem and Jericho, that the coming of the Teacher of Righteousness was soon at hand. Needless to say, this news had a profound effect on those who heard it. The rumour quickly spread that the advent of the long-awaited Messiah was imminent.

Now, if you can imagine John wearing the camel's hair tunic of an anchorite, with his own hair uncut, eating the most ascetic of Essene diets and delivering unfaltering sermons spoken with the voice of a lion, you can begin to understand the unforgettable impression he made on everyone who met him. To understand John more deeply is also to have an awareness of his orientation to life, which like most Essenes – especially those who lived in the Qumran community – was to be heavily influenced by a Zarathustrian or Nazarite 'warrior of light' perspective. Such ones were often nursing the wounds of political persecution, and it was easy for them to see this world through dualistic eyes. This view sees the Earth as a battleground upon which the sons of light and the sons of darkness wage eternal war. As with most warriors, however, they often were blind to the awareness that the real battleground within the consciousness of duality is waged within the breast of each soul. If the internal war is not acknowledged and harmonized, then it is often projected outward where it is seen reflected as discordant dramas.

John's temperament and adopted Nazarite bias, conditioned by the wounding he suffered as a child when his father was killed in the Temple at Jerusalem, resulted in an uncompromising attitude that bordered on militancy. So it was with passionate ardour that John implored the Jews to repent of their stubborn and arrogant ways. To fortify himself and to prepare his audience, John began his mornings in prayer and meditation. Often he was unavailable to the increasing crowds that began to press upon him until the sun had reached its zenith. When the sorrowful and anxious hearts of his audience were filled with eager anticipation, he began preaching his electrifying message. Every question was answered with undeniable authority, passion, sincerity, and forthrightness.

Just when he had his repentant petitioners ready to believe that he was the long awaited Messiah, he made it unmistakably clear that he was but his humble servant. He was a harbinger sent to prepare the way of the Teacher of Righteousness who was mightier than he ever hoped to be. It was the Messiah who would teach the people the rightful use of God's energy flowing through their bodies, minds, and souls. It was one greater than he who would demonstrate the resurrection of their true relationship to God.

John then introduced the uninitiated into the Essene purification ritual of washing themselves in water as a token of dying to their old creature nature of hatred, lust, and greed. For those made new in their consciousness, it was explained that they would be like the sun rising up from its nighttime watery grave and bringing forth its light to unconditionally shine its gift of life on all. The ritual John performed then you now call 'baptism'.

I will give a brief explanation to clarify the misunderstandings that some have regarding how our ritual washings were done. It was our custom, in circumstances where there was little water, to immerse our feet and hands in a basin or a specially constructed font, filled ankle deep with water. Then, we bent down and took a handful of the water, which we poured over our heads. We paid particular attention to cleansing our aura and the seven seals of our energy centres at our head, along the spine and front of our body. We also invoked the purifying and empowering presence of the angels of the elements, earth and sky, and those who govern the 'Tree of Life' in whose Sephirothic spheres we stood. In situations where there was plenty of water, we allowed ourselves to be fully immersed in deeper water with the assistance of a fellow Essene. The washing ritual was practised everyday, not just once in a lifetime. Nor was a mediating priest required for the ritual to be sanctified.

Because John was teaching the practice of ritual washing to many who had not experienced it, and because he preferred the symbolism of full immersion that was possible in the Jordan River, he acted as an assistant mentor for those who came to him. He insisted that he was here to help them to open and prepare their hearts for the greater baptism of the Holy Spirit's fire (the anointing of divine light that results in full enlightenment as a Christ) that Yeshua, not he, was capable of demonstrating. John never intended to create a ritualized dogma about how to purify one's heart in order to know the kingdom of God within.

For those who experienced his words and partook of the ritual washings, each person responded differently, according to their particular religious or political orientation. For example, those Essenes who were spiritually aligned with John felt nourished and uplifted by the courageous manner in which he boldly spoke the truth. On the other hand, those Pharisees, wise in their own eyes because they considered themselves to be experts regarding the law, felt challenged and perplexed. And those Sadducees who were currently enjoying positions of wealth and status felt threatened to the core. However, those Zealots who were feeling oppressed by Roman rule saw in John a saviour who could redeem Israel from the scourge of foreign governance and restore an independent Palestine. There were also those who chose to dismiss John's words altogether, because they simply were not ready to open their minds and hearts to a new way of life. They consequently rejected him as a ranting and raving madman, dressed in the attire of the outcast poor, who lived on locusts and honey in the desert and baptized endless numbers of people day after day.

For most, John was not easily dismissed. His dedication was intense, his attitude fearless, and his countenance fierce when challenged. Such was the force of nature that rested in Yeshua's forerunner. And, it was to John, now called The Baptizer, at Beth Barah on the River Jordan, that Yeshua and Mary Magdalene came in the autumn of AD28.

Yeshua and his companions had returned from the Orient the previous year. For the most part, they each went their own way, as they continued to prepare for the Great Work ahead. Yeshua and Mary Magdalene spent most of their time in seclusion at several Essene outposts in the desert where there were healing springs. They enjoyed giving their bodies and souls the deep nurturing that had been long overdue. Nathaniel and Mariam returned to Mount Carmel and rejoiced in their reunion with their son, Benjamin, who had been dedicated to the service of God within the inner sanctuary as preparation for becoming a rabbi. The others returned to their villages and began in earnest to court and marry appropriate partners who could support them in Yeshua's ministry when the time came.

The year had passed quickly and the time of the 'Opening of the Way' had come. After sending runners, Yeshua's companions with their married or betrothed wives gathered at John's camp at Beth Barah. New to the group of inner disciples was Andrew bar Jonah's brother Simon, also called Peter.

Because Peter is so widely known in your day and so little is spoken of him in my story, I will share a portion that may assist you in understanding his personality. Peter's focus, which had formerly been directed outwards on supporting his family as a fisherman, now drew inwards after he had had an almost miraculous change of heart when his brother, Andrew, who had returned from Egypt, encouraged him to spend time with Yeshua. In doing so, Peter had had a spontaneous quickening (a kundalini opening) that forever changed him. Peter's lack of experience with esoteric initiations and his very strong patriarchal bias that feared the feminine aspect of God, continued to haunt him the remainder of his days. Particularly difficult for Peter was his tendency to compare himself unfavourably with the disciples, especially the women and Mary Magdalene in particular, who had matured and exceeded him in their spiritual discipline and powers. However, his continued experiences of direct revelation and his leadership skills placed Peter in a position to be of great assistance to Yeshua.

So it was that in order to fulfil all things spoken of by the Prophets, my grandson Yeshua went forth with his cousin, John, who had prepared the way, until they stood together in a deep, eddying pool of the River Jordan. John announced to all that this was the Anointed One, whose sandals he was unworthy to unlace. Everyone pressed close. Filled with wonder and amazement that such a man, who looked no different than themselves, could be the Messiah, the crowd looked on with bated breath. Even the chattering of children and crows ceased. All was still.

Then, allowing John to support him, Yeshua laid himself back completely in the water as if it were a grave or sepulchre. At the moment my grandson stood upright, a large thundercloud overhead parted and the sun sent forth a brilliant ray of light directly over the place where Yeshua and John stood. The light was so dazzling upon the river's rippling water and the illumination of these two men so stunning, that a suppressed sigh escaped the lips of those gathered along the banks of the Jordan. Then a chorus of Hosannas was sung that unforgettable hour.

John solemnly raised his right arm, signifying that he was now acting as a witness to Yeshua's obedience and humility, which was an example for all. The sunlight continued to illuminate as though it were a stage spotlight. As the heavens opened, John announced that he had heard the word of God the Father saying that He was well pleased in His son. He also confided that God the Mother, the Holy Shekinah, had descended and rested upon the Chosen One as a dove.

So, in like manner, was Yeshua's baptism recorded in your Holy Bible account. However, no mention is made about Mary Magdalene. I, therefore, add my witness that she also went to be baptized by John and thereby to set an example that she was equal with her mate. Few recognized her as an adept or what she was doing at that time. However, many wondered when the same signs that occurred with Yeshua were seen and heard following her baptism when she rose up out of the water. Then all of the other disciples who were present were baptized with John's assistance.

Thus, a remarkable day ended and a new chapter in Yeshua's public life began.

After a time of solitude, cleansing and fasting, Yeshua and Mary Magdalene gathered their support team that you call the twelve disciples. However, it has been removed from your records that these twelve men also had female counterparts. As I indicated earlier, after their return from the Orient, those companions who had been preparing for their work with Yeshua, began to find their appropriate mates who could provide the required feminine balance that Yeshua and Mary Magdalene insisted upon having.

So it was that the number of the close inner circle began to grow until there were twelve men and twelve women. And, then, as the populace began to hear of the miracles and teachings that Yeshua and Mary Magdalene wrought, the circles of twelve men and twelve women multiplied so that the required assistance to those who sought healing of bodies and souls could receive in equal measure. Although I did not have a mate to whom I was married, I also became a member of the second circle of twelve men and twelve women disciples. Over the next four years, the twelve multiplied to total 144 – 72 male and 72 female dedicated disciples. What a joy it was to my soul to release my position at Mount Carmel and to be in intimate contact with Yeshua and Mary Magdalene, as well as others of my beloved family, as we travelled among the peoples of Palestine!

∽

✎ Chapter 34 ✎
Yeshua's Sayings

It brings me great pleasure to share some of my fondest memories of Yeshua's deeds and sayings that were accomplished during his last years on the physical plane. These remembered sayings are given to nurture the seed of light that has been placed in you from the beginning of the world. Thus, I share with you a few of the numerous experiences in which I was present to hear and bear witness to my grandson's life and teachings. This covers some of the highlights of his brief ministry in Palestine, which began in the late September of AD28 and culminated in the early April of AD30, just a year and a half later.

Of these experiences, I offer a small portion so that you may increase your awareness that there is a fuller meaning, power, and grace within his works and words that you have not yet received. Your Holy Scriptures reveal only a meagre portion of the bounty that Yeshua freely gave to those with ears to hear. For those whose soul is hungering and thirsting for love's liberating light, I invite you to explore those lesser known works, such as the Dead Sea Scrolls and the Nag Hammadi Scrolls, which reveal more of the Son of Man translated directly from the rich Aramaic language he spoke.

I will now share more fully about Mary Magdalene, who as a mature woman adopted three children. As you recall, I have told you that she had been the founder of a number of orphanages, hospices, hospitals, and sanctuaries for the homeless and society's outcast since she was nineteen. With the financial generosity of her father, Mary Magdalene converted his estate near Magdala into a hospital and orphanage. With her mother's assistance, my granddaughter also expanded her Bethany home into a sanctuary and refuge for the infirm of mind, body, and soul. As with Magdala, it was also a place where unwed mothers could birth their unwanted children and where their children could be sheltered until they were old enough to make their own way. Some of these children, who showed a desire for the Essene monastic life, were then taken to Qumran.

Yeshua and Mary Magdalene adopted three homeless children after their betrothal. These three children were called Joses, Judas, and Miriam. There always seemed to be many children closely gathered around my grandson and granddaughter wherever they went among the crowds of people.

One of my favourite memories that occurred at the time of the early ministry is that of Yeshua's and Mary Magdalene's marriage at Cana in December of AD28. To be sure it was a glorious event. The four years since the betrothal had allowed both families to accumulate a large dowry. There was also the dowry of John ben Zebedee and his betrothed bride, Abigail, who were planning to be married on this same occasion. (Abigail was the daughter of Mary and Cleopas, who were also Yeshua's disciples. Cleopas was a brother of Joseph ben Jacob, Yeshua's father.)

It was decided that the spacious ancestral home in Cana, which had formerly belonged to Jacob and Lois, Yeshua's paternal grandparents, was the best location for most of the guests who would be travelling from afar. The estate was now Cleopas' since his widowed mother, Lois, had died while Yeshua was in India.

Mary and Cleopas invited over one hundred guests. It had been years since our close and extended family had all gathered together, so it was truly a grand reunion. The several months prior to the wedding were devoted to preparations, and the following several weeks were given to celebration.

Just before the sharing of marriage vows, Mary Magdalene performed the first public anointing of her beloved with spikenard, a pungent and rare healing herb, that she had gathered on the recent pilgrimage to the Orient when she was in the foothills of the Himalayas. From the plants, Mary had extracted their essential oil, and made ointment that was placed in alabaster jars. Small glass vials were also filled with the pure oil. The containers were then hermetically sealed and carefully stored so that they would arrive in Palestine safely.

On this sacred occasion, she took one of the vials, broke the seal, and poured the entire contents on Yeshua's head and massaged it into his hands and feet. Her profound love was clearly demonstrated as she openly wept and dried her beloved's feet with her long, dark mahogany-red hair. We were all touched by her devotion and wept freely with her. And, clearly my grandson, who also openly wept, received so deeply of the supernal love that flowed through Mary Magdalene that his entire countenance began to glow with a radiance that matched the sun at mid-day.

As the formal celebration continued into its third day of feasting, dancing, and storytelling, Mary Anna learned from Abigail's mother that the wine was running low. Right away she went to Yeshua in the courtyard as he was enjoying a lighthearted exchange with John, the other groom. Then, as my beloved grandson looked directly into my eyes, I heard his mother say to a nearby servant, 'Whatever he tells you, do it.'

Yeshua asked to be taken to the wine cellar, where the casks of wine, both grape juice and fermented wine, and large earthen jars of water were kept cool. After ordering the servants to fill several of the water containers to the brim, he then asked to be left alone. I was not present while Yeshua worked with the angels of the elements to change the water into new wine or the grape juice that was preferred by those Essenes who kept a strict diet. But I did drink the new wine when it was served, which was sweeter by far than that which had been served previously. I was not surprised by my grandson's abilities with alchemy, since he had turned water to wine one season at Mount Carmel when the grape harvest had been shortened by a severe early frost. This was one of Yeshua's first public miracles, as his spiritual manifestations were called.

Come with me now as I recollect a dear memory of a glorious spring day as Yeshua spoke to a large crowd that had gathered on a hillside overlooking the community of Bethsaida. From our vantage-point we could gaze out onto Galilee's great fresh-water lake and the surrounding hillscape. Near the top of the knoll, there was a broad, open concave area, which created a natural amphitheatre. Those of us who were his close disciples assisted the growing crowd to find places where all could listen while reclining on blankets or sitting on stones.

It was one of those unexpectedly warm days that favour Galilee in the springtime. A gentle breeze blew across our faces, rippling the hillside grasses as if they were an extension of the sea below. Swallows and sea birds darted and winged overhead amongst wispy white clouds that floated past a dazzling bright sun. Yet this sun, which graced all with its warmth and light, could not equal the brilliance that I perceived emanating from my beloved grandson's face. I fixed my gaze upon him, eagerly awaiting his voice that moved through my heart as deep, silent waters.

Many who came were sceptical, coming out of curiosity or by the invitation of a friend. And then there were the ever present sick and lame brought by their relatives. Yeshua, Mary Magdalene, and the other principal twenty-four disciples – women as well as men – ministered to the infirm first. To assist in whatever way I could was my soul's greatest pleasure.

Even while I ministered, I could not take my eyes away from my grandson and granddaughter as they walked among the people. Yeshua's and Mary's simple robes were basically identical, both made of finely woven bleached linen. Their hooded outer cloaks were woven of finest white wool. Each kept a dark cloak to cover their white clothing, as well as a change of typical Galilean garb to put on when it was necessary to pass through the countryside incognito.

Thus, they travelled not out of fear for themselves but rather that their service to humanity be unimpeded. The women who crafted and washed the disciples' white garments considered their labours a great fulfilment to their hearts. Now, as I looked upon our master teachers and observed their radiant, tanned faces against the dazzling white of their robes, I felt as though I were truly gazing upon the purest of holy vessels.

Mariam and several other women sang and played musical instruments. Children as well as adults joined in the chorus, and where there was room, people danced. Our hearts were gladdened by the joyful feelings, which opened us to the light of the sun, sweet birdsong, early spring grasses and wildflowers, and the delight of having the Anointed One in our midst. He paused from time to time to pick up a small child, placing them on his shoulders. How the memories stirred in my breast as I remembered previous occasions when my playful young grandson had done this long ago!

So did we pass the early afternoon hours, until Yeshua was satisfied that everyone was ready to receive his words. Mary Magdalene was content to play her supportive feminine role, as was her custom during their ministering to a crowd. Silently, and with great power, she enhanced the energy for her beloved, as he invited us to sit down. He took his place where he could be seen and heard by all. By this time, many more people had arrived from near and far, filling the entire area of the natural amphitheatre and its surrounding ridges.

Finally, when everyone was calm and at peace, he began to speak, projecting his voice, as had the ancient prophets long ago, 'Children of the One God, it is your faith that has brought you here. Mighty, indeed, are the works of all whose faith is as a mustard seed. Though your faith may be small in the beginning, if given nourishment, it will grow into a great bush wherein the birds may nest. So it is that I am come unto you because your faith is sufficient for the hearing of my words. As with the mustard seed, may my words find a place within your fertile hearts and minds so that they may germinate and become fruitful in your daily lives.

'Thus do I speak to you that you may be glad of heart and strong of spirit. For, to walk in the Way of the Teacher of Righteousness is to remember no more your idleness, which yields a poor harvest, nor your rebelliousness against Father–Mother Creator whose strong arms bear you up from day to day. If you have ears to hear and eyes to see, you will know that I say only that which my Father gives me to say to you. What you see me do also comes directly from Him. And the Mother of Wisdom, Shekinah-Sophia, the Holy Spirit of Truth within you, shall bear witness that this, indeed, is so.

'Therefore, hear well these sayings. Let go those cords of guilt that bind you in judgement to another's trespass, and release your neighbours from the hidden snares of your judgement's clasp. Raise not your arm in protest when your cloak is taken from you, but give that which is your surplus also. Be not cast down in weariness when one who is needy asks of your supply, but be glad of heart that you may do unto others as you would have them do unto you.

'Know your true Self and the passionate depths of your innermost being. Gather up all the energy that your small self attempts to hoard or scatter, and offer up all that you are to the Giver of Life. This is the first commandment that empowers all others. And then likewise, with generous compassion bless that friend who is drawn to walk beside you, offering you a reflection. Bestow on your neighbour those good things that you would have the Father–Mother of All impart unto you. You are loved, even that shadowy self, who still practises arrogant separation and has not opened the door to our Father–Mother's hearth and the nourishment found therein.

'This is the creative principle out of which comes all righteousness, meaning the right use of energy. No other commandment is there than to love the One God within you and to love and serve the One creation you also are, so that you may have life more abundantly. I ask you: how else can you know peace and prosperity within your soul?

'Believe more so in the witness borne within your own heart than in that which you perceive to be miracles wrought at my hand. For I do nothing of myself. It is the Father–Mother Creator within me that does the works you see. Likewise, it is that same Creator within you who multiplies your fortune and who cares for you day by day. Consider the gentle lilies of the field. They neither spin nor weave. Yet their raiment is beautiful to behold. Observe our brother, the sparrow, how it freely wings through the heavens overhead. In innocence and trust, it glides upon the wind supported in all things whither it goes. Therefore, be not anxious. For with your worry, you cannot purchase more time against the morrow. Nor does your anxiety add credibility to your stature among men. Rather be still, and go within to the treasure of your heart, and you shall be given all things. Your Father–Mother knows wherewith you are needful and gives to you even before you ask. When in unity and gladness, you are merged with your innermost desire in the moment of realizing it is already yours, then surely is it given.

'Prove me herewith, that whatsoever you ask of your Father–Mother in the spirit of love shall surely be given to you according to your faith and works. Therefore, seek and you shall find. Knock and the door shall be opened. Ask and you shall receive, measure for measure multiplied without end. Look all about you and weigh in the balance of your heart all that is richly provided. For even in your trials there is a gift. Even in your stumbling block, you may find strength. By taking time to account for the seed you now harvest, you may find your way to return to the Master within who gives you the pearl of wisdom.

'Lay not up for yourself the treasures of the world, where moth and rust corrupt, and where thieves break in to steal. To do so is to become poor in spirit and aggrieved within a hungered soul. Rather than lamenting over that which perishes in time, lay up for yourself the imperishable treasures of that heavenly realm that moves and breathes you, wherein you may always find sweet refreshment and rest.

'Be bold enough to cast off your false self, who would enslave you within an illusory prison borne of your mortal senses. Refine your senses with love's pure light, and your body becomes heaven's earthly temple. Remember who you are, simple and free. As you seek first the kingdom of God within you, everything else will be added as you give.

'Rather than seeking to be seen and outwardly rewarded when you do your good works, turn inward in secret, and commune with the Giver of Life who openly increases the treasure within your heart. Likewise, do your almsgiving in secret and keep your own counsel. When the harvest of the Law of Life is given to you, reap of your good works in thankful silence, acknowledging God as the Giver. When you fast to cleanse yourself of defilement borne of fearful self-loathing and resentment, do it in a spirit of release and gratitude without false humility and self-righteousness.

'Judge not your brother, nor attempt to remove the speck of dust in his eye, until you have removed from your own eye the beam that distorts your seeing. Indeed, judge not at all. For, with the measure that you judge to invalidate another, you shall also be condemned.

'I am come to prepare my Father's banquet table, even as does the husband who invites his bride to come and have sup with him. Like my Father, I give forth every good thing that comes from the bountiful kingdom that has its foundation within you. You are the salt of the earth when you contribute your full essence to life's feast.

'I have not come to gather an army. Nor have I come to establish peace in this land. Rather, the sword of my mouth shall tear asunder the veil that covers the greater Law of the One. Do not follow blind guides who would have you believe that salvation may be found in the traditions of your fathers. To be a blind slave, chained to tradition, is to fall into a ditch. To see clearly, turn to the light of the sun that dwells within you, which forever lights your way. Reveal your light from beneath its covering where it may illuminate the path of those who otherwise would fall.

'Come to me, all you who labour and are heavy laden, and I will give you rest. For, my yoke of union in God is easy, and my burden is eternal light. I AM the light of the world. Come to the fountain of your own light and know the peace that passes all understanding. For, here with me, you may drink and find refreshment, until you have found your way to our Father–Mother's eternal spring. Cast off your wearisome burdens of guilt, false pride, and self-loathing. Stop kicking, as does a stubborn mule, against the pricks of self-condemnation, and reclaim your rightful inheritance as a Son/Daughter of God.

'Behold these, your children, who surround me and sit upon my lap. Yea, to be as one of these little ones is to be mindful of the present moment, resting in innocence, wherein all opposites are met in One and salvation abides. In the simple way of the lilies and in the innocent play of children, the keys to the kingdom are given and all its riches may be found.

'Verily, all that you seek is within you. Therefore, know your self. Your body is indeed the temple of God. Simply open the door of your heart, and enter in. Your Father–Mother awaits you. Even now, the Father–Mother runs out upon the stony path you have trod, and welcomes that part of your self you have judged prodigal and returns you to your birthright. Once you turn around, and begin to press homewards back into the light, you know this light is the Beloved you have futilely sought in the night.

The Beloved is the good shepherd who leaves the ninety and nine when he knows that they are safe at home and seeks the one lost sheep, to guide its return to the nurturing hearth of its Mother's sacred heart. Though a crown of thorns pierces her heart with the suffering of her children, still does she invite and receive each child without condition. So it is that I am come to gather and feed the sheep that my Father–Mother has given to me, returning even the stragglers home in my arms.

'You need not be surprised at my sayings nor doubt my words because I reinterpret the law of your youth. I bring you the good news that you are free to raise up an immortal body of divine light so that you may overcome the illusion of death. Not all who hear my words will understand that of which I plainly speak. Soon, however, all that was spoken of by Enoch, Isaiah, and John the Baptizer shall be made clear. I am come to make the Way of the Teacher of Righteousness plain for you, so that you might not stumble when the day that turns dark is upon you.

'Rest assured that when that new day comes you will not be left comfortless. For, on that day, I shall inaugurate a New Covenant. And when you are ready, I shall send my Heavenly Mother, the Holy Spirit of Truth, who is the intelligence behind and within all things, to be your second comforter. This, indeed, is the promise that I have received from my Father–Mother who is a God of Love.'

In the silence after Yeshua announced this promise there was a great quietude among those present, and I saw many tears on the shining faces of those who received these sayings deeply into their hearts. These words, and many more, did Yeshua speak to the multitudes that gathered over the remaining months of his public ministry.

෴

∽ Chapter 35 ∽

The Power of Yeshua's Healing

I will begin our sharing about Yeshua's healing practices by telling you how Yeshua assisted my great-grandson Benjamin, Mariam and Nathaniel's son, to heal his body that was born with a clubfoot and often shook with palsy. It was after the baptism at Beth Barah and their forty-day ordeal fasting in the desert, that Yeshua and Mary Magdalene came to Mount Carmel to receive counsel from the elders of our community, including me. It was an unusually warm autumn evening that Yeshua sought out Benjamin. Yeshua found him lying on his pallet on the roof of the men's dormitory gazing at the stars overhead.

This is the story that Benjamin, who was delighted to receive attention from the one he had looked up to as a hero throughout his young life, told me.

Lying down beside Benjamin, Yeshua held his crippled hands as they continued to gaze rapturously into the star-lit night. The moon had not yet risen. Gradually Benjamin's breath began to soften and deepen. As his mind stilled, his Book of Life opened to his inner sight. He witnessed many lifetimes passing before him with all the errors for which he had not forgiven himself. He saw how he had shaken tight fists, had kicked, and thrown himself at perceived enemies, cursing them to hell. He observed all manners of familiar patterns that he still repeated over and over, even though his intent was to be harmless and of service to his fellow beings. More than anything, he began to understand why his soul had chosen to heal itself through a body that shook and walked with crippled limbs.

As the night wore on, punctuated with Benjamin's deep sighing and suppressed sobbing, Yeshua gently placed his arms around the boy's slender body, laying his right hand over the boy's heart. Silently, their consciousness joined as they travelled through the astral planes, gradually lifting burdens of guilt and shame. Set free, Benjamin spiralled upwards into higher dimensions and greater light. They enjoyed a wordless celestial peace, as they lay cradled together beneath the witnessing stars and smiling moon.

Tears fell from their eyes as they turned to face each other. Benjamin's body no longer shook with palsy. He lifted his hands to look at them in the moonlight. They were no longer twisted. He stood and took a measured step or two. His clubfoot and twisted legs were straight and could support his full weight. Remembering that it was the time of communal silence, Benjamin suppressed a Hosanna, and knelt before a smiling Yeshua. Telepathically, he communicated that he would forever be loyal, just as his mother, Mariam, had promised from her youth. Yeshua gently reminded him to be faithful to his own I AM and to live in gratitude for all that life gives each day.

And so it was during those remaining years of Yeshua's ministry, after I had left Mount Carmel to travel with my grandson, that I continued to be one of his personal witnesses. Indeed, I often saw many acts of spiritual power that turned the populace to seek out or to fear my grandson and his close inner circle of disciples. I shall share with you now another recollection of one such memorable day that occurred at Bethesda, the pool of healing waters that was located just outside the Sheep Gate at Jerusalem. It took place on a Sabbath during the Feast of Tabernacles in the autumn of AD29.

I had come to Jerusalem with my great-grandson, Benjamin, whom Yeshua had recently healed. We were staying with my daughter, Mary Anna, her husband Ahmed, and their three children: John Mark, Thomas, and Matteus. They were now living northwest of the Jerusalem Temple, not far from the Old Gate in the second of Joseph of Arimathea's large homes. We knew that Yeshua, Mary Magdalene, and the other close disciples had returned to Jerusalem from a seven-day retreat in the desert, communing with the brethren of Qumran. It was said that they could be found at the pool of Bethesda. So it was that we gathered ourselves and went forth to the Bethesda pool, where many spontaneous healings had taken place over the centuries.

As the tradition of miracles had long promised, so it was this day that the sick, lame, paralysed, or blind had gathered around Bethesda's five porches on their pallets, waiting for the waters to move. The belief was that an angel stirred the waters from time to time, and that whoever entered the pool first when the waters were moving would be healed of their affliction. Hence, the name 'Bethesda', which in the Hebrew language means 'house of mercy'.

Word had spread all around Palestine about Yeshua's healing powers. And so it was that when he and the disciples came to the pool to refresh themselves, there were some of the afflicted who recognized him and pressed upon him to heal them. Indeed, when we arrived, a multitude of people, rich and poor alike, were waiting their turn to be seen and touched by Yeshua and by his beloved Mary, whose presence stirred their souls as if they were touched by the angel of healing herself.

As if upon waves, the energy of the throng would gather and ebb, hysterical frenzy followed by a hushed quietude and silent reverence. Yeshua's male disciples had their hands full maintaining order among the emotional crowd, as they assisted the infirm to come to the place where Yeshua and Mary Magdalene sat beside the pool. The women disciples moved among the afflicted, offering solace and preparation of their souls, so that they could be receptive to the healing energies they might choose to receive.

Many questioned among themselves how it was that the young rabbi from Galilee dared to work as a healer on the Sabbath. Whispered murmuring could be heard. I recognized that some of those who murmured were Pharisees; and when they suddenly took their leave, I knew Yeshua would be confronted before too long. As is the nature of this world, when the Son of Light comes among humankind, the Son of Darkness comes also. So it seemed that the false belief of duality always created shadowy patterns of fear wherever Yeshua went. I felt uneasy. Yet when I looked upon my grandson and granddaughter, and observed their calm compassion for these innocents, I too felt a desire that this be a day of healing, regardless of the sanctioned functions that were arbitrarily ordained. And so, forgetting the Pharisees, I joined the other women, and turned my attention to those in need.

Yeshua took crying babes into his arms, cradled aged and emaciated bodies on his lap, poured oil on the heads of the twisted and infirm, mixed his spittle with clay and placed it on eyes or into ears, all the while speaking gently with those who were being healed. Children stopped crying and the palsied stopped shaking, the lame walked, the deaf heard, the blind saw, and the sick became well. All the while, the healing energy came in waves, as if the angel of Bethesda had stirred the pooled water. So it was that the ebb and flow of the healing energy was reflected by the crowd's soft weeping and loud wailing, suppressed sighs and uncontrolled laughter, and occasional exclamations of, 'Hosanna, the Lord of Hosts is among us! Praise be to God most holy!'

Now, let it be known that it was not Yeshua who did the healing. He was like a hollow flute through which higher consciousness could orchestrate and perform these seemingly miraculous events. Before administering to each one, my grandson always paused to commune in the silence. While scanning each supplicate's energy field to determine the metaphysical cause of his or her condition, he communed on the soul level to determine whether a healing was the highest empowerment. Then, he empathetically tuned into the supplicant's heart to discover whether she or he was willing to lay aside the heavy stone of grievance that created the disease. He looked to see if there was an equally measured resonance with the healing power of Divine Love that was concentrated in Yeshua's heart and auric field. Only when there was an affirmative response to each of these queries did he proceed.

He began by holding each out-pictured soul in its perfected wholeness, no matter how deformed or diseased the body appeared to be. Next, he aligned himself with the over-lighting angels of manifestation, and tuned into the intelligence of the soul manifesting through the various axiotonal grids of the physical and subtle bodies. After merging with the soul's latticed matrices and assessing the soul's blueprint for this incarnation, he then inwardly struck a resonant series of inward tones (sometimes heard by the physical ears). These vibrations reverberated through the congested organs, tissues, and bones until all terror, grief, and rage were embraced and transmuted.

Gradually he lifted those discordant and incoherent fear-based energies into love's coherent expression of harmony. Skilfully projecting light, sound, and colour, he cleansed and purified the aura. Holding each individual in innocence, there was a release of fear. With the letting go of fear, there was room to breathe. And, with each relaxed, connected breath, the perception of time and space expanded into a greater awareness of the eternal presence of love. Through co-created harmonic resonance the Divine Healer, who dwells in every heart, worked miracles through Yeshua, Mary Magdalene, and the other initiated disciples.

It was my grandson's and my granddaughter's alignment together in unity with the Law of One, which made it possible for the emancipating love energy to flow. What appeared to be a miracle, caused by the transmission of a power from an external source was, in truth, a self-healing in the flow of oneness. There was a shift in ordinary perception of limitation as time and space expanded into the unlimited quantum realms. Mastery of the physical and spiritual planes comes when there is an alignment with universal laws. Miracles manifest when there is a matching resonance with love and the vibrational harmonics of creation.

Therefore, healing only occurs when the individual, on some level, consciously accepts, feels, and becomes one with coherent love-energy as it concentrates all around and through their body, mind, and soul. In that instant of merging with Divine Love, the entombed indwelling Christ rises into conscious awareness. The question then becomes can the error of misperceived separation/dis-ease continue to fall away and the newly emerged Christ remain in one's conscious choice for wellbeing? While many were healed, others continued to stumble and fall into the ditch of forgetfulness, grievance, and the familiar return of disease.

As the shadows of a long day lengthened and Yeshua and his close disciples were preparing to leave the Bethesda pool, a Temple priest, accompanied by a group of Pharisees, angrily confronted him after elbowing his way through the milling crowd. 'By what authority are you doing these things?' the priest demanded in a harsh voice that was curdled with malevolence.

Gazing directly into his eyes, Yeshua calmly replied: 'I do not seek my own will but the will of my Father who sent me. The son does nothing of his own accord, but only that which his Father shows him. It is my Father–Mother, the Birther of the Cosmos, who does these works that you see. I have come in the name of my Heavenly Parents, but you do not receive me because you do not acknowledge your own Sonship in God the Father nor do you feel the love of Mother God who gives you breath. He who does not honour the Son that he truly is, does not honour the Father–Mother who sent him.'

Shaken, but unmoved, the Temple priest persisted in his attempts to intimidate my grandson. He ignored Mary Magdalene with contempt as she courageously stood beside her beloved. Then with a shrill voice, the priest shouted, 'Don't you know that it is against the Law of Moses to do healing work on the Sabbath?'

Unperturbed by the hostility of this one who had assumed the role of adversary, Yeshua replied: 'Who among you would fail to respond if your servant fell into a well or remove your ox mired in quicksand on the Sabbath? The Sabbath was made for man, not man for the Sabbath. If you truly believe in Moses, then you would believe in me, because he wrote about me. But if you do not believe his writings, how will you believe my words? You search the scriptures; for in them, you think you have eternal life. I tell you, he who hears my words and believes in my Father who sent me and my Mother who sustains me, it is he who shall pass from death into life everlasting.'

Saying no more, Yeshua motioned to his mother with his hand and telepathically communicated that he would meet her in Bethany. Then he, Mary Magdalene, and his twenty-four close disciples took up their traveling bundles and made their way down the terraced steps. When Mary Anna and I took our leave a few minutes later, the Pharisees and the Temple priest were still arguing among themselves. Joseph of Arimathea met us at the Sheep Gate with three donkey carts for the short journey to Bethany, where we joyfully celebrated the Feast of Tabernacles with an abundance of savoury dishes that had been prepared for us by Martha.

Thus, I have shared with you another of the many examples that reaffirm my grandson's and, indeed, my granddaughter's demonstration of what it means to be a Christ. In so doing, I have pointed you in the direction of that great healing light that reveals the eternally open door to the kingdom of heaven that is within you. Now, my beloved friend, you stand at the open door that leads into the healing waters within your own House of Mercy. Will you, in a moment of effortless spontaneity, enter in?

He, who showed the way, has said: 'I do not seek my own will but the will of my Father who sent me. The son does nothing of his own accord, but only that which his Father shows him. It is my Father who does these works that you see. It is by my Mother's grace that you receive them.' He also said, 'He who chooses to save his life shall lose it, whereas he who chooses to lose his life shall save it.' So, I ask you once again, my beloved, will you exchange your small life of separation so that you may fulfil your Greater Part? By aligning your heart, mind, and soul with the Father–Mother of Life, you may freely claim the life you truly seek.

Know that you are never alone, nor the obstacles too great, though at times the journey of the Christ will seem too difficult to bear. Remember you will experience the Beloved of your soul as your inner shepherd who nurtures and protects you. You will walk in life's green pastures as long as you acknowledge and align your will with your indwelling Good Shepherd's rod and staff that eternally connect you with the Source of your being.

So it is that the eternal presence of Yeshua, as your friend and brother, will reflect back to you your internal Good Shepherd who cares for you each day. Perhaps unseen, yet often felt when you still your mind, Yeshua, Mary Magdalene, Mary Anna, and I are closer than you think. Know that we are ever present, applauding the progress you make. We will never interfere, for you are the lord of your life, which is your kingdom. Your free will choice is always honoured and your individual sovereignty is esteemed. And if, in an eternal now moment, you choose to come face to face with the God of Love, our co-created purpose shall be fulfilled.

৲৯

~ Chapter 36 ~

A Message of Hope

During this time of great chaos, as most of humanity feels despondency and despair, it is vital to instil courage and hope. Not just a hope that is founded upon intellectual inquiry or childish fantasy, but a courageous experience of that Greater Power and Eternal Life in which a certain trust and expectation of 'something better' can be fully grounded. From a more expanded viewpoint, you may, on a very personal level, bring Yeshua's and Mary Magdalene's eternal example of forgiving, empowering love into your present choices and life's experiences. Through doing so, you can effect harmonious change in the world and midwife the Earth into the next Golden Age of peace – a peace that passes understanding, because it fully comforts what has felt comfortless through the power of the Divine Feminine heart.

Have you, my friend, found a belief in your self and in a higher source of love that encourages you to live fully in this world and not be hopeless and despairing? The way back to hope always follows an adjustment of perception and attitude – an ability to align with the Divine Mother's capacity to acknowledge and feel emotion without judgement or reactivity. When there is appreciation, forgiveness and reclaimed innocence, there is courage and hope to live in coherent patterns of love, regardless of the chaos all around.

What I now offer you is a model or paradigm from which to view Yeshua's and your initiations, while being in the midst of chaotic planetary crucifixion and resurrection. This is a new model of coherency dynamics based on the science of quantum mechanics and chaos theory. In your day there is research being done that indicates that a person's wellbeing and actual state of health is enhanced when his or her mind, emotions, and body are in harmonious relationship with one another – a coherent energy field.

Those involved in this research have found that the most coherent field is subjectively called love and appreciation. When discordant, limiting time–space perception shifts into quantum, holistic awareness (spacious, embracing love and appreciation) there is healing, or reestablished order, balance, and wholeness. Another way to look at this is to see crucifixion, resurrection, and ascension as those processes that return incoherence to coherency.

You may choose to use this new perspective as an opportunity to liberate yourself from unquestioned, blind beliefs that have kept you ignorant and fearful. Some would call my coherency model of crucifixion and resurrection heretical. And some would call blasphemous what I will share with you about my interdimensional understanding of Yeshua's experiences. While what I offer is a kind of exposé, in order to unveil what has been hidden, it is most definitely not intended to replace one truth or dogma with another. My intention is to shake old limiting thought-forms and to awaken more coherent, self-empowering and loving ways to be in relationship with your Creator, your self, and your neighbours.

Today's ascension process that brings about global patterns of coherency or unity does not require going behind cloistered walls or taking prolonged sanctuary with master teachers, as we did in the old paradigm. Mother Earth and your life is your empowerment school. You have all kinds of support available to help you attain your self-mastery. There is the loving support of your ascending Earth Mother, awakening peers, books, seminars, alternative healing modalities, and a broad synthesis of 'what works' distilled from many spiritual paths. There is also assistance to be received from the incoming children who bring their immense love and mastery to the earthplane. Although unseen, you may also receive guidance from ascended masters and angels.

Your initiatory experiences will most likely be different from Yeshua's (such as being nailed to a cross), but, in essence, they are similar. Before we explore this further, let me offer a fuller explanation of what I mean by initiation. An initiation is that inner-directed experience that takes you over the threshold of irreversible change. In the initiations of resurrection and ascension, your former limited identity transforms into a more expansive awareness of inherent potential. This is illustrated in the transformational initiatory process demonstrated by the butterfly that emerges into a 'new life' resurrected from its crucified caterpillar life.

As you read the following five aspects of initiation that could be affecting your own life, please ask yourself which ones seem to have a personal meaning for you today.

1. A marked attitudinal change that brings a committed willingness to align limited consciousness with a higher Will and Purpose.

2. Physical changes in which toxins are cleared and dormant DNA codes, endocrine glands, brain and neurological functions are activated, all of which result in enhanced health and increased potential for demonstrating paranormal abilities.

3. Emotional clearing and greater emotional maturity and stability.

4. Changes in self-perception, in which there is a greater sense of divinity, sovereignty, interconnectedness, heightened creativity and/or superconscious abilities such as telepathy and clairvoyance.

5. More identification with the spacious unified quantum realms instead of only perceiving and reactively dramatizing the limiting transitory idea of being a separate mind located in a separate body.

Having reviewed these various aspects of initiation, are you seeing any of these initiatory benchmarks showing up in your own life? What are your reactions to your present-day transformational initiations?

There has been much misunderstanding about the nature of crucifixion and resurrection. However, these are the foundational initiations of empowerment that anyone who chooses union in God experiences. I offer you my perspective in order to bring clarity and to motivate more empowering choices. Christ ascension cannot be understood until the initiations of crucifixion and resurrection are recognized as those transformational events that may be already occurring in your life.

Have you, at one time or another, believed that crucifixion equals suffering – usually as a way for paying back a debt – original sin, guilt, shame? Do you insist that Yeshua, in order to be the Christ, must have suffered and died in order to redeem a fallen world? What feelings come up for you when you contemplate the Son of God suffering on the cross? What if Yeshua did not suffer? What if he did not die? What if his crucifixion was simply a demonstration of how you can align your will with Divine Will, release all attachment to a limited identity, and open the way to being the Radiant One you already are? Not the false self you think you are, entombed in the material world, but the Self who is looking and breathing through the mask of pretense!

Are you ready to take Jesus and yourself off the cross of endless suffering? Are you ready to shift your focus into resurrecting your consciousness into enlightened states of happiness, joy, and bliss, instead of justifying why you feel betrayed, abandoned, trapped, helpless, and hopeless? Are you ready to take back your power instead of blindly giving it to mediating priesthoods, saints, teachers, or unquestioned limiting beliefs? When it is time to allow growth and expansion of your inner authority and divinity, are you willing to fly free of self-imposed prisons that were the structures and teachers that once served you? If your answer to these provocative questions is 'Yes!' – then I genuinely celebrate with you!

Once you understand that Yeshua learned from his youth how to pass through crucifixion (dying to limitation) and resurrection (aligning with eternal life and original innocence), you can begin to allow for the possibility that he did not suffer to pay any form of debt. As you recall what I have shared with you about the Rite of the Sepulchre, you can also begin to understand that he did not die, even though all his vital signs ceased to support his physical body for a time.

Having mastered the physical and subtle realms throughout his life, Yeshua did not suffer in the gruesome way you may have been taught, or that some subconscious part of you may insist that he did. *He did not die for your sins! He lived to model love and forgiveness so that you could choose to live by the same qualities he demonstrated.* I encourage you to let go of the idea that transformation, change, and detaching from the nails of limitation or crucifixion has to be a hard struggle, full of tragic drama and fraught with suffering. As you allow your separated consciousness to 'die' into unity consciousness, you may pass much more easily through your crucifixion initiation into resurrecting and ascending yourself as a living Christ.

You may well ask, why did Yeshua and his close male and female disciples travel long distances to the mystery schools of Palestine, Egypt and India, in order to participate in arduous initiatory experiences? My experience was that the mystery schools, and being in cloistered community, provided the necessary support my peers and I required so that we could embody immortality and ascension while living in a disbelieving, dense outer world that was fixated on fear, mortality, suffering, and separation. Just as it was important for us to feel supported in our process of ascending our consciousness, so is it likewise important for you to gather the tangible harmonious support of friends and family who encourage your spiritual growth.

Perhaps, as you have read about Yeshua's and my family's extraordinary spiritual abilities and experiences in my story, you have felt as though you could never accomplish what we did because we were more 'special' – genetically endowed and more deserving than you are. However, if you distance us from yourself by thinking you are less or unworthy, you cannot bring our example and message of hope into your life. The truth is that all of life is equally endowed, even though external appearances seem to indicate otherwise.

At this point, I would also reemphasize that there is no one outside of your own divine Self who will save you or who will take away those empowering experiences your soul desires you to have. Especially, those challenging experiences that empower your ability to know and express enlightened love. The fact is you would most likely be angry with anyone you allowed to interfere with your sovereignty and your innate ability to attain all or any portion of what Yeshua demonstrated.

In whatever way you are choosing to be more loving, kind, forgiving, honest, and generous, you are realizing what it means to live as a Christ. When your consciousness has a very literal knowing that you are Creator expressing in all forms and beyond all forms, your consciousness has been Christed. You are the spiritual path you walk, and you cannot get off your path. If you would desire your way to be a path of expanding spirituality, then consistent commitment, discipline, and mindfulness is required (witnessing thoughts, emotions, actions), while aligning your human will with Divine Will – your Divine Father.

Your path also becomes more spiritual when you come into an alignment with Divine Love – your Divine Mother. This happens when you are having experiences in which you can literally feel love expressing in and through you, as expanding, embracing uplifting energy. Any devotional practice that helps you to experience humility (being open to love), wonderment, original innocence, allowance and forgiveness facilitates intimacy with your Divine Heart – the gentle merciful heart of the Mother of Life.

Just as you may have felt yourself 're-experiencing' many of the scenes I have already shared, so may you also 'find yourself walking with Yeshua' in my story's remaining chapters. To assist you to more easily integrate what may yet be catalysed, I desire to offer you a perspective or model from which to view Yeshua's crucifixion and resurrection. In this way, you can empower your own initiatory processes.

The way to gain a clearer alternative view is to imagine yourself seated comfortably and safely on a high platform inside a large theatre. From this high place, you can easily look down on the entirety of an expansive stage below you from which you can see Jerusalem, Gethsemane, and Calvary. Once you have shifted your 'normal', perhaps fixated, orientation that has seen only a portion of what is happening on the stage below; you may begin to see aspects of the drama that you missed before. In addition to experiencing a greater fullness of what is happening below, I encourage you to look all around you. From this heightened perspective, you can behold a most beautiful scene filled with peaceful people and all manner of life thriving together in harmony. This is where Yeshua and his disciples were focused, even though we appeared to be with the hysterical crowds who were enacting the discordant drama below.

This all-inclusive perspective that includes numerous levels above and below, is how enlightened beings, such as Yeshua, live life. Yeshua knew he was all of it: the inter-dimensional actors, including the stages, roles, settings, audiences, and the compassionate, though detached coordinating Director who was positioned 'above it all'. From this perspective, it is easy to note that there is more happening than one may have previously thought to be true. What Yeshua and his close disciples had the ability to do was to be on the stage where most of the intense action played out, while also being aware of more subtle realities or dimensions 'above' simultaneously expressing other potentialities. In other words, Yeshua exemplified, 'Being in the world, but not of it.'

Within which of these levels do you feel most at home? Below on the stage or in the peaceful realm Yeshua experienced? Are you finding yourself choosing to place your awareness more often into the coherent realm of love and appreciation? Think of a time when you felt hopeless, helpless, sad, angry, or afraid. How long did you stay in it? How do you go about regaining peace of mind, hope and courage for daily living when you have lost it? Can you do what Yeshua did by 'being above it' – an interdimensional director of the play of your life? Please understand, my beloved friend, that you are not left here alone and comfortless – choose to be connected – that's the key. And when the 'dark night of the soul' persists – do not resist the birthing process, but find someway to relax into the Divine Love that you already are.

I now offer you two simple spiritual practices that may assist you to 'be in the world, but not of it,' as you pass through your crucifixion, resurrection, and ascension initiations.

Find a quiet place in which to be seated comfortably. Putting your awareness in your present breath be centred completely in the NOW. There is no pondering of the past or peering into the future. In the present instant of breathing, you can step easily into the Truth of eternal Being. You and your breath are one continuous, uninterrupted flow of divine love. Know that you are allowing and expressing love, as powerfully as did Mary Anna, Yeshua and Mary Magdalene. With every breath be in the now, and then consciously step across the veil of disbelief. Come to know by feeling the energy of expanded love and light that you ARE a realized enlightened Christ–Magdalene in balanced wholeness of masculine and feminine energy! It is simply a matter of choosing to be more aware of where you are placing your attention.

A word to the wise: This exercise does not sidestep the crucifixion initiation. Understand that this direct action, when it is experienced with consistent repetition, may result in the transformation (crucifixion) of your limited identity as you thought yourself to be and your limited life's expression as you have lived it. Your ego, focused in a physical body, cannot stop your soul's inevitable spiritual growth, even if death of the body is required for its liberation. Whether you experience your soul's endless growth as suffering depends on how and where you are holding your consciousness. Mastering this exercise is not for the purpose of leaving the opportunities for growth on the earthplane behind. It does not remove you from the joy of practising being Divine Love embracing and ascending ALL your consciousness, including your body.

Although only you can step across the threshold of disbelief into the realization that you are a mighty 'I AM,' fully presenting yourself as a Christ, you are not alone while receiving the support you require. You are not alone when you realize the many opportunities that you have to share and express the power of your love with others. Remember where two or more are gathered there I AM – don't underestimate the power of unified prayer in action.

I will now share another simple exercise that was taught to Yeshua by his parents and grandparents. If you do not already have an ascension practice, I offer you this simple spiritual exercise that may assist you to let go of attachment to separation agendas that armour you against completely feeling and expressing Divine Love – your Creator as you.

Begin with five minutes a day, choosing to step into the resurrecting Christ conscious being you already are. Not trying to ascend, but actually feeling the energy shifting as you align with your 'I AM.' Then act from that empowered, kind, forgiving, and gracious place of resurrected love. When you can sustain five minutes of being fully present with love flowing unhindered through you, benefiting life within and around you, add another five minutes until you can do three increments of five minutes each a day. Then stretch the five minutes to ten, and so on, until you are effortlessly living the truth of your being in every now moment, day and night.

Throughout his life, Yeshua continued to choose to step into the true kingdom of his 'I AM' until every cell in his body knew and accepted union with its Creator. In this simple, direct way, Yeshua *simultaneously* passed through crucifixion, resurrection, and ascension, and so can you!

Prepared with this new lens through which to view 'The Greatest Story Ever Told', we will now enter the weeks of Yeshua's life when he demonstrated to the world how to become a realized, ascended Christ. As he exemplified the truth of eternal life and the power of love, so did many of his beloved disciples and so may you in this day! You are in an initiation process that is assisting you to be a willing and loving participant in a cosmic and global Divine Plan. My beloved friend, take notice – the very purpose for which you have taken birth is now happening!

ᨀ Chapter 37 ᨀ

The Storm Gathers

During those last two weeks before Yeshua's crucifixion and resurrection, I remained with him throughout, even into the following weeks in which his ascension process began. It was a most empowering time, for we all felt every possible emotion deeply. We were buried within the tumultuous waves of the most intense agony of despair and desolation, only to rise to the glorious heights of enraptured ecstasy. We wrestled so intensely with the collective fear and terror that found any resonance within our human consciousness, that there were moments in which we knew not if we could go on with the Plan.

While in those times of doubt, we trembled within the raging maelstrom of our personal hells of self-denial, guilt, abandonment, and judgement toward God, our Creator, and ourselves. How could the Realms of Light have ever contrived such a dangerous plan, as the one we had agreed to enact? I knew that what my grandson and granddaughter chose to do would most likely catalyse and expose all of humankind's most benevolent and hateful imaginings. I knew we would all be put to the test, as the extremes of duality, light and dark, life and death, would equally be brought together, so that all that was ever seeded might be harvested and returned to its Source, as one.

In those darkest of times, I recalled the days long ago, before Yeshua's birth, when I walked the burnt hillsides of Galilee. In the midst of the hot acrid dust and ashes, I felt similarly to what I now felt: 'O, my God, how am I to do this thing required of me?' Such were my thoughts and feelings. As I surveyed the souls who were among Yeshua's closest disciples, it was clear that I was not alone in what I thought and felt. I found comfort only when I completely stilled my mind and surveyed the world from a much higher perspective. I found peace when I felt Yeshua's and his beloved Mary's calm assurance that all was well, even though they also experienced personal and collective ambivalence. In spite of the internal wrestling of opposites, there was the renewed hope that every fragment of the Radiant One scattered across this burning world would be gathered home in God.

In the total embrace of that which we had most feared, judged, and cast outside of ourselves, we now had the promise of gathering all that we were into wholeness/holiness. Insofar as we also aligned our wills with the Divine Will of the Father–Mother who knows the Greater Part, as we watched Yeshua and Mary continually do, so in us was the hope of the world. Nevertheless, the weight of the separated consciousness, which contracts itself in order to preserve the illusion of duality, weighed heavily upon our shoulders. Our own sense of human limitation, and the collective density with which we were in empathy, was as a millstone upon our hearts. For you see, the heart of Divine Love is open to feel the energy of emotion that moves through all life.

Yeshua took us apart from the crowds as much as possible during those days of intense preparation. We each, according to our capacity to understand and to align our emotional and mental bodies, received Yeshua's counsel. In some of us, the pressure to immerse ourselves in the illusory world of chaos was so convincing that the full light of understanding was obscured. Fear increased in many of us because of the confusion and disillusionment coming from preconceived expectations of what we thought Yeshua would do as the Messiah. It had been prophesied that he would conquer Jehovah's perceived enemies. When he continued to emphasize that his kingdom was not of this Earth, many became anxious. Even some of the disciples who were closest to Yeshua began to nervously murmur among themselves.

It was a terrible time and truly a most wondrous time. We, who had been through arduous initiations, knew that everything we had experienced in all our lives – past, present, and future – was being gathered to this one pivotal point of choice. Would we remain true to the Christ light within us? Therefore, we sought to be as still as possible, in order to receive answers to the most profound questions that moved upon our deepest soul. We gathered up our accumulated wisdom and bolstered our courage through constant communion with God.

I sometimes saw Yeshua's and Mary's bodies tremble. Sweat poured profusely, drenching their garments as they were increasingly prepared on all levels to feel the collective flow of energy that moves through the entire planet and all her life forms. Then, as I followed their consciousness, it became as a web of light, extending as one pulsation moving on the currents of forever into the farthest universes. My grandson and granddaughter were stretched and stretched, so that they, as one, could embrace all life into the one true, infinite Self. Their gift to the world was to attain and imprint this cosmic awareness on subatomic levels while still maintaining an embodied state.

As the week of Passover approached, we went to Bethany, arriving in the night, so as to give ourselves a space of quiet from the press of the ever-present crowds. We passed the Sabbath there and prepared to go into the walled city of Jerusalem on the following day. Mary Magdalene and Mariam were particularly attentive to Yeshua's every need. Mary Anna was very still, rather withdrawn and pensive. At times, Yeshua came to her and buried his head in his mother's lap, his arms around her. Mary Anna's long hair fell around Yeshua, creating a molten gold veil behind which they both could weep and cleanse themselves of growing tension.

At such times, I gathered the little ones close to my knee, for I knew that they could sense, but did not know what was creating such unusual circumstances. I inwardly heard their questions, 'What would cause their mother, grandmother, and aunt, and their father, brother, cousin, and uncle, to be so apprehensive, withdrawn, and to cry so much?' I took the frightened children, one by one, to my bosom and soothed them with words of comfort and gentle caresses. As I assured them, the child within me was also reassured that all was indeed well.

Now, I will briefly reveal more of my understanding regarding Judas Iscariot, for he has been much maligned through time. I had noticed over the past weeks that Judas had grown increasingly nervous and apprehensive. He paced the floor, going out and then coming back in to look into Yeshua's face for reassurance. Sometimes Yeshua came to him, placing his arms around him, and Judas would break down in convulsive sobs or run out to the garden screaming, 'I don't understand! I don't understand! It is too much to bear!' He, of all the male disciples, was the most emotional. Although he had taken many Essene initiations, he was one of the most likely candidates to succeed and yet, at the same time, the least prepared to bear the burden of his soul's assigned role.

Now, I will share somewhat about Judas' background and personality so that you can begin to more fully appreciate him for fulfilling his dreaded task. Judas had spent most of his youth with John ben Zacharias in Qumran. His father, a widower, was an extremely learned man of the Law who ruled his sons with a stoic will. The elder Iscariot was also what you would describe in your day as a militant Zionist. As one of the leaders of the Qumran Zealots, every cell of his being cried out for a political Messiah who would remove Israel's cursed enemies and restore the Hebrew tribes and the Temple of Solomon to their full glory.

Judas, like his father, also had a bright mind and a great desire to win his father's respect and love. Like his father, he also desired a liberated Holy Land. He applied himself to his studies with a determined rigour. He excelled at his study of the Mosaic Law. He was a scholar of oratory history and debate, a scribe, and a trusted accountant of Qumran's and Mount Sinai's storehouses. Judas kept the purse for Yeshua, which contained necessary coinage for foodstuffs and other traveling expenses. After the traumatic loss of his beloved champion, John the Baptizer, who was murdered by Herod for publicly humiliating the despot for his lewd and immoral behaviour, Judas became one of Yeshua's heralding vanguard who defended him at the risk of his own life. He greatly enjoyed being one of Yeshua's forerunners, preparing villages along the way for his new messianic champion's arrival.

Few knew of Judas' inner nature, his restlessness, his need for recognition (especially by his father), and his sensitivity to things beautiful. Few ever read or heard his eloquent psalms, poetry, and discourses. There was one, however, who had won his confidence during his youth and young adulthood. In those years that Mary Magdalene visited Qumran, she became his enduring friend. Judas looked upon Mary as an older sister in whom he found a sanctuary of peace. In her presence, his sensitive and emotional inner self could be soothed and appreciated. They found in each other someone who could understand their propensity to feel emotion deeply. In later years, after Judas died during a bout of reoccurring suicidal depression, Mary shared with me some of Judas' remarkably passionate psalms to the Beloved and odes to Nature, as a memorial to his courageous loyalty.

As the last months passed, Judas had become slowly, yet increasingly, aware of the devastating, yet imperative role that was his to play. All of the inner circle disciples knew that the public demonstration of the archetypal hero and villain, required Yeshua to be publicly betrayed and put to death, in order to demonstrate the resurrection of the body and the eternality of life. Unlike the secret rites hidden within mystery school initiatory chambers, Yeshua and his close companions would openly reveal the Rite of the Sepulchre. Some of the disciples had enacted the role of Set or Satan, the betrayer, in their Egyptian initiations, and knew any of them was qualified to play that role now.

All the disciples, whether they had taken few or many Essene initiations, were to some degree familiar with 'the betrayer'. Yet, as all, save Judas, searched their hearts to see if their lot was cast to be 'the despised one', no answer came. No one knew for certain those last weeks, except Yeshua, Mary Magdalene, and Judas, who would be the catalyst to lift the curtain and call the cast to begin acting our parts upon centre stage.

Before we can be forgiving of Judas, it is helpful to have insight into his catalytic role. He played 'the despised betrayer', that part of self most judged and judging, that unforgiving, rebellious, zealous, and cruel one who lurks in the shadows of the human psyche. The inner loathed one, which is in the subconscious that the conscious mind projects outwards as the enemy with whom to do battle. That one who maintains the status quo at all costs. After all, is it not convenient for the warrior in duality to have a scapegoat to blame for causing incessant, bitter suffering? Who better to fault and condemn, than 'the betrayer?'

Have you noticed an aspect of your personality that is reluctant to forgive, holds resentment, and constantly looks for ways to aggrandize its position or conversely makes itself insignificant? Do you sometimes feel betrayed when this part of yourself sabotages the manifestation of what you truly desire? When this happens do you blame and judge others or harshly condemn yourself? These are not comfortable questions to ask one's self. However, to gain self-mastery, and to understand the crucifixion initiation that you may be passing through, this kind of inquiry is necessary. Then, it becomes possible to take responsibility for your thoughts and emotions as your creation. This is the truth behind the mystery school adage, 'Know Thy Self!'

We each have a perfect inner guidance system and an inherent capacity for love and expansion of consciousness. In truth, there is betrayal of self and Creator when one ignores or rebels against one's internal intuition, instincts, common sense, and wisdom. From a more expanded perspective, the oversoul or Higher Self guides the heart's purity of intent to be harmless, and assesses the soul's readiness for advanced levels of empowerment.

Your internal guidance system often acts as a kind of braking or accelerating system that assists every evolutionary step to be taken 'at the right time and place'. If you are forcing your spiritual growth, your soul slows you down by orchestrating obstacles to be placed in your way. Likewise, if you are resisting being more authentic and true to your power, love, and wisdom, your soul will uncannily orchestrate the necessary factors to have your fortressed life and armoured identity toppled seemingly overnight. When you understand that your soul or Higher Self is the captain of your life and that you are not a pawn victimized by outside forces, you can become an empowered team player with your life's divine director. Then, listening to and aligning with divine guidance can create more and more grace and ease in the flow of life's constant evolutionary changes.

When it is time for the transformational expansions of crucifixion and resurrection, you will be challenged to look at your attachments to beliefs, relationships, and possessions. Everything that limits you will come up for review. You may feel betrayed when your limited identity and world are falling apart, or, on the other hand, you may begin to realize that your soul is liberating you. When 'the betrayer', as the catalytic 'Judas' appears on your threshold and knocks, will you open the door and behold a welcomed friend or a foe? Yeshua recognized and welcomed Judas Iscariot as 'the friend little understood'.

Now, I remind you, my dear friend, that these understandings which often run contrary to accepted tradition, are given to you from the viewpoint that it is your responsibility to be discerning about what you accept as true, and how you will use this information in your life. Without hesitation, receive only what your inner being tells you is aligned to your soul's growth and evolution. And judge not the rest. Put the remainder aside and, perhaps upon taking up my story at some future time, you may find that what used to be Anna's 'blasphemous and heretical' sayings now have value for you.

I have come in this hour in response to our mutual call to reveal many things that have been concealed and hidden. May you likewise unveil yourself and remember who you are. In the empowerment that occurs through this self-revelation may you be increasingly comfortable, relaxed, and vulnerable to your soul's inevitable evolutionary changes. There need not be suffering during crucifixion's 'birth contractions' when your attention is on the caterpillar's true self taking flight as the butterfly.

ॐ

❧ *Chapter 38* ❧

The Last Supper

So it was that the greater tide of emotion among the populace had turned from jubilation to bitterness. The same crowds, shouting triumphant Hosannas and laying palm branches before Yeshua when he entered Jerusalem five days earlier, now hid themselves in the shadows. Fearing retribution by the self-righteous priests and Roman soldiers, especially after Yeshua's cleansing of the Temple, where the moneychangers and hypocritical priests were chastened, those who had once welcomed him now denied they knew him. Clearly, they reasoned, if Yeshua were really the Messiah, he would turn his anger on the Romans, not the priests who preserved the traditions of the Temple.

Seeing an opportunity to gain support from the populace and to turn them against the rebel from Galilee, the Scribes, Pharisees and Sadducees sowed seeds of discontent and doubt among the crowds, and like sheep, they followed. When Yeshua spoke with authority, they attempted to snare him in his teaching through their cunning and deceit. As my grandson spoke out against the priestly leaders' hypocrisy and arrogant pride, the agitated poor, who looked to Yeshua to save them, seemed to be caught in the riptide. Buffeted, they turned this way and that.

Looking for a Messiah who was a military leader strong enough to free the Holy Land from Roman oppression, the common people soon aligned with those in power when their lives were threatened. Yeshua's miracles, revolutionary teachings, and enigmatic example could be tolerated, even welcomed by a few, as a sign of the promised Messiah, but his persistent political passivity did not win popularity. Those whose bodies and souls had been healed with Yeshua's assistance, who had humbly turned their lives over to the God within, continued to support the Son of Man, no matter how they were chided for their belief in him. Those others who had also been healed, but could not handle the criticism and blatant attacks made upon them by their relatives and the priests, turned away in angry disappointment. All in all, the masses that pressed against the walls of Jerusalem became a seething turbulence that could not be contained.

The Roman sentries sent word to Pontius Pilate that civil mutiny was brewing. Annas, the Temple high priest, turned to Herod Antipas, demanding that something be done with this blasphemous heretic who threatened the Hebrew leaders' positions. The Sanhedrin was called to meet and put an end to this volatile situation. It was hoped that what had occurred with John the Baptizer would not happen again. After all, Herod had lost much sleep over it. But if this stubborn people could blindly follow such a wild man, then what might they do if they chose a revolutionary such as Yeshua ben Joseph to be their leader?

Annas and the other priests had heard the Zealots were saying this carpenter's son was the prophesied Messiah and the rightful heir to the throne of David. It would be better for all concerned, they reasoned, to do away with this impotent wine-bibber. This ridiculous imposter, who broke the Sabbath, railed against the priests who upheld the Law and the Prophets, and kept company with prostitutes, tax brokers, Gentiles, and the unclean! Never mind that he worked miracles. Any magician in hire to Beelzebub could do likewise. How could any one believe him to be the promised Messiah? So they argued among themselves.

Now, Joseph of Arimathea was present during all the pressing of charges and proposals for dealing with his nephew. Some knew Joseph was a relative and interrogated him until they were satisfied that he was not biased for or against the seditious troublemaker. If Joseph had not been an adept who knew the Greater Plan, he would have collapsed under the pressure. As it was, it took tremendous diplomacy and self-control to remain neutral. When crucifixion was discussed as the appropriate deterring example, Joseph had to muster all his faith in God. His memory returned to the multidimensional plan that the Councils of Light had shown him when he had teleported into the Great Pyramid where his daughter and nephew were prepared for the very atrocity now about to threaten their lives. Although Joseph shuddered at the thought that something could go wrong, he rallied his resolve to play his integral part as only he could. After all, mortals with free-will could change viewpoints at any moment when they were carrying out even a simple plan. Joseph knew the risks involved in this very complex orchestration.

As you may recall, it was in the Great Pyramid when Yeshua lay in the sepulchre, with Mary Magdalene holding the space that bridged the dimensions, that the hologram for planetary crucifixion/resurrection/ascension was first put into the Earth's crystalline grids. A holographic network was broadcast into the capstone of the Great Pyramid, into Yeshua's and his close disciples' bodies, and then into the Earth's subatomic matrix. Everything was now in place. Like an unfurling tapestry that had been rolled up and put in storage for awhile, so were the long awaited events unfolding very rapidly.

Now, as I relate the last days of that memorable week, I shall tell you, my beloved friend, that your inner Christ is with you. As the energy intensifies and your cellular and soul memory is stirred awake, you are not alone, nor have you ever been. The Christ light within distills a radiance all about you while you pass through yet another doorway to meet your Beloved Self.

Regardless of how your soul has held the Christ energies through many incarnations, know that the Christ is seeded in you, whether you are conscious of this or not. The seal, which has held the Christ energy dormant within, is now opening more fully than ever before. For some, this realization is welcomed, and for others it is feared and resisted. Each receives according to her or his soul's evolutionary design and timing. Judge not, nor be afraid. We will proceed gently and slowly in order that my words may have a place in you. As you choose to receive, so shall it be.

As we continue our story, let us go now to a spacious upper room in Joseph of Arimathea's residence near the Temple, where Yeshua and Mary Magdalene had come to spend their last supper together with their faithful families and companions. It was the evening before what you call Good Friday, the day of Yeshua's crucifixion. Mary Salome had taken residence here years ago, and during the past year, Mary Anna and Ahmed's small family had joined her. There were numerous rooms for the guests Joseph entertained. I had been given a particularly comfortable room, appointed with keepsakes from Britain. Yeshua and Mary Magdalene shared a nearby room with access to the inner courtyard garden.

Knowing that carefully concealed invitations had gone out to many, I had spent the past several days in the ground-floor kitchen, with Mary Anna, Mary Salome, and several assistants, preparing adequate food to feed all seventy or more guests.

The guests arrived discretely at designated hours and passed by Joseph of Arimathea, who stood sentry at the receiving door. I joined the last company of guests who slowly climbed the steep stairway to the upper reception room. Yeshua, Mary Magdalene, and most of Yeshua's intimate disciples had been waiting for several hours. Small grille windows along the stairwell allowed the rays of the setting sun to wash over our ascending bodies. The fragrance of sandalwood, frankincense, and myrrh greeted us from above and mixed with the sweet odours of the kitchen below, where flat bread and fruitcakes had been baked. Some, who had taken care of last minute preparations in the kitchen, carried a basket of bread or a platter of fruit and cheeses, while others carried jugs of water and new wine.

A long, low table was placed in the centre of the room, surrounded by reclining benches, as was the fashion of that day. Large hand-worked pillows, oriental rugs, and ornately carved hardwood chairs surrounded the innermost benches, and received the overflow. The high stone walls were covered with rich tapestries and tall grille windows and doors opened westwards to a balcony that overlooked an enclosed courtyard garden. The upper branches of palms, pomegranate, and fig trees silhouetted the sun as it slid behind the opposite dwelling across the courtyard. This adjoining building was Joseph's primary residence when he was in Jerusalem. Golden light and violet shadows bathed each of us as we quietly selected our places.

The men and women were invited to sit together as couples, friends, and equals. Yeshua, who was reclining on one of the low cushioned benches, sat up making room for others. Mary Magdalene comfortably sat beside her husband to his left. John ben Zebedee and Abigail accompanied him at his right side. Yeshua motioned for his mother and me to take a seat opposite him.

The air was filled with expectancy, awe, and great reverence – not a piety borne of tradition and propriety, but a genuine love and gratitude for being together to co-create a holy sanctuary. Soft whispers communicated brief greetings amidst birds' evensong, the rustle of palm fronds in the gathering breeze, and the rising chorus of crickets. Around the room, gentle hands rested easily on one another's knees or arms, or gently massaged tired, tense backs. Swollen red eyes evidenced recent crying as we lovingly gazed upon each other, drinking in the precious moments we now shared together. For some, tears continued to flow through the night, no matter how hard they were pushed away.

A very relaxed Yeshua sat with his arm around his beloved Mary, whom, from time to time, he openly kissed on the mouth. As his softly caressing, yet penetrating eyes rested in turn upon each guest, including his adopted children, Joses, Judas, and Miriam, he smiled his infectious smile, drawing out our most beautiful essence. When his familiar gaze fell upon me, it was as though there was no one else in the room, but the two of us dissolving into one another. Time stood still. Surely, looking into Yeshua's eyes was to feel the very gates of heaven swing wide open, to invite you in for the sweetest, intoxicating refreshment.

As I attempt to recall the events of that evening, it is as though I perceive everything that was said and done from a great distance, my mind too drunk in bliss to remember details. I do remember that after we sang psalms and prayed together Yeshua took a basin of water, removed his outer robe and wrapped a cotton bath sheet around his lower body. As you may recall from my explanation of our ritual washing in my story about Yeshua's baptism, he then stepped into the basin, and proceeded to openly demonstrate the Essene washing ritual.

When finished, he invited every guest to come forward to be cleansed and prepared for the anointing baptism of the Holy Spirit, which was surely to soon come upon us. We knew that this endowment of light bore witness to the truth of one's divinity and opened the windows of heaven to pour down miraculous blessings. Often, when this occurs it feels like every cell of the body, the thoughts of the mind, and the feelings of the heart are quickened by fire. Sometimes there is a sensation of heat, but always there is a great expansion of consciousness.

Yeshua gently poured a handful of water over our heads, and washed our hands and feet, which he dried with the towel that was girded around him. The last to come to Yeshua was Mary Magdalene, whom he lovingly assisted.

After receiving the cleansing ritual, Mary Magdalene removed the white hair band that caught back her thickly curled hair, letting it fall in a mahogany cascade to her waist. She invited Yeshua to sit on a chair in front of her, as she poured fresh water into the basin. Then Mary knelt before Yeshua, washing his feet. Her tears poured profusely from her eyes, spilling into the water basin and pooling on his feet, which she dried with her hair, as was her custom. Then, she gathered his feet into her lap and cleared her throat. Mary's contralto voice rendered Solomon's *Song of Songs* and David's *23rd Psalm* with such piercing love that a chorus of audible sighs rose up out of our collective throat. Even the doves that nested just beyond the balcony awoke and joined in.

When her singing was finished, she drew out one of her precious alabaster jars filled with spikenard salve. Ever so slowly and gently, Mary applied the sacred ointment to Yeshua's feet, palms and wrists, heart and head, paying particular attention to the crucifixion points in his wrists and feet. Then, Yeshua lifted his beloved to her feet, and they both returned to their places at the table. My grandson took a piece of flat bread that had been placed on a stoneware plate in front of him, prayed, and broke it into pieces.

He then explained, 'The hour has come in which all things that have been prophesied shall be fulfilled in me. For this reason I was born into this world. I have come not to condemn the world, but to bring remembrance of eternal life.

'Those with eyes to see and ears to hear, hearken to my words. Remember them well, for they shall comfort you. In this hour that we are met together, the long night that the prophets have foretold begins to descend. In the gathering darkness, there will be many of you who will forget my words and some of you will even deny that you know me. Woeful will be your hearts when you forget these words, for your souls will carry the agonizing remembrance of the appearance of my dying through time. Yet, I also say to you, rejoice, for in a day not far distant, when your soul is come again into the world, you shall remember my words, and be lifted up with all life around you. Therefore, be gentle with yourselves and judge not your limitation, nor your neighbour's.

'Now, it shall be that when the whirlwind comes to blot out the sun, the chaff of your ignorance may be shaken from your eyes. And I say to you that when your eyes are made new in Spirit, then raise them up on High. There, surely shall you see me as I AM, and know that I am in you as you are in me. And as I am one in my Father and

He is one in me, so it is likewise that you are in my Father and He in you. I have taught you to be one with the Father–Mother of the Cosmos, so that you can withstand the approaching storm. So it is that my beloved Mary and I have set an example for you that you love one another, as we, in eternal oneness, love you.

'I will now say to you, how you shall see me will be in accordance with the content of your heart. If your heart is filled with my Father's light and my Mother's holy love, then, so shall you see me also lifted into that same light and love. If your heart is pressed down in the darkness of the fear raging all around you, you shall see this body being broken upon the tree of crucifixion. My earthly body of flesh shall appear to be as this bread that lies broken upon this plate.

'Therefore, eat of this bread in remembrance of me and my words, so that you may be filled with that light and life that is eternal.

'Now, I pour out this new wine as an emblem of my Heavenly Parents' 'Covenant of Peace' that has been made new in me. This I do that the vessel of your body and the wine of your blood may become light, white as new fallen snow, through the awakening of your inner Christ who lies asleep within the tomb of ignorance. So, raise this communal cup of the Christ, who dwells in all, to your lips; drink, and remember this New Covenant. Partake of this light as if it were leaven raising the bread that is your body to rise up as a Christ. This same light that lifts you into the bosom of my Father–Mother gives eternal life to all the worlds and radiance to the heavens.

'Even as I raise the Temple of my body in three days hence, so may you witness all things unto the world, that what you have seen me do, so may you do likewise. Yea, my beloved children, in the holy name of your mighty I AM, even more than this shall you do.

'My hour comes and I shall leave you for a time. But know this, I shall not leave you comfortless. Were I not to leave you as you presently know me, you would not know the witnessing second comforter I shall send you, who shall bring all things I have spoken to your remembrance. This second comforter will be a baptism of the Holy Spirit as an expression of my Heavenly Mother's grace. My peace I give you. Not as the world gives, give I unto you. Be not troubled, neither be afraid. Know, my friends, I AM with you always. Amen and amen.'

Then, going to a trembling Judas Iscariot, Yeshua embraced him and said, 'Go, my brother, do that thing which now moves upon you.

In paradise I shall await you, that where I am you may come also. Now, go forth into the night, and do not look back.'

As Joseph of Arimathea let Judas out into the night, they shook hands in the handclasp that is understood by initiates. Although the handshake was a sign of fellowship, little comfort could be gained from it. Too much was at stake. A cold, bone-chilling wind blew through the open courtyard doors, banging them against the stone walls, compelling a now very pensive Yeshua to rise and close them. Standing still, gazing upon everyone with tear-filled eyes, my beloved grandson motioned to his close disciples that it was time to take our various stations. Mary Magdalene slipped her hand into his, and led her husband to their room to prepare for the appointed rendezvous in the garden of olive trees called Gethsemane.

Thus I have spoken my remembrance of what has come to be known as the Last Supper. Although the appearance of darkness will now gather thickly around the next words I shall share, let us remain resolved to know the unfailing light that is always present and brings life to all things.

৯

～ *Chapter 39* ～

In Gethsemane

We now return to the closing scenes of the Last Supper, after which we had exchanged our white clothing for street apparel. We secured hooded cloaks around us to provide protection against the night's early spring chill, as well as camouflage from unwanted observation. We exited Mary Salome's warm home located on the lower slopes of Mount Zion, just inside the First Wall. After passing through the shadows of a nearby alleyway we met Yeshua and Mary Magdalene who were awaiting us. Mount Moriah and the Temple complex towered to the east of us. We spoke in hushed whispers, as Yeshua raised his hand and beckoned us to follow.

We comprised a company of forty-eight members – four circles of twelve, plus Yeshua and Mary Magdalene who represented the circumscribing principle of the thirteenth. John ben Zebedee led twenty-four of us by an alternative route through the city to the Fountain Gate. We accompanied Yeshua down narrow, well-worn, cobbled passageways, until we arrived at the Valley Gate sentry point. Peter had gone ahead, paid the necessary bribe for silence, and waited for us in the shadows outside the city walls near the spring called Kidron.

After John ben Zebedee's group arrived at our designated rendezvous point, we ascended the well-worn path that crossed the Kidron Valley and took us up the Mount of Olives' southern slopes. We found cloistered shelter within the Garden of Gethsemane's oldest grove of gnarled olive trees. A cold, desert-borne breeze gently stirred the pungent odour of crushed, dry leaves underfoot. We silently took our places surrounding Yeshua and Mary Magdalene. Mary Anna and Ahmed sat beside me. We softly sang a litany of psalms, intoned Sanskrit mantras and the seventy-two Hebrew names of Father–Mother God, until we rested in a deep abiding calm.

Then Yeshua spoke. 'The hour comes for which we have long prepared. You are the chosen ones that my Father–Mother God has given me to hold the Way of the Teacher of Righteousness secure. While the world sleeps you have chosen to be awake, and so it is that we have come together to prepare all things.

'Even with all your knowing and wisdom, more shall be accomplished these next fifty days than you can presently understand. For, I say to you, my Heavenly Father–Mother has established a New Covenant in me and my beloved Mary, that you now know not of, but soon you shall be our witnesses. I testify that what we do shall be imprinted in you, even as the signs of crucifixion imprint my hands, wrists and feet as a testimonial that the old patterns of atoning for guilt through blood sacrifice are to be done away. So shall it be that every cell of your physical body will likewise be imprinted with the universal codes of light and truth that shall surely set you free.'

In the midst of serenading cricket song, Yeshua paused. Our attention turned to embrace the nocturnal sounds of nature around us. Then he crushed an olive leaf between his fingers, and allowed the gentle breeze to send the fragments aloft. Next, my grandson picked up a nearby clod of earth, which crumbled in his hands and slowly sifted through his fingers. Smiling and acknowledging each disciple, he softly whispered, causing us to draw close to him, 'Yea, even the least of these, which are of the Mother's earthly body, will be likewise imprinted with ascending light. No creature hidden in the deepest place will escape the irresistible pull of our cosmic Mother's love, when She brings all opposites together as divinely harmonious complements in Union. She shall surely bring down the Heavenly Father's cosmic light in order to give this earthly body a new form. We have come together at this time to assist our cosmic Mother and Father to prepare humanity and Earth for ascension's bright day, in a season yet to come.

'All of you, whether physically or in your light body, were with me as I lay in the sepulchre of the Great Pyramid of Egypt. I have taken you aside and have given you additional instruction these past six years. Therefore, understand that what was placed into your conscious and subconscious knowing is now being opened to you. Now you may release the Old Covenant of our matriarchal and patriarchal ancestors who believed that original sin required blood sacrifice to appease an angry, jealous god and to keep the Earth Mother fertile.

'Likewise, it is you who will usher in the New Testament or New Covenant of the ascending and eternally living Christ who proclaims all life as innocent and in eternal union with its Creator. It is that same Christ living within you, who whispers this irrevocable truth to you day by day. Seek and you shall find. Knock and it shall be opened to you. It is you, my beloved companions, as you are and shall be, in a day that you now know not, who shall join with humanity to unite the highest heavenly realms of our Father with this, our beloved Earth Mother, to birth the Universal Christ into your consciousness.

'If you would enter the kingdom of Heaven on Earth, allow the differences that provide contrast to inspire you. Make the two, one, by joining the inner with the outer and the outer with the inner. Allow your feelings of love to flow, giving and receiving as one. So likewise, make the upper like the lower and the lower like the upper, merging the Heavenly Father and Earthly Mother, male and female, light and darkness into a single One. In this way you shall enter the bridal chamber where the Bridegroom claims you as himself. Then you shall surely enter the kingdom.'

Now Yeshua stood in the centre of our intimate circle, lifting Mary Magdalene to stand beside him. With his arm securely around her, he said, 'Mary and I shall now go off a short distance to pray and prepare all things. Remain here, watch, and pray also with all your might, mind, and soul. The time is short that we have together. Soon I shall be taken from you. Let not fear overcome you, but do the part that you have long prepared to do. Though what we shall now pass through is indeed the partaking of the bitter appearance of death, humbly replace that illusion with the true sweetness of your Father–Mother's Will, which is eternal life.

'Remember this' said Yeshua, his lips trembling. 'As the sun is darkened and the Earth Mother quakes, keep your eye single and look into the heaven worlds. There you shall find me and know I have not left you. On the third day, this body shall rise, and you shall see me as I AM. So be it. Amen and Amen.' With these last words of comforting counsel, Yeshua stooped low and tenderly pulled his mother to him, kissing her forehead.

Yeshua motioned to Peter, John, and James ben Zebedee and his brother, James, and a small number of other close disciples, both male and female, to follow him. They could be seen about fifteen feet away sitting huddled in the shadows of ancient olive trees. Yeshua and Mary Magdalene went off a short distance further, sitting face to face, their cloaked forms barely discernable. We followed the example of the others and knelt on the ground, our bodies quaking with an ever-increasing intensity of energy. For some, the energy became so great that we fell prone upon the ground.

Below our bodies we could feel a low, humming vibration within the Earth that seemed to be rising to the surface from her core. As our consciousness expanded into a greater sense of oneness with the more subtle realms of intelligence that are often unacknowledged but nevertheless are always co-creating with humanity, we became aware of web-like patterns of light enveloping us, uniting with our hearts in profound unity and love. I witnessed legions of angels and ascended beings of this and other worlds providing us with their loving support should we choose to receive it. I was also aware of the ethereal city of light that we called the 'New Jerusalem'.

Our consciousness shifted with our deepening breath. A vista opened to us. All the Earth's history rolled past. All the golden ages of splendour, and all the dark ages of ignorance and bloodshed, seductively beckoned us to partake and to be distracted. With disciplined determination, we held our focus, each according to his or her capacity. As the amplitude of the energy increased, Mary Anna and I stood and went occasionally to our neighbouring companions, to place a gentle, reassuring hand on trembling shoulders, backs, or chests. One time I saw Mary Magdalene also administering to the bodies of those disciples who were now lying near her. Although their bodies had entered into a deep sleep, their minds were very lucid and awake. Then she returned to silently sit in front of her beloved Yeshua.

So we passed the next few hours, although it seemed an eternity. The energies were so intense that it literally felt as though the imploding energies of the Earth were sucking us down into her belly to be crushed. The upward attraction of the expanding ethereal realms of light which represented a refuge to escape physicality's increasing density, was so strong that it felt as if we were being torn apart. So it was that the immense push and pull of opposites were felt through our entire bodies. Although I experienced the intensity greatly, it is clear that Yeshua and Mary Magdalene felt the energies beyond my ability to understand at that time.

I will now say this, that when they returned to tell us to arise and prepare to leave, there was an extraordinary glow radiating from their eyes and bodies. And, upon closer scrutiny, tiny rivulets of blood-flecked sweat, where small capillaries close to the skin had ruptured, could be seen on their faces. Small red stains had also soaked into their damp clinging robes. So it is that you can begin to imagine the intensity of their internal experience of bringing the most extreme of opposing and attracting polarities into Union.

We then created several concentric circles, the men surrounding the women, and invoked our Father–Mother God and our ethereal companions to continue to support us. As we were finishing our last psalm, dogs began barking in the makeshift itinerants' camp below us. While the darkness began to fade in the east, we quickly embraced one another and then stood still, awaiting Judas Iscariot and the torch bearing soldiers, priests, and aroused curiosity seekers.

When the surly mob stopped within ten feet of us, Judas nervously came forward. With bowed head, he approached my grandson with an embrace and a kiss on each cheek, thus signifying that this was the one whom they sought. Then Yeshua stepped forward and asked, 'Whom do you seek?' The Temple high priest, Annas, had sent his chief steward to bring Yeshua to him for questioning. Annas' liaison, alarmed by the power of my grandson's words, fell back, but then recovered his composure and queried, 'It is said that you are called Yeshua ben Joseph of Nazareth. Are you he?' And Yeshua responded, 'I am he. And I say to you, if it is I whom you seek, then let these others go their way.'

The steward, after clearing his throat and motioning to his guard to take Yeshua into custody, said, 'Annas, who is the father-in-law of Caiaphas, the high priest of Jerusalem, has sent me to bring you before the elders for questioning.' Then, as the guard reached to take my grandson's arm, Peter reactively drew his dagger and cut the servant's right ear. Whereupon, Yeshua rebuked him. 'You have not understood, Peter. Return your blade to its sheath. I go willingly so that I may fulfil my Father's Will and receive the Greater Part.' Then he placed his hand on the side of the wounded guard's head, causing the bleeding to stop. As if startled out of a trance, the guard realized what had happened and roughly manacled Yeshua's wrists pushing him forward into the throng of soldiers.

Shocked to our core, we realized that the terrifying drama had begun. What remained for us now was to stay together and play our respective supportive roles as masterfully as possible.

So it is that I have further expanded upon the biblical account. I will also do this with Yeshua's crucifixion and resurrection, in the hope that an increased empowerment may occur as you pass through your Christ initiations. Yeshua and Mary Magdalene, in concert with the assistance of vast cosmic and planetary levels of consciousness, co-created a seeding for global ascension, which is coming into its full realization during your new millennium. They did not experience this assistance as coming from a rescuing agent outside themselves, taking their power away. Their consciousness was in unity with the cosmic realms. In this way, the assistance they received was experienced as their cosmic presence facilitating ascension through the physical aspects they represented. When you know this kind of co-creative unity, your initiations will be like doors opening to greater and greater opportunities for self-mastery and service to life.

✎ Chapter 40 ✎
The Secrets of Calvary

After Yeshua was taken from the garden, Simon Peter and John ben Zebedee followed immediately behind the guards. Judas Iscariot walked with Annas' steward and entered into Caiaphas' palace. Mary Magdalene was joined by a small number of the other male and female disciples on the steps outside the door. The remainder of us continued past and made our way to our various assigned stations both in and outside the walled city.

It was my lot to remain with Mary Anna and several of the women, until we were given further notice. One of Joseph of Arimathea's assistants had escorted us to another of his residences located northwest of the Bethesda pools. This small home was inconspicuous and few knew of it. We were brought here because it was relatively close to Joseph's expansive garden beyond the outermost wall. We knew he had ordered a large tomb to be excavated into the steep hillside that was not tillable for gardening. This would be the sepulchre site for the resurrection process.

Although I was not present to witness the interrogations of Herod, the high priests, or Pontius Pilate, I viewed and felt with my inner vision and empathetic heart the harshness and brutality of the flogging that tore my grandson's flesh. I could not help flinching occasionally when his back and legs were severely struck, even though I knew he could withstand it by transmuting his physical sensations through mastered spiritual practices.

Yeshua understood the higher initiatory meaning of the crown of thorns and the purple robe as representations of the spiritual sovereignty that was his rightful inheritance. He was not in any way humiliated, as his persecutors intended, when the crown and robe were derisively placed upon him. The debacle of mockery in the hall of judgement did not move Yeshua from his calm centre, but its sadistic effect certainly incited further mob hysteria in the growing crowd that began to take up the priests' wanton cry, 'Crucify him! Crucify him!'

Benjamin suddenly came to us with the news that Yeshua was being taken to Golgotha, or the Place of the Skull, which was one of several places outside the city walls where capital punishment was executed. Golgotha happened to be close to Joseph's garden with its recently excavated hillside tomb. We began to hear dreadful screaming, the pounding of drums, and the sharp repetitive sound of horses' shod feet

My task was to remain calm and centred. But how, as I acknowledged the vibration of fear knotting my stomach? I breathed deeply, grounded my body into the present, and prayed, 'O, my Father God, do not forsake me, for I know it is you expressing in me who shall do this thing required in this darkest of hours. Holy Mother in your mercy, transmute the hatred and suffering in the hearts of these, your children, who know not what they do. O, blessed Mother, Mother of all things, hold me steadfast in your compassionate heart, which is a clear fountain of forgiving love. May my heart, that has been broken open through my life's tribulations, love today as I have never loved before.' Then, remembering my beloved grandson's words whenever he calmed the raging elements, I stood tall and decreed, 'Peace. Be still, and know I AM God.'

Beside me, Mary Anna quaked, her face ashen. Then, she stood erect, resolutely smoothed her skirts, and pulled her stooped shoulders back. Her jaw was set, her lips skewed tight, as they used to be when a storm of anger moved through her little body as a child. She came to me and squeezed my hands, holding them to her heart. We looked deeply into each other's eyes, and dived into the bottomless well of the Divine Mother's love. Breathing together, we did not move until we firmly anchored ourselves within the core of our God presence. Although at first it felt as though our hearts would break at any moment, we were comforted by the grace of angels. Even though our feet felt riveted to the stone floor, our souls soared heavenwards. Uplifted, a peaceful calm came over us. As clarity came, Benjamin carefully escorted us out into the thronged street.

Joseph knew the Sanhedrin would most likely summon him, so immediately after Yeshua's arrest, he personally escorted Mariam and Nathaniel, Andrew, Luke, and their wives directly to the site of his garden tomb. Then, he went directly to the house of a confidante who was also an adjunctive member of the Sanhedrin. Together, they quickly joined with other council members and went to Caiaphas' palace in order to witness the interrogations.

The disciples who took their assigned positions inside the garden tomb assisted holding a powerful energy matrix from this strategic point. Although they were not physically present, they were well aware of the brutal scenes raging behind stone walls and on Golgotha's barren hill, as they waited to assist Yeshua's resurrection process within the sanctuary cave.

Mary Magdalene and other key disciples followed Yeshua to his various trials, and awaited him as he emerged from the hall of judgement. Mary walked behind her beloved as he slowly made his way towards Calvary. A crossbeam, the horizontal member of the cross, was tied to his lacerated back. Frenzied bystanders were swept up into the press of the crowd that pushed a stumbling Yeshua forwards. As he bore his heavy burden, they continued to scream hysterically, 'Crucify him! Crucify him! Yeshua ben Joseph, King of the Jews!'

The crazed mob mocked and spat upon Mary Magdalene, calling her a whore of the devil, demanding that she be stoned. Then, when Yeshua fell again, and could not be roused by the soldiers' whips, Simon, a Cyrenian, was commanded to come out of the crowd to bear the crossbeam that was untied and lifted to his shoulders. Simon, who had not known Yeshua before, carried the heavy slab of rough-planed wood the remainder of the weary way. Little did he know how this experience would change his life for ever.

By the time the small group of family members, including Mary Anna and me, arrived near the Damascus Gate, two other men had passed through carrying cross beams. They were being made to lie on the vertical beams that had not yet been hoisted to their upright position on Golgotha's highest prominence. Others of the disciples joined the two being crucified on the wind blasted knoll. Their places of crucifixion were on either side of Yeshua's. We awaited Yeshua inside the gate, and fell in behind him as he slowly passed through following a faltering and sometimes cursing Simon, who did not fully understand what he was being forced to do.

Time seemed to stand still as we watched Yeshua's body being crucified on the assembled cross. Then the vertical beam was hoisted and dropped into place. The wind suddenly whipped into a gale. Within a short time, sandstorms darkened the horizon and whirlwinds swirled around us, pelting our faces with unleashed fury. Ominous clouds darkened the sun, piercing the sky with bolts of lightning. Incessant rolls of thunder deafened our ears. The moon slowly slipped between the earth and sun eclipsing the sun's light. I remembered Yeshua's words, 'When the whirlwind comes and the sun is darkened, look up into the heaven worlds; there, you shall find me.'

I remembered Yeshua's words spoken as he broke bread at his 'last' supper, '... how you shall see me will be in accordance with the content of your heart. If your heart is filled with my Father's light and my Mother's holy love, then, so shall you see me also lifted into that same light and love. If your heart is pressed down in the darkness of the fear raging all around you, you shall see this body being broken upon the tree of crucifixion. My earthly body of flesh shall appear as this bread that lies broken upon this plate.'

I also remembered my promise to hold the way secure for those who would now publicly demonstrate the mystery school crucifixion initiation in an extremely violent and literal way. So it was that I continued to gird myself in the truth that 'All Is Well,' although the chaos around me told my physical senses and emotional body that I was deluding myself. Still I was determined to focus my attention on the greater reality held in the unity consciousness of the higher dimensions. I breathed – not as a third-dimensional mortal unconsciously breathes, but as an immortal adept consciously breathes prana/life force – through my central channel. Thus, my perception of time and space shifted. I knew my connection with my God Source. My inner vision opened and I witnessed Yeshua's consciousness separated from his physical body. He was completely unified with his immortal body of golden light, which he called Abba.

In his light body, he assisted the two men hanging beside him to journey into the underworld and paradisiacal realms. I saw that Mary Magdalene had bilocated her consciousness, and had joined her beloved in this mighty uplifting work that was being simultaneously imprinted into the Earth and into the atoms of every living thing.

What was required of me became increasingly clear. Although I was confronted by unbelievable atrocity, I was resolved to know the truth and to see beyond the illusion. In the midst of rolling

thunder and the hysterical crowd's bloodthirsty screams, I heard a
still voice speaking to my heart: 'It is finished! There is no death!
Release all fear!' On the inner planes I telepathically heard my
grandson proclaim, 'Awake and arise! Come forth all nations and
lay aside your weapons of war that plunder and divide. Claim your
inheritance freely given. Eternal life reigns within the kingdom of
each atom. Let go your fearful grasping. Be Love! Be peace! Amen
and Amen! And so it is!'

As our consciousness connected, I could feel that my grandson
registered no pain as his vital signs completely ceased. Yeshua was
not poisoned as some have postulated, but fully utilized the mastery
he had gained from many years of initiation and practice. I saw
that his silver cord connecting his physical body and soul were still
attached, even though he appeared dead to the uninitiated eyes of
the gross physical dimension.

I struggled with every fibre of my being to remain conscious and
connected to my Creator Source and Yeshua's consciousness which
was completely merged with his highest light body – the Sahu. The
primal emotions of terror, rage, and grief buffeted me from every
direction. I cried out, 'Oh, my God help me to love and forgive.
Surely these people know not what they are doing. Bear me up and
open my eyes to see the truth that sets all of life free of suffering!'

As it drew toward sundown and Passover was about to begin,
Joseph of Arimathea had gained permission to remove Yeshua's body
from the cross, so that he could be given 'burial' before the Jewish
Sabbath. The raging storm and earthquake tremors continued
to darken the sun although the solar eclipse had passed. The few
soldiers that stayed through the ordeal and the last obstinate,
entranced onlookers slowly turned away, leaving us alone with the
remaining disciples who wrapped Yeshua's unconscious body in
blankets. Then he was gently placed in a horse drawn wagon and we
carefully made our way to Joseph's nearby tomb.

So it was that Yeshua had allowed his separated self to 'die', as
he completely stilled his vital signs and placed his full attention
on his Mother–Father God, with whom he had fully merged in
consciousness. As I tell you this, my beloved friend, remember
that it was not the Christ who 'died' but the personality's illusion of
separation. It was through Yeshua's experience of his crucifixion that
his union with God as a living Christ was realized.

When you know that Yeshua did not suffer for your perceived separation from love, you can also release your need and attachment to suffering in your human life. With love, all things are possible. With mindfulness, discipline, and devotion you may come to realize that your Creator and your Christ presence are not outside of you, but dwell eternally inside your consciousness. As you experience this self-empowering and saving truth, any need for an external saviour lessens its hold in your mind. When it is time to pass into a greater knowing of God union, as it was with Yeshua, you will also have all the support you require. Accept that you are the beloved of God throughout eternity! You only have to release the past misperception that you are a body that dies to claim the truth that Yeshua did not die, nor will you.

As in the example of the theatre, in order to attain the realizations of a Christ, it is helpful to practise viewing your human challenges from a higher perspective. Now, breathe with me, and heal the anguishing misperceptions that have burdened your soul for centuries, even eons. Raise your awareness to another level, and view Calvary with new eyes. Forgive yourself, and the God within, of all outer appearances of suffering and damnation, powerlessness and betrayal, punishment and martyrdom, and human victim/tyrant dramas.

Breathe slowly. Relax... Relax... Relax....

Your soul has a permanent passport to eternity. Knowing you cannot go back to the limited self you once were, you are able to welcome the chaos of great planetary change that is occurring all around and within you. With confidence and ease, you can allow the birth of your ascending Christ consciousness that has been lying hidden and sleeping in your heart's womb/tomb.

The caterpillar cannot become the butterfly without its crucifixion initiation that brings about its liberating transformation. As the butterfly's chrysalis is its birthing chamber, so is the chrysalis also the caterpillar's tomb. And so it is that we proceed now with Yeshua into his chrysalis womb of resurrection.

༄

∾ Chapter 41 ∾

Raising the Immortal Christ Body

Yes, my dear friend, let us enter into the Rite of the Sepulchre and join with all the disciples who were gathered in Joseph of Arimathea's tomb on the night that you call Good Friday.

The storm continued to rage. Once the great round stone had been rolled into place, covering the low door, the screaming wind and violent thunder outside were barely discernible to our ears. Now that we were safely cloistered inside the spacious tomb we moved swiftly, without hesitation, into our next phase of the Great Work.

Luke, my son who was still a practising physician, had ordered ample linens, herbs, essential oils, salves and ointments, water, lamps and all the necessary medical tools for this high occasion. He had placed everything in his half-brother Joseph's tomb the day before. Those of us who had experience with embalming the dead and/or the ritual of the Rite of the Sepulchre took the initiative in leading the others who were less informed. These disciples became our willing assistants.

As I looked upon Yeshua's scourged body lying in front of me, memories returned of his blemish-free, twelve-year-old form lying in the sepulchre in the cave of initiation at Mount Carmel. Seeing into the future, there had been a part of me in those days that wished the bitter cup would not be drunk. Since then he had passed through twenty-one years of tasting, transmuting, and resurrecting his consciousness from the 'death-state'.

Yeshua's vital signs, which had completely ceased earlier, were now barely discernible as he lay in a very deep 'sleep' or state of samadhi. I could not help my tears that fell as I carefully washed my grandson's body. Kneeling beside him, Mary Anna, Mary Magdalene and I carefully removed fragments of lead and horsehair that had embedded into Yeshua's back and legs from the flailing whips. We also took out gravel, dung, and blackened pitch from the many wounds that covered his body. Next, we washed, purified, and applied healing ointments, compresses, and essential oils.

Seeing that we were ready for his assistance, Luke helped us to wrap the linen shroud that was saturated with regenerating herbal oils, much as Egyptian mummies are initially wrapped. Most of the head was covered, and then a cloth napkin was placed over the face. As I have shared before, the fluttering of the napkin served to alert the attending high priest or priestess attending the Rite of the Sepulchre that the body of the initiate was returning to animation. When they noticed this subtle movement, it was known with certainty that the animating consciousness of the soul was returning into the physical plane and the time for removing the shroud was close at hand.

So it was that after Yeshua's body had been cleansed, purified, anointed, and shrouded, we took our various positions around him within the tomb. Joseph of Arimathea began a deep, droning chant and those of us particularly skilled with sound vibration joined in. Others used percussion, string, and wind instruments. All of us moved our bodies, some very actively, others gesturing only with hands, nodding heads, or swaying backs. Sweet incense burned in censers. Most of the oil lamps had been put out, with only two remaining lit.

We invoked the presence of our Creator. We called in the healing angels, gods, goddesses, and the Councils of Light of this planet and beyond. We intoned hymns to the Great Mother, particularly Isis, because what we now were doing was being done in the same manner as her rite is performed in Egypt during the resurrection enactment of her beloved Osiris' resurrection.

In this way, we cultivated the highest and most coherent energies of healing through our hearts and voices. We circulated these energetic flows through our bodies, and wove patterns of light with Yeshua's consciousness. I was aware of Yeshua's consciousness, as he journeyed through the underworld realms of Amenti. The masters who dwell near its sun met and escorted him into many realms. I saw him journey into the astral planes where souls create their hells as a continuation of the tormented lives they had lived. I saw that Yeshua assisted their consciousness to let go of ignorant attitudes and limiting beliefs and move towards greater light. In the underworld, my grandson assigned more evolved teachers and way-showers who, rather than moving on into more harmonious realms, had chosen for a time to remain in order to assist consciousness to cease suffering, rise, and ascend with them.

I saw that Mary Magdalene's consciousness was present in all these journeys, and that this twin-flame couple was participating with the highest Councils of Light in matters that I barely comprehended. I sensed that they were being prepared for much more than a planetary assignment, but my consciousness at that time had not expanded enough to know what it was.

Once we began to sense that Yeshua's energies had stabilized, most of us chose to withdraw from the tomb in order to rest. Toward sunset of the second day, Joseph of Arimathea, after scanning the surrounding area with inner vision to make certain that no one was present, rolled back the heavy tombstone, with the use of sound as a levitation device. Those of us who knew our service was no longer required in the tomb went to Joseph's home in Bethesda to refresh ourselves. Joseph, Mary Magdalene, Mary Anna, Sara, and Mariam stayed on in the tomb.

Yeshua was very familiar with the incredibly powerful flows of resurrecting energy that transforms on all levels. Now, his more enlightened consciousness began to enter back into his physical body, through the crown into the central channel or pranic tube. With his vital signs returned, the process of raising the immortal Christ body of light (what the Egyptians called Raising the Djed Rod or Osiris' spine) began. As the energy increased, light began to be emitted. My grandson's body became highly radioactive, sending out subatomic, pulsing vibrations. These high vibrations penetrated the acoustic chambers of the tomb and expanded through the planetary crystalline grids. There was a cosmic alignment that facilitated a new matrix of ascension codes to be imprinted throughout the Earth Mother's body and atmosphere.

Once the resurrecting energies were raised in the physical body, it was necessary to allow it to rest for a time before we removed the linen shrouds. When we were prompted, we removed the highly charged linens, after which we washed, purified, and anointed Yeshua's body with sweet smelling oils and healing ointments. We placed a new robe on his body and allowed him to continue to rest in the silence.

Knowing that there was no further need for our attendance we departed before sunrise, leaving Yeshua lying on the altar with the large round stone covering the door. We welcomed rest and refreshment. After several hours of sleep, Mary Magdalene left her father's house just after sunrise and returned to the tomb. She was startled to find the stone rolled back, and when she stooped to enter in, was even more surprised to find that Yeshua was gone! Sitting calmly at the head and foot of the altar were two angelic beings of radiant countenance. Yeshua's shroud and face napkins were neatly folded on the altar by one of them.

They smiled, recognizing a weeping Mary Magdalene as fulfilling her Egyptian role as Isis when she wept because her beloved Osiris had been taken away. They rhetorically asked, 'Woman, why do you weep?' Whereupon she replied, 'I am looking for my beloved Master who was here and is now gone.' And then, when she turned back and stepped into the garden, still looking into the tomb, she again heard, 'Woman, why do you weep? Whom do you seek?' The words came from the mouth of a man whom she assumed was the gardener, because his energy felt different from Yeshua's. Again, she asked after the one who had been taken away, and she heard Yeshua say, 'Mary!' Then, she turned and recognized her beloved, although his form had changed somewhat. Now his body appeared to be much more translucent and luminous.

As she ran to embrace him, Yeshua raised his hand and said, 'Not yet, my beloved Mary, for I have not stabilized the ascending frequencies of my body. I will be with you in this resurrected form for an indefinite period of time. There are yet many more levels of ascension through which I will pass. Much of this time you will meet with me in the heavenly realms.

'You, who represent our Great Mother, still have an important work to do here on the earthplane. Together, we shall prepare humanity to enter into and realize the Way of the Christ. Although we will be together in our merged consciousness, you will be more focused on this side of the veil and I on the other, just as we have done so many times on other worlds. Let us be thankful that we have been given these years to walk together in these wonderful bodies of flesh and bone.

'You are my beloved disciple and into yours and John's care I give my blessed and beautiful mother. Go now and tell my mother and the others all that you have seen and heard.' Then, with great love, he smiled and gently passed by her, their fingertips almost touching.

These were the words I, Anna, heard from Mary Magdalene when she returned to tell us the glad news of Yeshua's full resurrection.

As I have shared with you, Yeshua and his companions demonstrated the Great Work of resurrecting the soul's consciousness into greater awareness of divine love and eternal life. And, in this instance, Yeshua's physical body was resurrected and lifted into a higher vibration that was preparing it for ascension.

You, too, may have experiences of resurrection in which you consciously bring more light and higher frequencies into your body. Then, your body's innate capacity to heal and regenerate through physical immortality can be realized, so that you can have more time to serve life and increase your self-mastery. You may also choose to consciously strengthen your connection with your immortal light bodies, and take your memories and self-awareness with you as you leave your physical vehicle's elements to return to the Earth.

Once the process of crucifixion and resurrection begins, enlightened consciousness is realized step by step as it ascends. This is often accompanied with a greater awareness of thoughts and behaviours that have not yet aligned with love. Having an increased capacity for compassionate love, you may embrace and bring these aspects of consciousness into union with their Creator. With the enlightenment of consciousness comes greater insight and opportunities to experience simultaneous realities and dimensions. This is the ultimate experience of freedom and union in the eternal NOW!

❧ Chapter 42 ❧

The Baptism of the Holy Spirit

My dear friend, as our time together draws to a close, your life awaits you to do with it what you will. This time is not unlike mine 2,000 years ago, a time both terrifying and magnificent. I have invited you to walk with me, in the hope that my experience might assist you in some way to fulfil a destiny that is entwined with that of the Earth Mother and all that she supports. Being with me has likely taken you across a threshold of no return. As we linger together, let us choose to view the future with an even vaster horizon, as we review the past. And, in so doing, may the eternal now moment be blessed.

Because you may be wondering what life was like after Yeshua's resurrection, I will now share my remembrance of the remaining years that I lived in Palestine before my departure to France and Britain. I felt as though I stood on a high precipice scanning an unknown that stretched far ahead of me. All that I had been through these many years, seemed to be pressed and distilled into a pearl of great price. Standing poised on the edge, it felt like the time of winter when life turns inwards, rests, and awaits the thrust of spring's new growth. So I abided on the precipice for a time, until I received a clear impulse from within that assured me that it was time to take flight and create a new life.

For Yeshua's support team of family and friends, it was a very introverted time, a time for assessing, tending, and nurturing the sleeping seeds we had sown over the previous years' active service. For quite a period after Calvary, hearts continued to be troubled, minds oppressed, and bodies tortured. During the fifty days immediately following Yeshua's crucifixion and resurrection, the sun remained darkened for weeks because of the wind-borne ash that had erupted from distant volcanoes. The ground below us still trembled with aftershocks. And for the most part, Yeshua's inner circle of disciples had gone underground. Few who were not a part of the original small group of disciples ever saw Yeshua in Palestine after his resurrection.

Persecution continued to ferret out those followers whose lives had reached out, touched, and had been healed within the auric hem of the Christ mantle that my grandson had worn during the year and a half before the crucifixion–resurrection experience. Trying on the mantle of the Christ, in order to follow Yeshua's example, was not easy. For those whose spirits were willing, but who found their flesh unprepared for the increased responsibilities and the unavoidable tests of empowerment that came, there was a scattering to the winds.

For those of us who had known Yeshua behind cloistered Essene community walls, had journeyed with him to near and distant lands to participate in initiatory preparation, and who in some way carried the same family lineage, it was a time of intense purification and reassessment. It was a time of secret council meetings where there was heated debate, attempted resolution, and deep soul-searching in which we prayed to know our next steps. It was a time of dissolution and a time of reorganization. And most of all, it was a time to go inward and integrate all that had happened. This was the only way to know any form of peace or to gain any hope of clarity, as the outer world fomented chaos.

It was agreed among the intimate disciples who had walked with Yeshua that we would commit what we had heard and seen to memory, in much the same way as master storytellers pass on oral traditions from generation to generation. It was also agreed that much of what we had witnessed would be inscribed in a cryptic fashion on scrolls. These writings would be sealed up and hidden away with earlier texts, and most would be carried abroad to many lands east and west. So it was that, as we were scattered, we also took with us the oral stories and the written word, which we shared with those willing to hear and to allow their lives to be transformed. It was known that this would be an ongoing project for the remainder of our lives.

Shortly following the crucifixion and during the following fifty days, Yeshua was often with us. These were usually unexpected encounters that occurred in extraordinary ways. Sometimes he simply appeared in the room in which we were gathered for meals or for a meeting. There were times that we saw him walking on water beside our boat, whereupon, after greeting us, he would then levitate and join us in the boat. One time he walked through the stone walls of an underground cavern where we were gathered avoiding a potential arrest. Often when we were traveling incognito on the dangerous roads of Judea and Galilee, he would appear as a beckoning stranger resting beside the road, or would simply fall in with us as we walked. On the occasions when he joined us during meals, he would also partake and grandly enjoy whatever was served.

Except for those meetings that occurred on the roadways in which he wore the dark, sombre apparel of the natives, Yeshua always wore white. There was an unearthly glow that radiated from his flesh and robes, and, when he walked, it was as though his feet skimmed the ground. His appearance was of translucent light. To be touched by him was electrifying and rarely experienced by those who came into his countenance. Yet, when we were sufficiently prepared, Yeshua would come to us individually, take a hand and tenderly kiss it, or he would cup our face in his hands, and continue to look into our eyes until every tension drained away.

We greatly missed Yeshua's presence when he was not with us. How joyful we were when he did unexpectedly appear! We delighted to hear his stories about being in the heavens aboard benevolent lightcraft and visiting all the Earth's continents and islands of the sea. He sadly told us about the many volcanoes that had erupted, the earthquakes that had lifted and sunk landmasses, and about tidal waves that had swept cities out to sea during the three days of his crucifixion and resurrection.

The people who had been the most affected by these earth changes were, for the most part, humbled and ready to receive Yeshua's healing energy and comforting words. It felt good to connect with humanity all around the Earth. Many of us who knew how to bilocate our bodies joined him, and delighted in establishing ties with our brothers and sisters with whom we continued a conscious connection through our prayers and meditations.

It was at such a time, when we were gathered together seeking solace and deep healing, that we were taken by surprise by an energy field unlike any we had known before. It was not that this energy was unfamiliar. It entered into everyone present to such a degree that our minds were completely silenced. Our hearts were ignited as one collective bonfire and our physical and spiritual eyes were opened to the heavenly realms. Mary Anna was particularly lifted up, and upon her return to normal consciousness, she told us that we were invited to gather together so that we could receive the New Covenant of Love from the Great Mother presence of the Godhead.

So it is that I will now share with you about the descent of the Holy Shekinah, or the Holy Spirit of Promise, as some call this energy field, and how the Great Mother's mantle of flaming light enveloped us in a baptism of spiritual fire. Yeshua had told us that she would come as our second comforter, witnessing in our hearts everything that was required to be known and remembered, so that we could also accomplish our own Christing. As I tell you this, my friend, I remember well his saying, 'All that you see me do, so also shall you do, and even more shall you do.'

After a week of fasting in complete solitude and silence, Mary Anna called a special meeting of the disciples who were scattered about Palestine to come quietly to Qumran. Trusted messengers sent out the word, and a rather large group of us came together in the night. Several of us who had been visiting Qumran at the time made preparations and kept vigils over the tired pilgrims while they slept before the ceremony began. Just before dawn, a sound as of rushing waters began to be heard and felt. Everyone arose from their makeshift beds and followed Mary Anna and Mary Magdalene in a procession to the ancient grotto in a large cave that had served the Divine Mother for millennia.

Although the cave had been desecrated by profane worship over the eons, it was still imbued with the energies of the Great Mother. Because of the male Qumran leaders' increasing patriarchal bias, the main entrance had been closed for many years. Thus, very few knew of the secret entrance that still gave access to those who chose to continue to enact the Great Mother's rituals. Most of these spiritual ceremonies were associated with the ancient Sumerian goddess Ishtar/Inanna and the esoteric practices of the Magdalene, which is an Order of Isis. Because of our association with Yeshua, the leaders of Qumran opened the main entrance to us on this occasion.

Mary Anna had done most of her fasting and prayer in the grotto. She had cleaned the ancient altar and placed a few flowers, herbs, and incense on it, along with a basin of water containing precious oils. After we had taken our seats inside, we sang psalms and ancient chants to the Divine Mother of all things. After a lengthy time of silence, Mary Anna went to the altar, anointed herself, and then invited each of us to come forth.

One by one, we knelt before her. She crushed flower petals and herbs in her small hands, scattering them over our heads and shoulders, and then she burned the remainder in the flame of a brazier on the altar. After we parted our outer garments to expose our hearts, Mary Anna then dipped a small gauze cloth into the perfumed water that had been poured into the simple Celtic cup used by Yeshua at his last supper. She gently washed our faces, hands, and chest. Her right hand lingered over every heart, until a warm glow could be felt. She kissed teary cheeks, solemnly gazing into each wet eye. Before she turned to the next supplicant, Mary Anna selected a long strip of cloth from a bundled sheaf. She then placed a cloth, as if it were a scarf, around each one's neck. These torn strips were from the cloth that had been Yeshua's robes. It was not for the sake of worshipping Yeshua that his mother performed this ritual. The cloth was a token of love and our willingness to accept our eternal union with God, even as her risen son exemplified.

Then, Mary Anna quoted one of Yeshua's sayings, which was told when Thomas, who had not been in the tomb during the resurrection process, asked that he also see and know that the one who appeared before him was indeed of flesh and bone. Although visible as before, Yeshua's body was now much more refined and translucent. He said to Thomas, 'Look, see and feel for yourself, that it is I, your brother, and that I have come to fulfil all things that my Father–Mother God has given me to do. I have set an example, so that you may know how to worship the One God who breathes life in All. Make of your body also an emblem of light and an instrument of peace so that all in the world may have light and life more abundantly.' So did Mary Anna assist us to remember the purpose for the trials that we were continuing to pass through.

When everyone had taken their turn, we came together to sit in concentric circles, the men surrounding the women. The children were seated in the centre, except for the small babes who suckled at their mother's breasts. We sang several hymns, and then an awesome silence came over us. Some bowed low to the ground, others raised their heads skywards, eyes rolled back. Many spoke the 'Languages of Light'. Some began to rise up, levitating towards the ceiling of the great cavern. Again, there was the inner sound of the rushing of waters, and then it was as though the stone ceiling above our heads opened.

Everyone had their own vision and experience of the Holy Shekinah's many gifts, not the least of which was the unmistakable presence of the Mother of All Life. Regardless of her many names, the Holy Spirit came, according to each one's belief. She was felt within every heart and body, according to each one's capacity to hold her mighty presence, which was like being consumed in flames of light. Then, when that capacity was reached, each was stretched and stretched, until all in equal measure received the gifts of Spirit their soul had long awaited since beginning to incarnate in flesh.

The feminine creative aspect of the Godhead came down and alighted upon each of us with the softness of a white dove. Her embrace was both incredibly sweet and terrible. Sweet, because her Divine Love is the milk of eternal life. Her countenance was only 'dark and terrible' to those who chose to resist her embrace. For it is that when her intoxicating nectars are drunk, everything dissolves into formless being. In the moment of her coming, we became one with the Birther of All Life. We became one with God, the Mother-Father! In those precious hours, we knew only the One.

It was that fiery, consuming anointing of Holy Spirit that sustained us throughout our remaining days! Regardless of our outer circumstances on the earthplane, whether we witnessed joy or suffering, the Holy Spirit, like a dove of eternal peace, carried us into our destiny, each in our own way.

ᴖ Chapter 43 ᴖ

The Passage of the Holy Grail

Come, my beloved friend, it is time to share our departure from Palestine. Although Yeshua visited us from time to time in his resurrected body, most of our ongoing experiences with him were occurring on the higher dimensions.

Our lives passed through much tribulation over the following years after Yeshua's resurrection. Mary Anna's husband, Ahmed, died during the winter of congestive heart failure. My great grandson, Benjamin, was later stoned to death by an angry mob, as was Stephen. Joseph of Arimathea had been expelled from the Sanhedrin, and even imprisoned for a short time under false charges. Soon after Joseph's release from prison, he took Mary Magdalene and her children to a monastic community south of Alexandria to keep them from harm's way. None of us escaped being deeply touched by the blind hatred that opposed us from every side.

Saul of Tarsus and others sought to imprison us with an unexplainable compulsive vengeance. It became increasingly difficult to conceal our identities and whereabouts. All of us took aliases and used every possible precaution, including code names, special handshakes, and cryptic messages, in order to secure our lives. So it was that we moved about frequently, spending most of our time in the Essene communities along the Dead Sea south of Qumran or secreted away in Jerusalem. Very rarely in those two years did I return to my beloved Mount Carmel. Most of its monastic inhabitants were evacuated when the Romans began to use its strategic promontory overseeing the Great Sea as a sentry point. Even our simple Essene sanctuary was rededicated to the Roman god, Zeus.

We used the name Damascus as a code name for Qumran. And so it was that when Saul of Tarsus had learned that many of us were staying in Qumran for the winter, he sought to find and kill us. It was when he was on this journey to Qumran (Damascus) that Saul was stopped by Yeshua on the roadside. Saul was taken up into the light and his heart was softened. He returned back to Jerusalem a changed man. The company of soldiers that had gone with him scattered in fear instead of carrying out orders to burn Qumran and imprison Zealot fugitives.

Saul later changed his name to Paul, and began to enlist those disciples who felt a resonance with him and his vision of changing the hearts of humanity to believe in Yeshua ben Joseph, as the only Christ, their personal, mediating saviour. Paul's strong charisma and more easily understood spiritual practices began to win him increasing popularity and support. His cause also attracted a number of the inner circle of disciples who desired to proselytize Yeshua's message by organizing a hierarchical priesthood in order to accomplish this endeavour. Peter was especially aligned with Paul, and consequently, there began to be a division among those of us who had held leadership positions over the previous years.

Often a division comes relatively quickly among the followers of enlightened beings who have had direct revelation of the more subtle spiritual realms. The group with the larger numbers adopts a body of beliefs and practices that are based on interpreting the experiences of a perceived mediating redeemer or prophet (often martyred) who is no longer on the physical plane. With those disciples who followed Paul, authority rested outside – either in Yeshua or in the mediating priesthood organized to proselytize him.

Others of us, including myself, who had come to know through direct experience that all that we sought was already within us, honoured and maintained an inward authority. Though the way was more hidden and not readily apparent to the physical senses, we were willing to pass through the same transformational disciplines and revelatory processes, as did Yeshua whose example catalysed our ongoing Self-realizations.

While the lesser travelled path of the mystic is my preferred choice, I do not invalidate the journey of those pilgrims who have not passed through the internal door of gnosis. It is not a matter of one path being better than the other is. The question becomes: is there a readiness to embrace the same experiences that enlightened Yeshua and his close companions?

Now let us go to the dramatic and dangerous scene of our expulsion from Palestine.

Since our lives were endangered because of our close association with Yeshua and because of our adherence to esoteric practices, we were forced to seek a refuge away from Palestine. Joseph of Arimathea had returned from his journey to Alexandria and Britain, and was alarmed by the increased violence that threatened our lives. Without fully resting or replenishing the supplies and crew that he usually took with him on his voyages, Joseph was ready to depart again within two weeks. Those family members who were choosing to leave Palestine had gathered our few belongings and made our way with Joseph to the port of Joppa. By the close of the second day, we had set sail for Alexandria.

Instead of the usual three or more boats, Joseph only enlisted two of his freighting fleet for our journey. One would primarily hold passengers, and the other carried supplies and trading items that had been ordered for Joseph to bring to Gaul and Britain on his next return. Our intention was to arrive in Alexandria within days, stay there for a few weeks, and, depending on sailing conditions, arrive on the southern coast of Gaul well within two months of our leaving Palestine.

Beside myself, there was Mary Anna and her four younger children, Mariam and Nathaniel, Sara and Phillip, and Joseph of Arimathea and his children Lois Salome, Martha, and Lazarus, together with their children. We made good time to Alexandria, and quickly found shelter with relatives.

We rejoiced at being reunited with Mary Magdalene and her children. Mary informed us that she was very eager to move to Gaul where she had been told telepathically by Yeshua that he would be waiting for her. As I have said, Yeshua had told Mary Magdalene at the time of his resurrection that she would continue to assist his enlightened body to pass through additional ascension processes. He had made it known to Mary that much of this higher work of alchemy would occur in Gaul and Britain.

Once we were comfortable, Joseph and the men set themselves to the task of gathering the necessary supplies and crew that would see us all the way to Britain. Initially, it felt like a great relief to be away from the constant stress and vigilance that had coloured the past years. While there were many Romans in Alexandria, Yeshua was for the most part unheard of, except for the stories that circulated among the Alexandria Essene community and relatives who were very eager to hear all the news we could tell them.

For almost a week, we enjoyed the hospitality of our hosts. However, the sense of welcomed rest and relaxation soon evaporated when a transport of one of the Roman legions, which had been previously stationed in Jerusalem, was transferred to Alexandria. One of the centurions within the legion had been present during Yeshua's trial and crucifixion. Not only that, but he was the same centurion, who for some unexplainable reason, had resented Joseph of Arimathea for meddling in the situation. Several weeks after the crucifixion, he had had Joseph arrested and jailed, under false accusations that he had been planted in the Sanhedrin by the Zealots in order to aid and abet Yeshua's 'revolution'. Fortunately Joseph's powerful connections had seen him released within a week.

It so happened that on the very day the legion arrived in Alexandria and the officers were given offshore leave, the centurion saw Joseph, Nathaniel, Lazarus, and Phillip in the marketplace gathering stores of food. Recognizing them and thinking that Joseph had escaped from jail, the resentful centurion arrested him without trial, and put him in the dungeon of Alexander's old fortress.

Wasting no time, Lazarus convinced a lower magistrate that his father had certified credentials showing that Joseph had been granted the rights and privileges of a Roman citizen. They were then granted audience before the Roman governor, to whom they presented Joseph's papers with the stamped seal of Augustus Caesar. These showed that their leader was a Minister of Mines in good standing, who commanded a fleet of ore boats that served the Roman Empire.

Incensed and humiliated, the centurion had Joseph beaten, reluctantly released, and dragged to the wharf where Phillip and Nathaniel were waiting for him. Then he insisted that Lazarus, under military escort, immediately gather everyone in our company and come to the dock, where only one of Joseph's boats could be seen. We were forced to proceed onto the smaller boat, which had had all its crew, supplies of food and water, and trading goods confiscated. As we looked about the boat, we also saw that the main sail had been shredded, most of it gone. There were no oars, no wheel, no rudder, and no anchor. Once we had all been shoved on board and the mooring ropes removed, we slowly slipped away on the outgoing tide.

In a state of shock and disbelief, we watched Alexandria slowly fade into the distance. As the cries of the children became more incessant, I paced the deck assessing our deplorable situation. Joseph sat in deep meditation, his bruised head in his hands. All the children were huddled around the women who held them, offering them comfort and reassurance. Nathaniel and Lazarus were looking to see what could be used to improvise oars and a rudder. Phillip had dismantled the tattered sail to see if it could be repaired. I took Mary Anna and Mary Magdalene aside and asked them to gather any supplies of food and water so that they could be rationed among us.

Although our desperate situation invited hysterical fear, I could see that each adult, in our own way, was resolved to meet this challenge with a resolute faith that was born of the many years of initiation that had taken us victoriously through equally arduous circumstances. I went to Joseph and invited him to go with me down into the hold where we privately discussed how we could best meet this extraordinary trial that threatened our lives. As we talked we realized that some of the children could very easily die within the next hours. It was determined that we would encourage everyone present to be calm and, as soon as the sun set and the children were put to sleep, we adults came together in prayer and counsel. As the children slept in the night, we brought ourselves together to quietly discuss our increasingly critical plight. In spite of our disciplined training, we could not help but feel our impotence.

So it was that we counted ourselves fortunate to have our lives, even though the vengeful Roman had intended our boat to be a floating tomb. We knew that the power of unified prayer and harmonious collaboration with the elements would turn the tide of our fate. However, a situation that normally we could have mastered within hours was not responding to our commands.

It became increasingly clear as the long dreary hours of that first day continued into the next that this was to be an initiation for everyone, including the children. Those of us with the mastery of an adept were humbled, and we were all redirected to a sense of unified purpose that had been somewhat diffused over the past years, when so many disciples were scattered to the winds.

We elders also realized that in all our focus on Yeshua's ministry and the chaos that followed his resurrection, we had overlooked teaching and preparing the children in the Way of the Christ initiate. None of the children had been exposed to the arduous tests that lead to mastery of the physical plane. Very soon, those of us who knew the path of the initiate quite well, recognized that our boat must become a floating mystery school if we were to survive.

The overhead sun blazed like a furnace on the Great Sea's molten surface and a cooling breeze was almost nonexistent. Swimming in the cool water, or having a bail of water poured over us, was our only relief during the day. Although surrounded by water, it was too salty to drink.

So it was that we passed several days in the hold with no cooling wind and no clouds to give us shade, as the prevailing currents of the Great Sea carried us in an easterly direction back toward Palestine. Our meagre clothing provided little protection from the day's blistering sun or the night's damp chill. The small store of water that we happened to have with us was almost gone. The dew that was collected during the night was barely enough to wet the parched lips of the children.

Before our little company could come into sufficient empowerment and unity, it was the children who humbled us. Most of the children had seen us work miracles, and pleaded with us to do so now. It was a sorry state of affairs to experience that we were powerless to change the boat's course. It became clear that we had an opportunity to heal any lingering issues of feeling powerless. As we watched the children suffer, and listened helplessly to their pleas, it was a painful test to surrender and align our wills.

Even though my heart ached to personally intervene for the children's sake, I knew little could manifest to save our lives until our entire group had come into some kind of cohesive unity. If there were to be a miracle, it would be done as a co-creative community with Father–Mother God our commander.

By the time we were into the third day, the children realized that the adults could not save them, and they were willing to hear our counsel. They began to really listen instead of shrugging off the stories we had been telling them about our own initiations, and especially those of Yeshua. Inspired, instead of complaining, they began to look on our plight as an adventure. With humility and courage, everyone was ready to come together in mighty prayer and conviction that our destiny lay ahead of us in Gaul and Britain, not being hopelessly adrift on the sea.

Having brought ourselves into a unified resolve to turn the currents, we began a nonstop vigil of prayer. After several hours of incessant silent prayer interspersed with strong vocal decrees, our little company had generated sufficient momentum for manifestation to occur. First we noticed a cool breeze rocking the boat, subtly shifting its course. Then we noticed dolphins swimming all around us, leaping into the air, and making a chorus of joyful sounds. Next, we saw that the colour of the water had changed, and with it the direction of the current. Slowly, but surely, our little boat turned its direction, as if carried by a force that was more than the current or wind.

Joseph and Nathaniel had earlier fashioned a kind of rudder, which they had attempted to use, but the prevailing current had been too strong for it to be of any use. Now, the little rudder offered more precise steering as we followed the course of the stars by night and our dolphin navigators by day.

Clouds coalesced and sent forth a gentle showering of rain. We collected the blessed water into every possible container. Although I realize my story must sound quite far-fetched, fish began to jump into our boat. And the flimsy nets made from the remnants of the sail, which we had attempted to use before with little success, now began to catch all the fish we could ever want and more.

With our physical needs met, our spirits high, and our course struck, we continued our voyage beyond impossible odds. We chose to stay away from any landmasses, knowing that we would reach our destination best by maintaining our unified focus, rather than dissipating our energy by engaging another encounter with the Romans. Although we were seen by a number of passing boats, the appearance of our crippled vessel told them we were fugitives put on the water to die, with nothing of value to pirate.

Joseph knew the coastline of Gaul very well. When he recognized that we were drawing close to the little port that has become known in your day as Saintes-Maries-de-la-Mer, he and the other men began to guide us toward the inlet. We found that our boat moved easily upon the incoming tide into the estuary, where several small wharves hemmed the banks. Beyond was the welcome sight of thatched, stone cottages, with smoke curling up into the sky from their hearths' chimneys. Before long, we ran aground in deep silt, and waited for the tide to turn back to the sea before we climbed down the makeshift ladders that had been fashioned from the mooring ropes.

Some of the local villagers, primarily fishermen, curious to find out who we were, had ventured out to us in their small skiffs. Seeing that we were mostly women and children, they returned to their wives, who then prepared shelter and food for us. Once the water was knee deep, we joyfully waded to shore, ravenously ate our first real meal in over a week, and tucked our weary, stiff bodies into warm beds to sleep as long as was required. The village continued to welcome us with wonderful hospitality.

Shortly after we arrived, a messenger sent word to a nearby wealthy merchant with whom Joseph had done commerce over the years. He was also a trusted liaison who had provided protection to the Essene initiates Joseph had brought to the Languedoc region. As soon as they received word, it did not take long for Jacob, Isaac, and Tabitha to join us. They welcomed the return of Sara and her recently married husband Phillip, whom they had not yet met. A feast was prepared in the village to celebrate our safe passage, and a warm invitation was extended to stay as long as we liked.

Gratefully, among the very few things that we were fortunate enough to still have with us, was the communal cup Yeshua used, at what has come to be known as the Last Supper. It had been in Mary Anna's safekeeping ever since that night. This simple wooden cup which was crafted in Britain, with its simple Celtic knot overlay of gold and silver, had been used frequently when the disciples gathered for communal supper, prayer, and meditation. As time passed, and we had fewer and fewer visitations by Yeshua, this cup gathered more and more significance for each of us who remembered him. With each use, it became increasingly charged with energy. For those with inner sight, a very distinct golden glow could be seen emanating from it. As we held it, we felt tingling warmth in our hands, and a feeling of love expanding our hearts.

With gratitude for all the bounteous gifts that were poured out on us, we slowly gathered strength and renewed peace of mind. Jacob and Isaac guided us to their homes situated in a small village nestled in a valley of the northern Pyrennes foothills. The land was fertile and the water was pure. Our simple Essene way of life easily blended with that of the rural natives whose language we gradually adopted. There were enough emigrants from Palestine that we felt an immediate sense of family and community.

So it was that a new life received us. We had taken flight and now we could find rest from our long labours. We had seen the Son of Man come and walk among us, we had given him shelter and nourishment, and we accompanied and comforted him when the hour of greatest darkness stole the light. He, in turn, gathered us to him and showed us the Way of eternal light within all forms.

All that Yeshua did, we came to know that we could also do. Perhaps we would accomplish even more before our time on the earthplane was finished. Yeshua had continually emphasized and supported our sovereign empowerment as Christ initiates. He reminded us that we could also be Christs and that, as a brother and a friend, he was equal with us in the sight of our Creator. I will further add that as the years passed, Yeshua told us that he never intended to be worshipped nor create a religion centred around him, nor did he desire to create a dynasty of earthly rulers.

Across many spiralling thresholds we have waltzed, weaving many coloured threads into a seamless tapestry. What I have shared with you may have raised many questions. My hope is that I have catalysed the answers that rest within you. As you know, my intent is to shake yesterday's unquestioned crystallized structures, loosen that which hoards energy, and invite a more empowered life into every moment's free flow. My desire is to create space and movement so that the Christ that you are may be birthed.

As I bring my story to a close, you may desire to know more about my family's remaining years on the earthplane. You, like many, may have questions, such as: What became of Mary Anna, Mary Magdalene, and other key characters in my story? Did we leave our physical bodies or ascend them? What is the true meaning of the Holy Grail? Answers to all these questions and more, I will share with you at another time as we walk the verdant fields of France and pass through Avalon's misty vales. An additional two hundred more years of my life as Anna still stretch before us with many interesting adventures. Know that when you have integrated the energy couched within the words that I have shared, and you are ready to ask for more, it surely shall be given. Be at peace, my beloved friend, and know I AM always with you.

Anna

∽

～ Afterword from Claire ～

My dear friend, it has been my joy and honour to serve you with the empowering and loving presence of Anna, the mother of Mary and the grandmother of Yeshua. I will now conclude this portion of her story by sharing with you how *Anna, Grandmother of Jesus* came into being.

In the fall of 1987, near a waterfall in the Grand Tetons, I experienced a completely life-transforming physical encounter with the ascended master Saint Germain (previously Joseph, the father of Yeshua). Shortly thereafter, I was informed that I had a close connection with Yeshua's grandmother. Almost a year later, while I was in deep meditation, Anna appeared to me on the inner planes and informed me that she desired to share her story with me. And so it was that I began to experience Anna telling me telepathically about her life and taking me holographically into her experiences, which I then sporadically recorded.

On January 11, 1998, Anna and the Councils of Light informed me that it was time to dedicate myself fully to the task of bringing Anna's transformational words to those souls who were calling forth Christ Consciousness. I was in great resistance. After all, who was I to tell Anna's story? The responsibility and scope of this project seemed far too overwhelming and the risks too great as cellular memory of persecution manifested in my body. I wanted to run away. But then I was gifted with a series of three computer upgrades and financial donations. I had no excuses! The relentless calling of my soul and the support of beloved friends have seen me through the travail of giving birth to what you now hold in your hands.

The writing process became one of aligning and stilling my mind until I could feel, see, and hear Anna's distinct presence and voice. Often our spiritual journeys together took us flying over the terrain of Palestine, Egypt, and Britain. Many times we zoomed in close enough to see great detail. As I was having these experiences, I wrote what I saw and heard. My favourite experiences were those in which I entered fully into Anna's life as if I were in a holographic virtual reality; touching, smelling, emoting, tasting, and seeing through Anna's senses. Often during these times of merging our consciousness, I could sense Anna looking through my eyes at the computer screen, marvelling at this much more convenient way of being a scribe!

The first channelled, very right-brain transmissions were completed in seven months while I was homebound undergoing two cataract surgeries. Since then it has been a process of collaboration with Anna and the Councils of Light, ongoing initiations, and deep integration, interspersed with extended periods of writing/ rewriting. It became clear from the very first encounter with Anna that writing her story was to be a major empowerment initiation. These past four and a half years of fulfilling this labour of love has involved learning something about how to consciously integrate channelled transmissions and creative writing. It has required a steadfast willingness to align my human will, to be patient, and to persevere while fulfilling a Greater Design.

Writing this book has been a process of high alchemy as Anna's lingering patriarchal paradigm was slowly but surely transmuted. Equally present from the beginning was Anna's new paradigm of egalitarian unity and the balancing of polarities. My job has been to bring that new model out of obscurity and into greater clarity and grounded application. Gratefully throughout, it has been your presence calling forth Anna's wisdom and love that has sustained me. May this book serve your Christ journey that returns you fully to your Self. May my example inspire you, my friend, to bring forth your story and highest destiny.

As Anna has promised, there is more to come as we pick up the trail of the 'Feminine Christ' and the Holy Grail. May the Divine Mother's love rise up to embrace you this beautiful day!

Claire

௸

Appendix A

Relationship Chart

Anna: Anna is born as Hannah in 612 BC in Etam near Bethlehem. She is of the tribes of Judah, Levi, and Joseph. Her parentage is unknown, except that her father was a rabbi.

Tomas and Anna's Child

Aurianna: Born 23 May 596 BC in Etam near Bethlehem. Lived in Jerusalem, Mount Carmel, and died in Heliopolis, Egypt about 500 BC.

Hismariam: Anna's great-granddaughter through Aurianna, who left Egypt with Anna and took her ascension from Mount Carmel c.150 BC. She later reincarnated as Mary Anna, the mother of Yeshua.

Matthias: The son of a Levite high priest at Mount Carmel. Matthias married Anna in 57 BC. Their marriage was annulled five years later. Matthias moved to Qumran and died there in 37 BC.

Matthias and Anna's Children

Joseph of Arimathea: Born in Mount Carmel in 57 BC. Married Eunice Salome in Jerusalem in 29 BC with whom he had two daughters, Lois Salome and Susannah Mary. Eunice died in 20 BC. He married **Mary of Magdala** in 5 BC.

Martha: Born in Mount Carmel in 55 BC. She never married and later managed her brother, Joseph of Arimathea's, country residence in Bethany.

Joseph of Arimathea and Mary of Magdala's Children

Mary Magdalene: Light conceived and born in Bethany in 4 BC.

Lazarus: Born in Bethany in AD1. Moved to France in AD32.

Martha: Born in Bethany in AD3. Moved to France in AD32.

༄

Joachim: Born in Persia 86 BC of the tribes of Judah, Dan, and Ephraim. His mother was Persian and Sumerian. He met Anna in 52 BC and they married in Mount Carmel in 49 BC. He died in 4 BC.

Joachim and Anna's Children
(All born in Mount Carmel except Mary Anna who was born in Ephesus.)

Ruth: Born in 48 BC and moved to Ephesus where she married Titus.

Isaac: Born in 47 BC, moved to Heliopolis in 22 BC, married **Tabitha** who gave birth to light conceived **Sara** in 4 BC. They moved to the Languedoc region of southern France. **Sara** was one of Yeshua's key disciples and the wife of Philip. She and Phillip moved to France in AD32.

Andrew: Isaac's twin, who never married. He moved to Britain in 22 BC.

Mariamne: Born in 45 BC and moved to Heliopolis in 22 BC where she married Adolphus. They had two children.

Jacob: Mariamne's twin. After going through initiations in Egypt he moved to the Languedoc region of France. He never married. After escorting Yeshua to India, he returned to France.

Josephus: Born in 43 BC, moved to Britain in 22 BC. He never married.

Nathan: Born in 41 BC, lived near Cana and later in Nazareth. He married Miriam and Leah who gave birth to 14 children altogether, some of whom were Yeshua's disciples.

Luke: Nathan's twin, became a physician, married Abigail, had six children and lived near Bethlehem.

Rebekah: Born in 38 BC, married Simeon, gave birth to light conceived **Mariam** in 4 BC. Died of leprosy in AD5 in Mount Carmel.

Mariam was adopted by Mary Anna and Joseph after her mother died. She married **Nathaniel** and gave birth to **Benjamin** in AD14. She was one of Yeshua's key disciples.

Ezekial: Born in 35 BC, moved to Egypt in 22 BC where he studied music.

Noah: Born in 33 BC, moved to Britain in 22 BC, married Ariadne, who light conceived Vivian in 4 BC.

Mary Anna: Born in 20 BC, married **Joseph ben Jacob** in 5 BC, light conceived **Yeshua ben Joseph.**

Joseph ben Jacob. Born in 37 BC in Bethlehem, the son of Joachim's brother Jacob and his wife Lois. Joseph was a widower and an adept before marrying Mary Anna. He made his ascension in the Himalayas in AD20.

Joseph ben Jacob and Mary Anna's Children

Yeshua: Born in Bethlehem in April, 4 BC
James and Jude (Judas): Born in Heliopolis in 2 BC
Joseph the Younger (Joses): Born in Heliopolis in AD1
Ruth: Born in Mount Carmel in AD4
Thomas and **Simon:** Twins born in Nazareth in AD7
Mariam: (Adopted, light conceived daughter of Rebekah born in 4 BC).

✎

Ahmed: An Egyptian Essene born in Heliopolis, married Mary Anna in AD23 in Nazareth. They moved to Jerusalem in AD27 where Ahmed died in AD31.

Ahmed's and Mary Anna's Children

John Mark: Born in Nazareth in AD24
Esther Salome and **Matteas:** Twins born in Nazareth in AD25.

✎

John the Baptizer: Light conceived and born in AD3, son of Zachariah and Elizabeth, a sister of Joseph ben Jacob and the niece of Joachim.

Yeshua and Mary Magdalene's Adopted Children:

Joses, Judas, and Miriam

෴

❧ *Appendix B* ❧
Chronology Chart

Anna of Mount Carmel

Hannah and Anna's soul merge occurred 23 May 596 BC, at the time of Aurianna's birth. Anna's betrothed husband, Tomas, was carried captive into Babylon in 597 BC.

Anna in Jerusalem: 583–559 BC

Anna in Mount Carmel: 559–510 BC

Anna in Egypt: 510–207 BC

Anna in Mount Carmel: AD207–28

Anna travels with Yeshua: AD29–30

Anna and family moved to southern France: summer AD32

Yeshua ben Joseph

Yeshua born in Bethlehem: April, 4 BC

Yeshua in Egypt: 4 BC–AD4

Yeshua in Mount Carmel & Nazareth: AD4–9

Yeshua in Britain: AD9–12

Yeshua in India: AD14–21

Yeshua in Egypt: AD22–24

Yeshua and Mary Magdalene's betrothal: AD24

Yeshua in the Orient: AD25–27

Yeshua's ministry in Palestine: AD28–30

Yeshua's ministry after the resurrection: AD30 – unknown

Mary Magdalene and Yeshua's children – Joses, Judas, and Miriam – were taken secretly to a monastic village south of Alexandria by Joseph of Arimathea in June of AD30. They moved to southern France in the summer of AD32 with other members of the family.

∽

∽ *Appendix C* ∽
Glossary of Etheric Terms

Anointed One: A being who has attained enlightenment – a Christ or Buddha. The etheric anointing oil produced by the pineal gland in the brain has been fully activated.

Aramaic: (derived from an ancient Middle Eastern origin) Aramaic is Yeshua's native tongue and the common language he used to express his teachings. The Aramaic worldview is holistic, interdimensional and nondualistic compared to the Greek translations of Yeshua's sayings that are the basis of the *Holy Bible*.

Ascension Initiation(s): The processes that ascend consciousness into full enlightenment, unity consciousness, immortality and union with Creator Source.

Atlantis and-Lemuria: Ancient, highly evolved civilizations whose land masses sank respectively into the Atlantic and Pacific Oceans.

Ba Body: The Egyptian light body equivalent to the causal body or universal I AM Presence, who neutrally witnesses and directs the soul's evolution and physical life.

Beloved on High: A name for the God Self who is absolute Love, Lover, and Beloved.

Book of Life: In the etheric realms all thoughts, actions, causes and effects, and wisdom are imprinted upon a kind of holographic grid of light, sound, colour, and sacred geometry. This psychically accessible light grid is also known as the Akashic Records.

Breath of Life: Life force breathed in a conscious way so as to amplify its effect.

Brotherhood of Tat: An Atlantean (and perhaps more ancient) fellowship comprised of men and women adepts, high initiates, priestly scientists, and artisans who knew and practised the Mysteries that ascend and immortalize consciousness.

Brother–Sisterhood of Light: This is a planetary and cosmic association of conscious ascended beings who have attained mastery of the physical and subtle planes. They often remain on or near the earthplane to facilitate Earth and humanity's evolution since the beginning of time until all life is ascended.

Christ: An office of planetary service in which a man or woman has attained fully enlightened consciousness. Every soul has an indwelling Christ presence.

Christ Consciousness: Experiencing the Absolute Oneness while simultaneously embracing transitory forms and energies.

Crucifixion initiation: The Rite of Passage in which the initiate's separation consciousness is fully acknowledged and its transmutation has begun.

Divine Androgyne: The original and natural state of consciousness before 'the gender split' in which masculine and feminine attributes are merged, balanced, and harmonized. The goal of the initiate, whether male or female is to regain the consciousness of the Divine Androgyne.

Divine Mother: The intelligence behind and within all emptiness and form. She is equal with the Divine Father. She is the coalescing glue and the force that dissolves all things. She is personally approachable and unconditionally all-embracing of her creation.

Egyptian Light Bodies: Depending on the system, the ancient Egyptians perceived five to ten light bodies that comprise those of the most dense physical body to the most subtle spiritual bodies.

Enlightenment: Separation consciousness is transcended and expanded superconscious brain functions are realized.

Feminine Christ: A woman who has attained Christ Consciousness.

Garden of Paradise: The natural state of unified consciousness wherein the fruit of the Tree of Life is freely eaten in a state of original innocence. The fruit yields wisdom gained from the experience of choosing between and harmonizing contrasting polarities.

Gnosis: Direct revelation of the Absolute without a mediating saviour or priest.

Grail Ascension Codes: Subatomic patterns of light in the DNA that come directly from Creator Source ensuring the ascending evolution of all its emanations.

Great Plan: The ascending/descending blueprint that Creator Source conceives and uses as co-creator with creation so that there is eternal expansion and evolution.

Halls of Amenti: The psychic underworld and higher dimensional realms of 'Inner Earth' in which luminaries reside, teach, and facilitate planetary evolution.

Hathors: Interdimensional ascended masters of love and sound healing who came to Earth over 850,000 years ago to assist Earth and humanity's evolution. They facilitate coherent creation through high alchemy, which transmutes discordant fear-based emotions, thoughts, behaviours, systems, and structures.

High Alchemy: The Great Work of the Soul, or the Magnus Opus, in which base, instinctual consciousness is transmuted and then ascended into Christ Consciousness.

Holy Grail: The immaculate, eternal container of consciousness that holds and preserves coherent patterns of cosmic intelligence as light, sound, colour, and sacred geometry. It is also the void that perfectly births, sustains, and mirrors Creator in all creation. It is an aspect and function of the Divine Mother as her womb/matrix from which the Holy Child is born – the Christ is risen – matter is spiritualized. Yeshua's communal cup was a symbol for this greater cosmic Holy Grail.

Holy Spirit of Truth (Promise): An aspect of the Mother Godhead who witnesses, reveals, and guides. Her presence comforts and is the peace that passes all understanding.

I AM Presence (Lord God of My Being): The causal body who directs and manifests through its soul extension and physical lifestream. It is the Beloved on High.

Immortality – Physical and Spiritual: Physical immortality is the capacity to consciously engage the pineal and pituitary glands' hormones in such a way that the physical body continually renews itself. In this way the soul has more time for attaining self-mastery and for rendering service. Spiritual immortality is the soul's ability to retain conscious awareness of personal identity and memory while ascending into higher light bodies during its transition from the physical body.

Ka Body: The Egyptian light body, which is also the physical body's etheric twin.

Khat Body: The Egyptian light body, which is also the physical body.

Ladder of Light: The illumined seven-chakra system that facilitates enlightenment.

Languages of Light: Communication vibrations that originate from the Music of the Spheres or sounds of creation. Some languages of light on Earth have their origins in other universes, galaxies, and worlds that have seeded humanity.

Law of One/Life: An ethical code of relationship in which all life is perceived as interconnected, interdependent Oneness.

Light Conception: The conscious conception of children in which ascension light codes are deliberately cultivated and anchored into the mother's egg and father's seed, so that the incoming evolved soul's DNA can receive its highest possible 'service destiny blueprint'. These children enter Earth with few, if any, veils of forgetfulness. The processes of enlightenment and ascension are also forms of Light Conception.

Matri-Christic Grail Lineage: A spiritually resonant lineage, that may include but is not limited to a genetic bloodline, through which evolved souls incarnate with an agreement to assist planetary ascension as Christs. Women hold and pass on the Grail codes as wisdom teachings, transmissions of energy, and genetic material. Initiated men function as guardians of the code bearers and activators of the Grail ascension codes.

Mer Ka Ba: A interdimensional vehicle comprised of coherent unified consciousness and a counter-rotational field of electromagnetic energy that makes ascension of the physical body, time travel, and teleportation possible. Elijah's 'Chariot of the Sun' was a Mer Ka Ba vehicle.

Mystical Marriage: The horizontal union of Divine Masculine and Divine Feminine attributes within consciousness. It is also the conscious union of Father Spirit with Mother Matter on the vertical axis that conceives the enlightened Child.

Osirian-Isis Mysteries: The ancient Egyptian wisdom teachings and practices that culminate in the enlightenment of consciousness.

Resurrection Initiation: The Rite of Passage that fully transmutes separation consciousness and brings about enlightened unity with Creator Source and creation.

Rises of Civilization: There have been twelve previous rises or cycles of evolution on Earth during which many millions of years have passed. We are presently in the thirteenth rise.

Rite of the Sepulchre: The resurrection process by which initiates and adepts, such as Anna, stilled their vital signs and regenerated their physical bodies for extended periods of time. This practice facilitated physical immortality.

Rod of Light: The central column of etheric light that connects the cosmic and physical planes through the crown, centre of the physical body, and perineum.

Rosa Mystica: A mystical Order of the Holy Grail whose symbol is the rose.

Sahu Body: The Egyptian light body that holds the highest possible frequencies and most expanded states of consciousness. When one attains the Sahu there is full enlightenment and spiritual immortality. Yeshua attained his Sahu body during his resurrection and ascension initiations.

Seed, Flower, and Fruit of Life: All life is patterned after the intersecting spheres that create the 'Vesica Pisces'. Depending on how many spheres interpenetrate one another precise mathematical/ dimensional harmonics and sacred geometric shapes are created. The Fruit of Life (such as an apple) is the sphere with its central channel that circulates energy vertically and laterally. The human body follows this same pattern.

Shekinah: In Hebrew, she is the Divine Mother Godhead who is equal to God the Father.

Sound Current: All form is sound vibration. There is a current of sound that arises and moves out of the Creator's still void – the source of all emanations. 'In the beginning was the Word and the Word was God.' It is possible to inwardly hear and follow the Sound Current to its Source.

Staff of Life: The endocrine glands and their hormonal elixirs that bridge the spiritual and physical dimensions.

Tantric High Alchemy: Internal energy practices that cultivate life force and sexual energy for the purpose of enlightening the self so that one may be of greater service to life. Tantric practices may be done in celibacy or with a sexual partner.

Teacher of Righteousness: An adept who exemplifies mastery of the physical and subtle planes through the 'rightful (or harmless) use of energy'.

Tree of Life: Mystical wisdom teachings and practices through which consciousness is lifted and transmuted from the temporal and transient realms into the supernal and eternal realms. This body of wisdom is of ancient origins and was more recently synthesized into the mystical practices of the Hebrew Kabbalah.

✎ *Anna, the Voice of the Magdalenes* ✎

If you loved *Anna, Grandmother of Jesus* the journey continues in the sequel...

Claire Heartsong, in co-creation with Catherine Ann Clemett, has brought forth the sequel to *Anna, Grandmother of Jesus*. In the sequel, *Anna, the Voice of the Magdalenes*, Anna and 18 other Magdalene adepts and initiates bring forth intimate messages about their lives in France and Britain after Jesus' (Yeshua's) resurrection. They disclose their personal and deeply transformational experiences with the resurrected Yeshua, which occurred over the course of many years. Discourses on a variety of spiritual topics are offered, including material that some may consider heretical and controversial. Long-held secrets are revealed in such a way as to assist the lifting of the suppressed Divine Feminine/Magdalene voice in our time.

Join Anna, the holy family, and the Magdalene-Essenes as they carry their work forward into new regions and new experiences. Enjoy hearing intimate details from the Magdalenes' own lips as they lift the veil of silence that has concealed their exemplary lives of compassion and spiritual mastery. Receive a greater understanding of the Christ drama 2,000 years ago and its relevance to present-day humanity and your own awakening.

Through Anna, the Voice of the Magdalenes you'll...

- Continue the journey with Anna, the Holy Family and 18 other Magdalene-Essenes as their work is carried forward into France and Britain after Jesus' (Yeshua's) resurrection

- Uncover the 'lost' years after Jesus' crucifixion and resurrection

- Meet the Magdalenes who witnessed and walked with the resurrected Jesus in France, Britain, and India

- Discover long-hidden secrets concerning Jesus' intimate life, relationships, and children

- Understand the vital importance of lifting the suppressed Divine Feminine voice in our own time of great chaos, so that all beings may flourish and be brought into harmony and balance

- Grasp the importance of the 'Seeding of Light' – how the dispersion of Anna's, Mother Mary's, and Jesus' 'bloodline' of enlightened descendants may be carried within you, acting as a living catalyst for awakening your own Christ–Magdalene potential today.

ABOUT THE AUTHOR

Claire Heartsong raised her family in Idaho and taught at Boise State University before the inner planes were opened to her consciousness in 1986. Pivotal experiences then began to unfold with St. Germain, Yeshua, and Anna. She moved to Mount Shasta where she received Anna's invitation to tell her story. After passing through intense preparatory initiations for 10 years, Claire and Anna joined together to bring forth *Anna, Grandmother of Jesus*. This labor of devotional love continued unabated from January 1998 to October 2002.

Claire finds her current experiences expanding upon the mystical, gnostic Christianity demonstrated and taught by Anna, Yeshua (Jesus), and the Carmel Essenes. Once the *Anna* books were completed, Claire knew the next step in her spiritual awakening process would be to find teachers and teachings to assist her in bringing Anna's ethereal teachings into direct, embodied experience. Claire has found Tibetan Buddhist teachers and direct, experiential teachings to be the open door that Anna was always pointing to during the years she heard and felt Anna's guiding voice in her heart.

Since 2006, when Claire met her spiritual partner Lorenzo, she has been out of the public spotlight. They live a contemplative life in a remote northern California mountain hermitage where they practice essential Buddhist meditation. They are committed to awakening in this lifetime and bringing benefit to all beings.

CONNECT WITH

HAY HOUSE

ONLINE

 hayhouse.co.uk   **f** @hayhouse

@hayhouseuk   **X** @hayhouseuk

@hayhouseuk   @hayhouseuk

Find out all about our latest books & card decks • Be the first to know about exclusive discounts • Interact with our authors in live broadcasts • Celebrate the cycle of the seasons with us • Watch free videos from your favourite authors • Connect with like-minded souls

'*The gateways to wisdom and knowledge are always open.*'

Louise Hay